*By the same author*

---

NOTEBOOKS OF A DILETTANTE

# The Rosa Luxemburg
# Contraceptives Cooperative

A PRIMER ON
COMMUNIST
CIVILIZATION

# THE
# Rosa Luxemburg
## CONTRACEPTIVES
## COOPERATIVE

*A Primer on Communist Civilization*

by Leopold Tyrmand

THE MACMILLAN COMPANY
NEW YORK, NEW YORK

Library of Congress Catalog Card Number: 73–160083

FIRST PRINTING

Printed in the United States of America

*To Jacob and Maria Lewit—*
*for their help*
*in acquiring simple wisdoms.*

# CONTENTS

# CONTENTS

# CONTENTS

"Thought makes the whole dignity of man; therefore, endeavor to think well, that is the only morality."

BLAISE PASCAL, *Pensées*

# FOREWORD

THIS BOOK does not have any scholarly, publicistic, or journalistic pretensions. It has literary ambitions. Despite this, it is neither prose nor fiction nor a literary essay. It is a pamphlet, an intentional hyperbole of an existing reality. I personally regard communism as the worse plague that ever befell mankind and I nourish the deep hope that this book mirrors my feelings to a sufficient degree. Does this mean that the pamphlet distorts the truth? Not in the least. Communism is a phenomenon toward which objectivity as an interpretative method is absurdly helpless. I believe that a pamphlet is the only method, at least for the time being, of giving a correct interpretation of communism. In my opinion my book is truer than a hundred objective treatises, and I am sure that millions of people will agree with me.

Can one objectively explain a legal system in which the prosecutor is *always* right? Can one objectively discuss a psychology the cornerstone of which is the concept of class consciousness, which means that if someone orders someone else shot without a trial, he has displayed his class instinct? Can one objectively describe the institution of a political police whose *raison d'être* is to create culprits where none exist? Can one objectively write about a society in which drunkenness is the only form of epicureanism and a sign of humanism? Can one objectively investigate an economy where the shortage of bread is explained by the fact that every year more people eat bread? Can one objectively examine the morality of people who build careers by hunting down and destroying the slightest manifestation of free thought, while in London, Paris, and Washington they deliver speeches about

13

their struggle for freedom and the independence of the human spirit—and their Western listeners believe what they say?

Many who read this book will say that I am overstating, distorting, lapsing into the grotesque, and producing a surrealistic effect. I suppose they are right. But realism is as useful for explaining communism as a bicycle is for flying to the moon. Democracies lack a system of reference for so many of the phenomena that are commonplace in communism that talking about the adequacy of social or ontological processes, which is so fashionable in the West, is simple intellectual gibberish in the ears of people living under communism. Much in this book that will seem incredible to many arises from the fact that I am trying to talk about things about which nothing or very little is known in the West, while I am omitting what has been amply spoken of and written about here. Also, my interpretations are those of a person *from there* and may often appear to people *here* as deformation, irrationalism, and exaggeration. But people *there* for the most part see things in *this* way and know *this* about things. Writing about people who believe that communism represents the only prospect for good, justice, and structural meaning, and who, in the name of this belief, exercise a power based on unheard of cruelties, the utter destruction of the human individual, and complete contempt for rationality, does not by nature have much connection with logic. My ambition in writing this book was to look for a skeleton of the truth, a recovery of the structure of reality under the complexity of the expressions of life. To this end it was necessary to eliminate much of what life accumulates and all that muddies the transparency of the outline. I also believe that the changes occurring in the image of the Communist world—and they surely are occurring and in a visible way—affect to all intents and purposes only that external ornamentation accumulated by practice on the very surface of the phenomenon. The actual pattern and the fundamental principle by which *e pur se muove* always remain the same.

People who do not live under communism do not understand why those who do say "soup in communism," "Communist billiards," "a writer in communism," or "Communist tomatoes."

The phrase "they" is also in daily use and refers to Communists and rulers alike as well as to people who only *profess* communism as a world view. Perhaps the reader of this book will have trouble at first with the obvious anthropomorphization of the term "communism." But this is how communism is felt *there,* as some horrible and unbearable creature who actually lives nearby. Purists will accuse me of using the word "communism" to signify a host of imprecise contents and will add that the term denotes something fairly exact, and nothing apart from that. However, it seems to me that this term is at the present historical moment ambivalently loose and precise at the same time. Above all, it denotes what is happening *there.* The Communists maintain that what is happening at the present time behind the Iron Curtain is not yet communism but rather represents the stage called "socialism" on the way to a Communist society. But people there are not disposed to dialectical subtleties; they have pressed ahead and do not use any other word to describe the existing state of affairs. They are seized by despair at the thought that if *this* is not yet communism, then one can imagine what it will be like when communism does come. Here it is worth noting the words of a certain salesgirl in a Warsaw food store who shouted in response to the bitter complaints of the customers about the lack of bread, butter, meat, and other goods, "People, for God's sake, what do you want from me? I didn't order them to shoot from the *Aurora!"* *

My attitude toward communism is the outcome of my life under communism. During those years I learned to hate communism for the evil it contained. And also to fear it for its metaphysical power to hold more and more and more evil.

---

* According to the official history of the USSR, the firing from the guns of the cruiser *Aurora,* which had been taken over by the Communists, on the Winter Palace in St. Petersburg was the signal for the outbreak of the October Revolution and made its victory a foregone conclusion.

# 1 · How to be born

**B**OTH THEORY and experience now indicate that it is best to be born into a worker's family. This hint seems contradictory to any pragmatic observation; it appears a little heedless, even light-minded, at first glimpse. Everyone knows that workers do not do well in a Communist society, which is perfectly natural in terms of the inner logic of every revolution. The Communist Revolution was carried out in the name of the worker's needs claims, aims, and ideals, so it is fully coherent that the workers are the last to benefit from its success, as no revolution in history ever fulfilled its promises. Once communism is established, workers work harder and make less money. They are deprived of many social facilities and satisfactions workers enjoy under capitalism. Capitalism, the worker's fiercest foe, is constantly frightened of him and, therefore, forced to respect his labor organizations and pamper him with all kinds of modern social improvements. Communism, which is the worker's staunchest friend and ally, is consequently relieved from any such obligations. Thus, a worker's fate is not to be envied and, quite naturally, an infant in his house lacks all the luxuries a Party dignitary can easily obtain for his child. Nonetheless, regardless of evidence to the contrary, it is still the best approach to be born into a worker's family.

It is obvious, after more than fifty years, that communism has restored the basic feudal rule of privilege by birth and people are no longer born equal. They are born better or worse, according to their class affiliation. The effort of four hundred years of European thought to establish the principle of evaluation of the individual on the grounds of his personal qualities has thereby been wiped out. Current Communist society is strictly a class and hierarchic affair. People are rigidly divided into better and worse, superiority being determined not by the old traditional, but by the new, Communist set of values. One's profession determines one's social recognition, while one's position within the hierarchy is the basis for privileges uncorrelated with one's social worth. It is more important *what* one does than *how* one does it, or in what effective gains—for society and for oneself—one's activity results. The symbols of social status dominate universally and have the same meaning and power as did aristocratic symbols in feudal society, where poor, stupid noblemen always had better opportunities than rich and talented middle-class offspring. To be born a worker's child has a tremendous promotional force, even if it doesn't implement any actual benefit or prosperity. Worker origin doesn't assure automatic advantages but may be a source of endless profit, facilitation, and maneuvering, if skillfully exploited. Above all, it provides a special feeling of security when facing any misfortune later in life. And this is priceless in communism.

Marxist-Leninist theory and all Communist constitutions constantly use the term "people" (and every derivative of that noun) in the sense of a sovereign entity, empowered in a Communist state with all possible privileges and dominance.

Theoretically, "people" is the highest autonomous value.

Dialectically, "people" consists of three social classes: workers, peasants, and so-called working intelligentsia.

Nominally, they are equal, share the same rights and duties, and are impartially represented by the Communist Party.

The reality is more *nuancé*. The Communist Party, according to doctrine, was in its origins a worker's party, and this has an impact on the mythology of current evaluations and new social snobbery.

It institutes a new infrastructural texture of inequality.

To be a worker is *much* better than to be a peasant, and con-

siderably better than to be a representative of the working intelligentsia. When three persons of the same individual quality,
but of three different descents, try to get the same job, the one
who is of worker's origin will be offered it. If three writers write
three novels about three characters descending from three different social classes, the one who writes about a worker will be
most abundantly rewarded and receive the noisiest publicity. A
new baby is supposed to have *that* in mind. Moreover, when
later in life one is on the make and drifts into the higher regions
of success, it is excellent form to accentuate one's worker's origin, provided it is done in a subtle and refined way. There are
several circles of high society in communism and all of them accept worker's progeny with delight; one has only to know how
to stress this feature according to circumstances. Should it be an
intellectual or artistic milieu, it is advised to emphasize worker
origin with a touch of sophisticated irony and a bit of heartfelt
self-deprecation, intimating that personal success has been
achieved *despite* such descent. In official, governmental, or Party
circles it is advisable to reinforce carefully their theoretical and
totally unrealistic belief that a worker's condition is the *best* in
a Communist society and his children the ablest and most forceful human stock in the nation. Consequently, it is politic to maintain that all one has achieved is *because* of, and thanks to, one's
worker origin—thus supporting the illusions of the political
rulers to assure some further benefits, which, after all, are always welcome to a young man from a poor worker's family.
Finally, should a descendant of a worker, in his mature age, try
the way of an anti-Communist, public opinion would acclaim
him with double force. "You see, even he, the flesh and blood of
a proletarian . . ." would be repeated, thus increasing his popularity. His origin makes his decision more esoteric, therefore
more valuable from the literary point of view. However, if persecuted and arrested, he would face additional harm and an-
guish. The interrogating officer might throw a few supplemen-
tary punches at his jaw, accompanied by the bitter remark,
"Even *you,* you bastard, are against us." A newborn must
be strictly aware that it's very tough to be a nonconformist, a

real rebel, in communism, even if one is genuinely a worker's son.

To be born a peasant is not bad, but confusing. As the scriptures say, peasants are divided into three categories: poor, middle, and rich; this classification is based upon rather hazy measurements. For example: A rich peasant who accidentally happened to render a service to the Communists before the Revolution, after it is instantly classified as poor, which makes him ultimately very prosperous—for his possessions do not diminish, but his capacity for economic maneuvering does increase. He is granted both the privileges of one who was exploited and the permission to rake in the advantages of an exploiter. However, an infant should be aware of the perils of peasant descent: if later in life he should get involved in politics or strive for fame, honors, and awards, his competitors will always attempt to prove he is the son of *rich* country folk—and it will not matter if he actually grew up in a most miserable cabin where he slept with domestic animals and ate grass. It is difficult to operate convincingly with one's prerevolutionary poverty because misery is, for a Leninist faithful, not an objective condition but one dependent for its worth on its usefulness to the Communist cause. Thus it is not satisfactory to have been poor without proving how that poverty contributed to the victory of the proletariat, the Revolution, communism. One is *always* suspected of being the son of rich persons who is making himself out to be the progeny of the poor. The enemies of peasant offspring will never miss an occasion to use masterfully this credibility gap. Thousands of village gossips will topographically specify where a man's father buried golden dollars, even if the latter possessed neither one square acre of his own land nor a shovel. And to be a rich peasant is, for an orthodox Communist, next to sin; it exudes a smell of vice like that which promiscuity of the clergy has for a devoted Christian.

The same applies to the working intelligentsia, which, in the hierarchy of social opportunities, is estimated a grade lower than the peasantry. It represents a much larger notion than that of the white-collar worker in America and includes all intellectual professions, such as science, medicine, law, art, etc. Working intelligentsia has a very ambiguous socio-moral value and constantly serves as a scapegoat and easy denominator of all kinds of accusations, the most popular of which is duplicity. Thus a newborn in a working intelligentsia family, apart from enjoying quite early in life the company of cultured, intelligent, sometimes charming people, must count on, a little later in life, much friction and many worries.

There is no special difference in future opportunities whether one is born an heir to a Party membership or not. It is difficult to draw a line between what is a burden and what is an advantage in a Party member's life. The matter changes when we deal with a man who has the status of Party dignitary, administration bigwig, or high government official. The indisputable convenience of having oranges and foreign-made toys to one's heart's content throughout infancy is challenged by the dark, real danger waylaying a prominent Communist at each step. In communism, political failures and defeats are irreparable. They are not setbacks, but catastrophes; they do not result in misfortune, but in ruin and they tend to strike one with the unexpected abruptness of a thunderbolt. Rarely do they pass without marking the loser's progeny for the rest of his life.

In addition to these possibilities there is an immense variety of bad origins. The diversity of traps is effectively smoothed by the physiology of the lie in communism. The lie has a special function and is a new element in the new social order. Morally, the lie is the most ambivalent factor in the Communist "esse"— at the same time an evil distortion, or annihilation, of truth, and the blessed rescue and sole shelter for millions of human beings. The use of the lie as an instrument to compensate for fate's blindness is as old as the world: history is filled with people who knew well how to correct the unacceptable locations of their birthplaces. What communism introduces as new is the scale and insolence of the lie: it is not seldom that the Communist press describes a Marxist saint as having been born under a milling machine at which his exploited mother had to sweat with no time for decent delivery—even if everyone knows him as a son of a prerevolutionary blood-sucking grocer.

## 2 • How to survive a maternity hospital and a state-controlled nursery

FROM THE very first moment of his life a newcomer to the Communist world is supposed to be extremely watchful. Nursing is one of the worst, most underpaid jobs; nurses are tired and inadvertent, and there have been a few widely known scandals involving exchanged infants in the mammoth state-owned hospitals in Communist cities and towns. As a result, a new Communist citizen learns from the beginning that it is more sensible not to rely on the state's service, but to take care of oneself.

Quite early, while still in the nursery, he is first given clues to the fundamental attitude toward him as a human being and an individual. A story was told in Warsaw about a young mother who calls at a state nursery, impatient to see and pick up her baby after a long working day's separation. The nurse brings the child, the young mother hugs her little thing, then exclaims, "But, Comrade Nurse, for God's sake! This is *not* my daughter!" The nurse smiles indulgently. "What's the big fuss about? What's the difference? You'd bring her back tomorrow in the morning, before going to work as it is, wouldn't you?"

# 3 · How to be a child

THE PROBLEMS of awareness, of consciousness, which vex a person throughout his entire life, begin disturbingly early under communism. It follows, therefore, that being a child in a Communist society is difficult, even without one's being aware of it. In a democracy a child is untroubled by things that don't concern childhood; it enjoys the priceless right of nonawareness. The problems of choice, differentiation, and value judgments possess an exclusively pedagogical significance for it. The unique pleasure of childhood is precisely the freedom from the intimidations of criticism that belabor the adult at every step. The child has the right to enthusiasm and faith uncontrolled by reason, the instinct for self-preservation, or irony. Under communism, however, this right is denied the child; it is annulled by the very structure of daily life.

After its seizure of power, communism assumes all the features of a state religion. The consecration of ideas and customs is both the right and the privilege of state religions, and communism takes abundant advantage of it. In general, the beatification of people and events does not become a source of anxiety for the human masses subservient to communism; societies produce derisive antitoxins, wit exposes the hollowness of false liturgies. Children represent the one social group defenseless before the hypocrisy of artificial deities.

23

The child is sensitized to holiness; it yearns for it, its consciousness is fertile ground for beings elevated by piety, goodness, nobility, and beauty, and destined for adoration. The child longs for nothing so much as for charisma, unction, and adoration, and among communism's most passionate ambitions is the desire to be adored in conceptual structures raised by it, in temples of its own significance, in the figures of charismatic and consecrated leaders who rule in the name of communism.

From the earliest moments of awakened consciousness the child is thus surrounded by symbols and signs which it is obliged to worship. The frequency of their repetition at each step drums mercilessly on the child's soft little cerebrum. And so the child worships, adores the color red, scythes and hammers, and state dignitaries. At a relatively early stage it begins to perceive godlike figures. Whichever direction it turns to, it encounters a plethora of Marxes, Lenins, and the host of lesser, local saints. They stand erect on monuments, hang on the walls of public places, flutter on banners; books, papers, and television are full of them. They arouse pious respect by their appearance of holiness; from the very beginning they become associated in the child's mind with some superior order and some indeterminate power. If communism went no further than this stratification of impressions and their reflections in the child's consciousness, children would experience no great damage; in all social systems the child is given colorful official figures for the purpose of naive rapture. But communism has other goals for children that go much further than the inculcation of esteem and adoration. Communism wishes for love; it wants the child to love it.

To realize this end it employs unusual equipment for the activation of the child's consciousness and perception. With the help of the talents of retouchers it transforms worthy and dignified Lenins and Stalins into beloved and tender Lenins and Stalins. The child knows nothing about the existence of special retouching agencies whose prime task is the remaking of the expressions of the faces of Party and state worthies. In Soviet Russia entire regiments of specially trained retouchers have worked as diligently as ants to remake the face of Lenin, which

24

radiated a rare maliciousness and shrewdness, into the face of a beloved old uncle whom children are wild about, the type who would hand over to them his gold timepiece for certain destruction. Stalin, as we know, was distinguished by the kind of face that would have stopped Al Capone dead in his tracks; the wildness of his nature, the baseness and cruelty of his character, leap out from every uncensored photograph. But then, that's what skilled retouchers are for. In millions of nurseries and elementary schools throughout the entire imperium a fatherly portrait of Stalin used to appear, embellished with so radiant a smile that it would be hard to imagine a child who wouldn't dream of climbing up on the generalissimo's lap and tugging his moustaches. And what remains to be said of the veritable army of sycophantic and servile artists and illustrators who in hundreds of millions of children's books have portrayed Stalin as the personification of everything delectable? In time it even reached the point where it was possible to discover the features of Lenin, Stalin, Ulbricht, and Mao in the cherubic little faces of Orphan Annie, Snow White, and Little Red Riding Hood, while the Big Bad Wolf always seemed to have something American about him.

Someone will say: Well, after all, presidents, senatorial candidates, and ministers in democratic capitalism in order to win the approbation of the crowds also like to be photographed patting the golden curls of little children or taking them into their arms and kissing their chubby cheeks with false smiles of pseudo-kindliness on their cunning lips while their shrewd eyes ferret out the voters. That's a fact, to be sure, but that sickly-sweet little smile is an easily discernible mask concealing a natural repulsion for damp noses and unpredictable little behinds. Democratic men of state do not as a rule employ the services of retouchers to disguise their true natures. Western statesmen and politicians do use makeup, usually when facing a TV camera; they do it to look younger and better, which bespeaks their weakness for vanity, but cannot be deemed a sinful lie. And children somehow, in their own special way, sense this. They don't take the politicians and statesmen seriously, nobody discourses about love, trust, and submission, and the whole business is merely a pleasant and honorable kind of game. It just happens to be a convention of life, as it were, that at certain moments politicians need children, but there are no speeches about feelings and no mutual self-deception.

In order to preserve psychic well-being the child ought to demand the restoration of his rights to a neutralized Puss-in-Boots and Ferdinand the Bull, but what talk can there be of demanding rights in a system in which the writ of habeas corpus does not exist? The child thus remains robbed of his privilege of nonawareness. He still adores and loves with his whole, pure little heart, but the first awkward doubts begin insinuating themselves. Why does beloved Uncle Stalin of the portrait in the nursery suddenly become the downright stern Stalin of the picture in the post office where you have to go with Mamma? How is it that adults don't see in him the magnanimity that the child perceives and speak about him unsympathetically or try instead to say nothing and keep putting off questions on the subject? In Party families the child comes into contact with a directed adoration which in turn arouses understandable suspicions. "Why do I have to be polite and love Stalin?" Wherever it turns there appear signs of an oppressive and puzzling ambivalence, which shatter the delights of nonawareness.

In a certain small Hungarian city, immediately after the suppression of the 1956 insurrection by Soviet tanks, the Communists—with a tact unique to them—erected a monument to Soviet-Hungarian friendship. Passing by it, a little boy asked his father, "Daddy, what's that?" "That's a monument to Soviet-Hungarian friendship," replied his father in concord with the appearance of reality. "But why in our country, Daddy?" the boy asked, desiring further explanation. At a relatively early stage in his life the boy has already taken a stand in the struggle against the ambiguity and equivocation that will in time poison his life; he has entered the unequal battle with all-crushing falsehood and the omnipotence of appearance. But this historical moment of the awakening of his critical faculty has ended, or at least shaken, his childhood world. Antitotalitarian social systems, on the other hand, respect the sovereignty of this world. Its silly little bears and rabbits perhaps do not contribute outstandingly to the development of the child's intelligence, but they do not rob the child of the sole area of autonomy and nonengagement in his life. The issue of Santa Claus is a characteristic case in point.

In Russia Santa Claus has been replaced in his annual functions by a certain Grandfather Frost, a figure drawn from Old Russian folk mythology. For many years Grandfather Frost effectively carried out his duties under the watchful eye and control of the security organs of the USSR. But somehow he still failed to arouse a warm, sincere response, perhaps on account of his name. On some metaphysical principle or other, children denied him tender affection, even children born long after the Revolution, whose parents would have been afraid to formulate so antistate a slogan as "good Saint Nick." In Khrushchev's time people began to speak about returning his old title to this important functionary. The old Catholic countries which were occupied by Communist armies after World War II were forced to accept Grandfather Frost along with the beneficences of economic planning. From the very beginning the enterprise was destined for trouble. Launched intensively in the press, on radio and television, and by official performances and parties for children, Grandfather Frost became exclusively an object of malicious jokes. Children overwhelmingly rejected all emotional ties to him—but at what cost? At the cost of the subsequent destruction of the sovereignty of their world. Once a year children fell into the despair of schizophrenia. How was it possible to reconcile the mass-media–sponsored propaganda campaign in behalf of Grandfather Frost with the Santa Claus stubbornly supported by the rest of society? "Santa Claus is coming to see you today," a mother would say to her offspring in the morning, while in the afternoon, at some children's ball, the saint would introduce himself officially with the words, "I am Grandfather Frost." When children called him Santa Claus in harmony with the mood of the entire nation, he would wink knowingly as if to give them to understand that there were people in the hall at the time who were not supposed to know his true name. And sometimes, when tugged too rashly by the sleeve and importuned about other saints, he would mumble wryly, "Beat it, kid, or I'll have you pulled in for whispered propaganda." Something clearly wasn't right here, in the children's eyes, but what? It is difficult to determine without first reading *Problems of Leninism,* but a person who reads this work at the age of five is indeed rare.

During the period of the Stalinist degradation of great masses of human beings, children in nurseries or even in the poorest orphans' shelters were summoned, or as it was said then, "organized," to offer up their miniscule savings to buy presents for beloved Grandfather Stalin. Such an appeal fell on receptive ground, for it is easier to approach a child with a request for an act of dedication than for the cessation of senseless shouting. And so the children gave, extracted coins from the pockets of their pinafores, bought plasticene, and made and sent forth little figures for the Savior and Patron of Humanity. And they doubtless would have been shocked had they been told that their devotion and dedication were planned by Party economists as an important element in the struggle against inflation and the extravagant consumption of chocolate, which is so difficult to produce and supply to the market in the necessary quantities. But once upon a time when a little girl was summoned to a drive for presents for the murderer of Marshal Tukachevsky, she is supposed to have said, "But why don't I get presents from him?" This is the answer she got from her conformist schoolteacher: "Stalin gave you everything you've got—your country, your freedom, your happy childhood." But the little girl couldn't be put down and replied coldly, "I want a pair of shoes!" This little girl surely deserves a place in the pantheon of great champions of the sense of contemporary civilization, and perhaps not without reason this event is said to have taken place in Königsberg-Kaliningrad, the city of the author of the *Critique of Pure Reason.* For under communism the cultivation of this critique is frequently in the hands of children.

A child does not know how and does not like to hate, but it

knows how and likes to be afraid. This is something communism doesn't overlook. To the extent that communism has a subconscious, its libido is the desire to sow fear and a perverse longing for love in the souls of its victims. Like a system of codes, this desire and longing are concealed in various euphemisms. The child becomes a superb partner in all this. It does not know how to defend itself, is easily terrified, and willingly and trustingly seeks protection in the arms of the person frightening it. The science of terrifying children is a delight of communism, and the dreams of Communist sorcerers of implanting fear in a person for his entire life represent the libidinous sublimation of this delight. How many future propaganda successes can be carried out on people with degenerated reflexes and perceptual paresis as the result of childhood fears? The whole matter boils down to knowing how to operate skillfully with symbols of fear.

Once upon a time one such symbol was the pig-faced bourgeois. Today it's the terrible lean American with an awful hooknose and a star-covered top hat perched on his head, looking remarkably like the devil of Christian iconography. In remote out-of-the-way collective farms the American is used to frighten children. Not because an American means anything to people who have never seen one with their own eyes, but precisely because he means nothing and functions as no more than a symbol established by an occasion not subject to control.

Radio, television, and the press replace the priest and the sermon in the formation of psycho-conceptual hideousness and teach, in the aureola of supernatural technology, that the American is an eater of children. Once upon a time superstitious nannies used to threaten, "The devil's going to come and carry you off to the woods." Nowadays, however, burdened by want and toil beyond her strength, the village mother says, trusting in the power of the celebration of slogans pressing in on the child from all sides, "If you don't behave, I'll hand you over to an American who'll take you away to America." In the light of Party exegesis this is an apocalyptic ultimatum, but later on in life one learns it would have been worth being such a horrible child in order to receive such a true reward. In this respect the

29

Christian system of punishments demonstrates its incontrovertible superiority and finesse.

In fairness it ought to be pointed out that American children's comic books are full of terrifying creatures called Reds. They possess sharply etched ethnic features, chiefly conveyed by upsetting faces, loose-fitting Russian blouses on men instead of shirts, or slanted eyes characterizing the latest polycentric deviation in the bosom of the Cominform. The difference in the method of indoctrination does not seem great, yet somehow I never recall having heard of children in America being frightened by Russians or Communists. There exists a profound analogy between the Red of the comic books and the dragon of ancient fairy tales. It's as though one really *should* be afraid of him, but there's something in him that's not quite for real, so it is possible to permit oneself a lack of hatred. This arrangement mirrors, it seems, some sort of profound correctness. As long as there is no military confrontation, Russia faces a greater danger from America than if the obverse were true. Russia must propagate fear of the American among its children, while America can allow itself the luxury of pleasant contempt and the pulp-magazine victories of Batman over Smersh. The use of fear is, after all, a double-edged sword and submits to the variety and richness of life itself.

Informed by radio and television, the child in a Communist state demands supplemental explication. "Daddy," he asks, "what's a warmonger?" Inasmuch as the parents are not Party people and accurately informed, they themselves don't know and try to extricate themselves by means of a convenient but obscurantist idiom: "That's an American, or someone from the West"; or still less precisely: "That's someone they write about in the papers." And the child again sets sail on the sea of muddied distinctions. Lack of trust in the newspapers, radio, or television is an imperative scattered in the very air one breathes; one meets it in every word, gesture, glance, and sigh of older people. If they speak ill of someone on the radio, then perhaps he really isn't so bad? Perhaps he's different from the way they write about him, perhaps he doesn't have financial problems like everyone else, perhaps he's even got a car? Such are the discomforts of an awakening awareness.

Not being prone to doubt, the child is sentenced to a lost battle with communism. "Let's play Five Year Plan!" children call out in a yard or on the street, in the same tone in which they used to say to each other, "Let's play store." But under communism a store is unattractive, gray, barren, a place of boredom and torture for those who as a rule cannot find in it what they have come for and what should be available in it. On the other hand, the Five Year Plan exists everywhere in colorful posters which take the place of the lighthearted cereal ads of capitalism. The child does not know that the Five Year Plan is one huge mistake precisely thanks to which there is nothing in the stores. That is why it yields to mystification against which the sole defense is derisive doubt.

Cynicism is a real help. The child who can manage to be polite and cynical at the same time is in the best position to thrust back most effectively the assaults on his consciousness and the plunder of his childhood world. But it is easier for a child to be a vandal, a barbarian, a murderer, a rapist, a torturer, a sadist, a liar, than a cynic. Entering a Communist toy store demands considerable strength of character and only extraordinary individuals avoid giving up and fleeing in panic before the concentration of ugliness accumulated in the squint-eyed dolls, sadistic teddy bears, rheumatism-twisted giraffes, clowns made of velveteen used, in civilized countries, for sitting in trains, tops that in the name of some unknown sabotage refuse to spin, and balls that lack the energy to bounce back from the floor. Set face to face with such junk, a cynical child won't dissolve in tears but will just smile understandingly.

Toys have been the subject of animated discussions in the press since the dawn of communism: nobody seems to be able to understand why the toy-making industry is not in a position to produce goods that do not evoke an immediate groan at the very sight of them. The error doubtless lies in the theory that insists on the principle that a toy should instruct and not amuse. In the hands of the same planners, who believe in the instructional value of presents for Stalin purchased with the pennies scraped together by children, pedagogy observes that a kitten is not something that one ought to love, but a member of the socialist animal world and that a child should have the proper attitude toward the kitten befitting such membership. The "Komis" shops (commission shops where Western goods are sold), collectively one of the most potent economic institutions in Communist society, are full of toys from the capitalist world; everyone knows, to be sure, that it pays to import them. The ordinary child lets loose the wildest sounds of delight and greed at the sight of a Komis shop simply because he wants to have at once everything that's inside it. The cynical child, on the other hand, conducts himself calmly. He knows that the prices in the Komis shops are absurdly high and that relatively few people can afford to purchase the toys in them, and for sure not his own parents. Even from the wealthiest parents the cynical child does not ask for oranges; it understands that oranges in a store are a miracle of nature, appearing once a year, and that one should not demand miracles—one has to wait for them. It's good to be a cynical child under communism; everyone loves such children and their own parents speak about them with pride. "Such a wonderful child," they praise, not knowing that the kid is simply a cynic trying to make life easy for himself.

# 4 · How to go to school

THE COMMUNIST SCHOOL looks very much like the school in a democracy. Many of the schools, in fact, look even better, since schools represent favorite visiting places for official guests from abroad, hostile journalists, and excursions of Communists from countries where the Party hasn't yet come to power. The schools are attractive, modern buildings planned by the very best architects, endowed with spacious classrooms, impressive windows which admit much sun and air, and desks and other school aids all in accord with the latest findings of pedagogy. Children, as we are well aware, can express a host of feelings except irony, from which it follows that they can be of inestimable assistance in all acts of propaganda. The child shouts "Yes!" or "No!" but cannot give voice to his disapproval in a melancholic and ambivalent way—as any worker does who knows how to avoid the risk of repression. That's why it is better to show guests around schools than factories.

A keen and attentive observer, if he can escape the solicitude of his tour leaders for a while and peek into a classroom unprepared in advance for a formal inspection, or visit, will immediately perceive a drastic divergence between the smartness of the architecture and the general state inside the building. One can say it's a state bordering on devastation that gives pause for thought. Even the most exemplary school, delivered over to the dynamics of hundreds of young creatures the imperative of whose life is an extreme disdain for everything belonging to the state, is soon transformed into a junk heap. The poor quality of Communist products—and this includes building materials, methods of construction, and outfitting—utterly unfit for the struggle with time, plays a great role in the process of disintegration.

The press and television adore showing the schools to the rest of society, hoping to demonstrate by them the magnificent attainments of communism. They do this, however, with considerable skill and, one is forced to admit, charm, always remembering not to show what they don't have to. Tactically, this is a splendid move, and because of it many students are led to believe that only their particular school looks so awful, while all the others in the country look just the way they show them on television. This simple method of indoctrination possesses, theoretically, features of genius; in practice, however, the results are completely the opposite of those intended. In the beginning the students ascribe the physical downfall of their own school to local imperfections. From early childhood they develop a firsthand knowledge of the paltriness and wretchedness of the life around them and its discordance with the symbolic representations of that life in the press, films, and propaganda posters, but they think that it's so bad just *here,* in their particular school, and that somewhere else things have to be better. The conviction, though, that *nothing* is being done to save their school, that it's just not being photographed and filmed since a new, *exemplary* school is doing to be put up in its place, forces them to reflection. They still don't know that under communism it's easier to build something new than to maintain something already built in a state of good repair, to say nothing about improving it. The question of repair and renovation is the key problem, in a spiritual as well as a material sense, since communism still remains paralyzed by the magical impossibility of correcting something that has lost its ability to function. So it is that when the pupil ceases to be a pupil but hasn't yet reached the age of maturity, he learns—unless he's an exceptional idiot

—one of the basic laws of existence under communism, namely, that what is promulgated as a rule is always the exception, while the apparent exception is really the rule. He then grasps once and forever the first commandment of propaganda, which under communism is the sole instrument for shaping human consciousness sanctified by theory and which will accompany him the rest of his life.

The metaphysical injunction demanding a predatory relationship to everything governmental, which assumes the form now of appropriation, now of a disinterested destructiveness, represents something on the order of the instinct for self-preservation, a kind of *élan vital* with which one comes into the world under communism. It would be easy to call it vandalism, but vandalism is rooted in a senseless delight in annihilation, while what I have in mind crystallizes in a dark, almost biological, injunction to redress wrongs whose source is the unfathomable, mysterious concept of the state. Government officials, police, and soldiers, or, in other words, the oppressors in the name of the state, although hated, arouse inexplicable evil passions in the ordinary person less than the state itself, which takes on the semblance of an element always directed against man. The humanness of the individual oppressor and his struggle with life are perceptible, whereas the impersonality of the state evokes a mystical hatred, like sin in the Middle Ages. Home life nurses this impulse and cultivates, sometimes with sedulous frankness, the saying, "It's only the state's." This has the effect of absolving every excess, while the only moral precept is the effective avoidance of being caught redhanded and, of course, being punished. The leaders of communism are aware of this state of affairs, and that is why the school must be the first stage in a person's life where the attempt is made to uproot the vice. In a democracy the task of the school is the preparation of a person for life in general and the transmission to him of a sufficient quantity of knowledge to enable him to continue to develop. The Communist school, on the other hand, has as its goal the preparation for life *under communism,* or the transmission exclusively of information essential to the formation of a person whom communism will be able to use to its own advantage. Officially, this is called the formation of the individual capable of sacrificing his life for his society. In practice, it looks like this:

History textbooks have nothing in common with history, their prime task being the glorification, not the codification, of facts. This leads to some amazing results. To take one example: The thoughts and deeds of medieval national heroes, kings, and clergymen are explained and motivated in the language of contemporary press reports proclaiming the accomplishments of Communists. It turns out that the Crusades were the undertaking of Catholic warmongers attempting thereby to direct the class anger of a downtrodden people to the path of imperialistic adventures.

From the study of literature it appears that Goethe's *Faust* is an expression of the poet's attachment to folk tradition and the idea of progress, since the ancient legend about Faust's conflict with Mephistopheles reflects the aspirations of the laboring masses for independence from religion.

In the days of the Stalinist tyranny, schooling, together with all culture, plunged into the chaos of a neobarbarity which didn't even bother about the appearances of probability. Thus it was taught in the schools that during World War II the Allies had a secret accord with Hitler and that only the stunning victories of the Soviet Union under the leadership of the genius Stalin inclined them to deceive Hitler and join up with the triumphing Red Army.

Because the Russians were the first to bring about a Communist revolution, it is therefore a logical deduction that they are the source and chief motivating power of the whole of contemporary civilization. Moreover, science and knowledge, monopolized by the capitalists, falsified facts, which now demand rectification. In consequence of this rectification, it appears in Communist schoolbooks that a Russian invented the steam engine, that radio was also a Russian invention, that it was the Russians who erected the first Gothic cathedral and who were the first people in history to open a store.

In Polish schools quick-witted students eagerly asserted in

36

examinations that steps were the invention of a Russian named Ivan Stepov, that Kristov Timofeevich Kolumbov discovered America, and that electricity was given to the world by a certain gentleman named Beniamin Franklinienko.

As we know, it is the school, from one end of the globe to the other, that strives to inculcate the first loyalties. In democracies such teaching centers on the relations of man with man, as well as with the social community surrounding him, frequently designated as the nation but not treated as the highest value. Manifestations of skepticism toward implanted truths, or ways of thinking and behaving, are regarded as proof of mental activity and even intelligence. In Communist schools pupils are inculcated above all with the dogma of the Party absolute, which must confirm their conviction once and for all that the Communist Party is the blessed giver and equitable regulator of *everything,* that the coincidence of the interests of *all* citizens, as well as of their dreams, plans, kitchens, hats, dogs, cats, and razors, with the interests of the Party can never be doubted. From this it follows that even the faintest sign of skepticism or reservation concerning any aspect of the Party or its policies is immediately taken as a manifestation of revolt against inviolable truths and sanctities. In order to finish school and receive official certification, which is indispensable for further studies and essential for numerous accommodations in life, one has to:

—listen, but not speak, unless absolutely necessary;

—agree, when speaking becomes necessary, with every official point of view and praise it as the only one that is fair, wise, and good;

—pay no heed, when praising, to any criteria of rationalism, erudition, probability, or even common sense.

In Stalin's time the use of such expressions as "Stalin, our omniscient Father, who created all of us, animated us, gave us eternal happiness and was the first to formulate the Pythagorean theorem" guaranteed the best grades in mathematics. The skillful villification of an enemy of Stalin as "a Trotsky vampire unsatiated even by the blood of the working people" or "a Tukhachevsky fascist murderer of workers" gave proof of consider-

37

able political industry at a young age and indicated that the speaker read newspapers, since the enemies of Stalin did not even exist in textbooks. The October Revolution is described in such textbooks without even a single mention of Trotsky, but in accounts of the hardships of the first Five Year Plans and the famous Moscow trials of the thirties the term *Trotskyite* appears all of a sudden as the embodiment of demonic evil. Each pupil was made to understand that only Stalin, with the help of Lenin, brought about the Revolution, that he alone won the Civil War, built up industry and socialism, after which, again all by himself, he perfunctorily vanquished the Germans, Italians, and Japanese.

Such a striking abuse of truth and probability (strongly rationalized and modified in the post-Stalin era but comprising still a methodological foundation in schools) leads to basic divisions in the school community. The school age is an age of awakening curiosities; young boys and girls begin to take an ever wider interest in the environment around them, and what they see and perceive inclines them to contradictoriness—the first form of criticism. At home they become aware of endless difficulties, a constant lack of money and the most necessary household things, the primitivism of existence, the murderous overworking of their mothers and fathers in pursuit of mere subsistence. In school they are taught that they live in the most perfect of societies where people *must* be happy. In Party families they see an all-embracing fear before power, authority, and responsibility; they hear the servile slogans of prayers prescribed by the Party. In school they learn about how capitalism stifles, humiliates, and degrades man, while socialism elevates him. But in this age of technology and electronics nothing can prevent the penetration and circulation of even the simplest news. The school age is the time when one first hears a French or American song in which the *complete* absence of a note of propaganda is discovered with stupefaction; when an illustrated magazine from the West falls into one's hands, full of pictures of things, clothes, people, cars, all of which look immeasurably *better* than what one sees around one or in domestic publications; when a film is seen the subject of which is *exclusively* love or adventure. The school, however, moves at once to counter these impressions, teaching that Western democratic tinsel and publicity in fact mask the boundless misery of huge masses of people. In one school textbook, at the beginning of the fifties, there was a picture of emaciated children lying on a sidewalk, illustrating how children were dying of hunger in the streets of New York in the vicinity of Wall Street. But one would have to be an exceptionally weakly developed individual intellectually not to grasp the catastrophic contradictions among the assertions disseminated at school. Gaps in reasoning increase, while one is not free to ask questions because to do so would arouse the suspicions of overzealous teachers or companions in political organizations. For this reason there occurs a stratification of the school community into three basic groups.

The first group are the silent. They make up the overwhelming majority. They question nothing, they never express personal opinions. They just want to get through school as quickly as possible and receive their diploma.

The second group are the cynics. They talk a lot and in a tone of marked servility, but you can see that they absolutely don't believe what they are saying. While they go through the motions of accepting everything they are asked to believe, their acceptance bears features of a patent mockery, but a mockery so cautious that they can't be faulted on anything. They early came to the conclusion that the only freedom they could acquire under communism was the freedom not to have faith in anything, or the right to an unbounded, odious contempt for the price of ostentatious agreement. Their goal is the acquisition while still in school of a reputation which later will guarantee them a career and material success. That is the reputation of someone submissive, though unconvinced, willing to serve any cause in exchange for the appropriate recompense.

The third group are the idealists. Their youthful need for faith is so strong that they even believe what the school teaches them. There are very few of them. Usually, they come from families of devoted Party members in high positions, from a sphere, in other words, isolated from the rest of society. Their parents sometimes are people of a high personal caliber, which determines their idealism. In school these idealists constitute the pillars of political organizations. Standing behind them is the might of the state, the social system, and the apparatus of power. A consequence of this power is that their youthful awkwardness in operating with such a fund of strength becomes a source of numerous misfortunes and abuses for other people. Naturally, representatives of the third group are surrounded on all sides by universal hatred, which frequently they don't deserve, but which only strengthens their conviction that ruthlessness is wisdom.

The question arises: Doesn't anyone ever oppose? Doesn't the basic disharmony between the explanation of the world and the world itself arouse opposition, protest, resistance in anyone? From time to time there do appear rebellious youths who take the floor during lectures and childishly formulate their blundering *veto*. In Stalin's time such a performance qualified one for immediate expulsion from school and this was tantamount to the mandatory abandonment of all further formal education. There are well-known episodes, in Eastern Europe as well as in Russia, where the political police hauled teen-age students out of schools and held them in jail for years, without trial, simply because they dared raise doubts about who first started the war in Korea. In the post-Stalinist era such practices have undergone considerable modification; nevertheless, the principle of the pitiless suppression of "doubting Thomases" still prevails in the schools. Its most fearsome instrument is the complete isolation and silencing of the facts of resistance. When students in a democracy express their dissatisfaction, the mass media gives them broad coverage; any of the repressions that may follow are likewise made public knowledge, with the result that sympathy for the disaffected is aroused. Sometimes this sympathy becomes the foundation of their victory, if simply as a triumph of fairness. In Communist societies the act of defiance in school, even if supported by several hundred pupils, is tightly silenced by the mass media. Repression follows, usually very severe and brutal, but nobody makes any prideful fuss about it either. The repression remains in force until the resistance is crushed, and the gratification of fame never occurs. There is nobody to whom appeal may be made, since the press, courts, and police are in the same hands of those who do the suppressing. The strange symbiosis of Marx and centuries of Byzantine-Asiatic perfections in the exercise of tyranny has shaped the Communist belief that the only truly effective repression is that which is not trumpeted or publicized. Thus very early under communism the student learns the *impossibility* of struggle against wrong, from which follows a general esteem for apathy and inertia as the sole road to success.

The chief instrument of punishment in schools is the political organization. In Stalin's time belonging to it was mandatory. Whoever was lucky enough to find himself outside it had no chance of getting good scholarships or continuing his studies at a university since only the recommendation of the school political organization assured entry into the required qualifying examinations. The youth organization then was a cross between a scouting club and the Holy Inquisition. Its prime responsibility was concern for the purity of the students' souls; its fuel, devotion and bigotry. If the organization arranged a little dance or an excursion into the country, those who were unable to participate for one reason or another automatically became enemies of the system, or agents of the CIA, or victims of the perfidious propaganda of the Voice of America. When the young people who did participate enjoyed themselves, the spokesman for the organization explained that their pleasure was to the credit of the Revolution and the class struggle; when the snacks were tasty, he called for an expression of gratitude to the Party and its leaders.

Everything that was done, everything that was served, attested to the existence of a Communist super-reason. Accompanying the helping of little old ladies across the streets was the observation that the act of assistance was executed to the praise of Lenin, the Protector of Humankind. The school organization arrogated to itself complete judgment over the soul of each and every student. A harsh injunction obliged public confession at

41

plenary sessions and an inviolable system for the expiation of sin existed. Boys and girls confessed or accused each other mutually of a base passion for chewing gum and with tears in their eyes swore never again to submit to such devilish temptations of capitalism. When someone learned poorly, it meant that the CIA had sunk its feelers into the school. Informing was elevated to the level of the highest virtue. Everyone had the right to accuse a friend, or a teacher, of "wrong-think." Proofs of guilt were not demanded, since the fate of the accused was decided in advance. A boy in too colorful socks or a girl in a nonregulation hairdo were denounced as counter-revolutionaries and expelled from school, without the right of enrolling at any other. The charge of listening to jazz records or foreign radio programs frequently ended in arrest by the political police. Certain organizations demanded the reporting of private family conversations, after which they proudly turned over the acquired information to the secret police, all very much in the spirit of so-called social action or voluntary work for the betterment of socialism. The police patted students affectionately on the cheeks and awarded them prizes in the form of works of Lenin and Stalin. Obviously, even in this period of the complete degeneration of mind and instincts, mankind was still capable of producing humanistic antibiotics against degradation and stupidity. The speeches of juvenile zealots were a source of intoxicating humor and everyone knew how to laugh at them in such a way as not to invite arrest. The clandestine enjoyment of Louis Armstrong, Ella Fitzgerald, or Elvis Presley assumed the character of so sophisticated a pleasure that there are people to this very day who consider those conspiratorial sessions huddled over radios the most charming moments of their lives.

The school organization forejudged the fate of pupils and teachers alike. Unless they demonstrated eagerness in serving up the necessary commonplaces or were influential members of the Party, teachers lived in constant terror and dread. A stupid or bad student who enjoyed the support of the organization had guaranteed good grades—otherwise the organization accused the teacher of repressing young Communists. To this very day the teacher's life in a Communist school remains a hell, even if he is a conformist or an opportunist with no desire or intention of fighting for truth or justice. He is poorly paid, works in chronically overcrowded classrooms, and constantly faces humiliation at the hands of his own pupils. Even the dumbest nitwit can force him to submit, declaring coolly, "I advise you, sir, not to annoy me too much. You don't know who my daddy is and what he can do." If it so happens that Daddy is an influential member of the Party or a high official in the administration, he can, in fact, do quite a bit. Cases where the children of state and Party dignitaries received diplomas with distinction after committing crimes in school for which one is normally packed off to jail have been and continue to be in the daily order of things.

Post-Stalinist leaders made a bold effort to improve conditions in the schools. Membership in the school organization, outside of Russia, ceased to be obligatory. However, the basic principle of the supremacy of dogma over intellect, or even common sense, never was abolished anywhere. There are no longer any restrictions against publicly dancing to rock 'n' roll music or wearing miniskirts, but the student is still constantly taught in school that the inhabitant of a Communist country lives more freely and better than anyone else on the face of the earth. The better he learns, though, the more effectively does he reach his own conclusions about that.

43

# 5 • What to do after school

A SOCIALIST ECONOMY doesn't develop, it gemmates. By this I mean that each sector of the economy doesn't experience organic changes dictated by human needs and the logic of supply and demand, but is shaped by a so-called economic plan, or theoretical foundation, evolved from political and propagandistic criteria and set into motion by centrally formulated decrees. In this way, a factory, or any other enterprise, does not receive as many workers as it needs in order to function efficiently, but as many as it *must* employ in accord with a plan. Apropos of this, Communist official offices are filled with small armies of people whose only chore is sealing envelopes addressed in advance by people other than those who wrote the letters. Of course, each of these workers receives a salary offering no possibility of subsistence—1000 *zlotys* a month in Poland, for example, where the poorest quality suit of clothes costs 800. As a result, he achieves the height of artistry in the indifference with which he approaches his job and carries it out with a negligence bordering on the awesome. Thus when any of the aforementioned letters falls on the floor on its tortuous route from one desk to another, nobody ever bends down to pick it up. This necessitates the hiring of new employees whose task will be the picking up of letters that have fallen on the floor and the eventual (though

44

not inevitable, since new, unforeseen difficulties can arise) dispatching of them further on their journey. Such a process of multiplying the work force of the country is called gemmation.

Gemmation has the virtue of permitting the employment of any quantity of people supplied to the labor market, without assuming any responsibility for their subsistence. Reasoning correctly, this eliminates the problem of unemployment, but correct reasoning never got anyone anywhere under communism. The number of jobs paying salaries *impossible* to subsist on is so large that people avoid them, preferring not to do anything rather than work for a salary out of which at the end of the month it's not even possible to pay the rent and buy food and cigarettes, let alone three shirts. Moreover, in every Communist society there exists a certain number of citizens who "are not employed." In Stalinist times the reasons for such unemployment were exclusively political; if someone had fought against the Germans in some non-Communist partisan organization, or came from a family which had exploited workers before the war (the muddiness of this formulation permitted its applicability to anyone the new leaders disapproved of, including the exploited workers themselves), it was enough to preclude the possibility of getting any work. After the fall of Stalinism the political criterion lost all meaning, but a person's social views still remained a consideration. Let's say, for example, that someone protested too loudly against poor working conditions and a miserable salary, or against the high-handedness of Party superiors, for which he was dismissed from his job. The stigma of "antisocial agitator" clings to him wherever he goes and makes it impossible for him to find new employment. There is no way such a stigma can be removed, even though it be most unjust, because professional unions are fictitious institutions in Communist countries as far as the rights of workers are concerned; they are directed by trusted members of the Party or the political police and their operating principle is the unbending defense of their state employer.

A young person who finishes school in such a system has several roads open to him. He can try to be admitted to higher studies, for one. Getting into a university certainly is no easy job, but it's well worth every effort.

If he happens to possess technical abilities, he can go on to a trade school. Specialization is in great demand and assures better working conditions and remuneration. Trade schools do not require the completion of a full secondary school education; they accept students earlier and grant further educational opportunities up to and including the degree of engineer. Industry still continues to be the best-paid branch of the economy, but specialization in the service trades, apart from the fact that it leads to the depths of a chaos whose dimensions nobody in the West is in a position to imagine (a Communist airline can only be compared to the suffocating *nightmare* of an American airline employee), can still become a source of relative success. Of course, a young man may enter the job market as an ordinary worker in industry where he will be able to earn well in proportion to the outlay of labor and immeasurably better than in other trades. That is because socialism, as practice has shown, and despite the assurances of the theorists, turns *against* the interests of workers once it assumes power. For that reason it fears the worker in very much the same way that capitalism does and strives to maintain with him as correct relations as possible.

But a young person doesn't share this attitude. Today socialist societies are the most hierarchical class structures in the contemporary world. Social position, separated from any economic determinants, has very much the same significance as it did under feudalism. It is not fitting to be a common laborer, and whoever can possibly help it does not become one. This explains all the better the neverending supply of individual talents for addressing envelopes or any other occupation, no matter how sterile, that can be considered pseudointellectual or at least nonphysical, even if the earnings from it aren't enough to cover three square meals a day. Nevertheless, punching index cards in an office continues to be considered a springboard for some other, better destiny, whereas physical labor, except where it is undertaken in pure snobbism by a young writer anxious for

46

self-abasement, remains a hopeless, wretched dead end from which there is no escape.

There exists, however, another possibility, which depends entirely on a human quality known as enterprise. Contrary to the myths disseminated beyond the sphere of communism, the source of which is Marxist ethical theory, money is still one of the basic regulators of life in Communist societies. The possession of money does not, to be sure, guarantee the attainment of whatever one desires, but it does assure all possibilities for acquiring advantages. Everything inevitably leads, therefore, to ways of getting the money necessary to assuring oneself a comfortable niche in society. When he leaves school, a young person sees well-dressed and well-fed people, unburdened by material worries, able to acquire an automobile or a trip out of the country with remarkable ease—the twin acmes of success beyond the reach even of the daydreams of millions of people. When he asks, in keeping with the ideas inculcated in him in school, what *important* and *useful* contributions these people are making to society to warrant such exceptional recompense, nobody is able to come up with a precise explanation. Their elevation seems as inexplicable as it does natural, since social contrast, that element of communal coexistence which the Marxists and Communists swore to eliminate from the picture of *their* society, has become in practice the most striking feature of *their* society. The degree of elevation is a relative thing. Where there is one automobile to several thousand people, naturally the ownership of a Volkswagen is tantamount to the ownership of a Rolls Royce elsewhere. Thus for a young person endowed with an enterprising spirit, the basic thing is to find out what the permissible field of maneuver is. He has to search for it, of course, along the outer limits of legality.

In democracies the concept of legality is precisely defined but at the same time very broad. A citizen is permitted anything that is not a transgression against the law. Under communism "legal" means whatever the Communist Party recognizes as legal, wholly independently of officially codified and binding laws. The Party, moreover, has the habit of ceaselessly changing its principles of legality, forever creating and multiplying new laws and requirements which very often run counter to and result in conflict with those already in existence. The abrogation or annulment of the latter, needless to say, disturbs no one. If one year, for example, it is illegal to own a house larger than two stories, and the following year the regulation is modified to three stories, people still will be punished for violating last year's regulation, which is no longer in force, only to have the Party reverse itself once again and go back to some regulation promulgated a few years before. In the chaos that inevitably results from such a state of affairs, the owner of even a one-man tent can find himself in violation of the law and subject to penalty. Consequently, the person living under communism is permitted almost nothing, and what little he is allowed gets lost in a fog of ambiguity and looseness of interpretation which gives each and every official and policeman the opportunity of extracting the greatest advantage for himself. Not having one's personal identity papers, which might have been simply forgotten at home, can be regarded as a serious offense by some unfavorably disposed representative of the law, while the theft of several machines from a state factory may be interpreted as streamlining production.

To be sure, Communist constitutions proudly assert that work is a privilege and nowhere declare that idleness is prohibited. But the fact remains that when someone doesn't work who isn't retired or sick, an aura of illegality clings to him. Nobody will ever willingly confess that he isn't working, and every crook and pimp carries around in his pocket a formal document, plastered with countless official stamps, attesting to the fact that he is a mechanic or a salesman in a state store for baby carriages and kiddy carts. The coffee shops in Communist capitals are always filled with people in the prime of life at hours when the rest of the country is pulsating with feverish work. But one has to suppose that each of these citizens sprawled indolently around the tables has in his pocket an appropriate document bearing evidence of his participation in the productive efforts of the nation.

It is clear that these local playboys and epicureans dressed in

Western clothes and drinking Western drinks have to get the means for these luxuries somewhere. They get them from the skillful exploration of the limits of legality. The possession of so-called connections is the simplest method by far. Under communism people are forever in need of something: the assignment of an apartment, the acquisition of a hospital bed for a sick mother, a passport to go abroad, help in the fight with an absolutely insane bureaucracy, assistance in getting one's son a decent job or admission to a university. Everything can be pulled off by means of bribes and payoffs, and specialists in the quiet, easy, and efficient accomplishment of these things are precisely the people in the coffee shops, elegantly attired and equally handsomely protected against possible harassment from the law.

From the moment the first post-revolutionary society divided itself into *pays légal* and *pays réel,* which happened immediately after a successful internal upheaval or the imposition of a revolution from outside, two currencies began circulating in each Communist society. One, surrounded by universal distrust and contempt, is the official state currency—the ruble, zloty, forint, crown, and so on; the other, which enjoys a mystic reverence and boundless confidence, is the American dollar. The dollar is the symbol of plenty and solidity, the one link between the world of want and uncertainty about the future and the world of stable and assured values. For dollars, certain objects and services can be obtained which are otherwise unobtainable. The result is that the acquisition and possession of dollars is prohibited, and dealing in them is severely punished. But again, this is a prohibition the coffee-shop crowd thrives on. They take on themselves the burden of dollar transactions and the consequent dangers of arrest and punishment, and their reward must relate proportionally to the risk involved. But the risk itself may be considerably reduced, depending on the individual's capacity for moral compromises, which seems to be their professional qualification and at times even the prime indicator of their true nature. Their persecutors are the regular police and the political police—and what could be simpler than to try to work out correct relations with these persecutors who are forever hungry for

49

information concerning the citizenry committed to their trust? The very simple arrangement looks like this: The police know quite well who deals in currency and in exchange, and for a certain reticence on the part of the long arm of the law they expect small favors from the dealer. The latter, on the other hand, doesn't hesitate to disclose to the police the most precious secrets of his profession; in addition to securing his personal liberty, he counts on the fact that a policeman, especially a higher ranking officer, also has his share of material desires, and so perhaps he too will buy something from him. Apart from individual transactions, the political police sometimes work out mass deals for the financing of their agents in the capitalistic West, which once again demonstrates how good and advantageous a thing it is, from every point of view, to be on friendly terms with the police.

In the capitalistic West you have to really exert yourself and display plenty of flashy ingenuity to be a successful operator. Only monetary-legal calculations come into the picture. But communism is a paradise for operators. Under communism the cheat and crook enjoy a fantastic field of operation which their Western counterparts couldn't imagine even in their wildest daydreams. A few slogans about the proletariat, the imperialists, and the class struggle are enough to arouse fear, force trust, terrorize, and rake in the spoils. The jungle of a fairly loosely defined legality is a reserve of inexhaustible riches. The Communist swindler doesn't sell wonder-working medicine, good for all ailments, to people in some out-of-the-way part of the country, or phony diamonds to country hicks, but delivers to them instead thunderous speeches about warmongers and organizes collections for the Viet Cong and the victims of American militarism. In capitalist countries the con artist is afraid of both the people he cheats and the police, while under communism it's the people who have been cheated and the police who are afraid of the con artist; beyond his lies stands the powerful and holiest authority of Faith and Ideology.

Communism is swarming with Gogolian Inspector-Generals. But with this difference: instead of pretending to be noblemen or state officials, they pretend to be idealists. This sort of a make-up opens limitless possibilities, especially if one is acquainted with the skill of writing. One can, for instance, write poems about mankind basking in the sunshine of socialism. A certain young man in Rumania wrote to one of the Bucharest newspapers requesting accreditation as a field correspondent. He received it without any trouble because the Communist press enthusiastically takes advantage of the help of thousands of unpaid reporters whose job it is to inform the central offices that in such and such a local park, for example, three new benches were constructed for the celebration of Lenin's birthday. With accreditation in hand, our young Rumanian friend made for some God-forsaken village where he presented himself to the local council as a correspondent from the capital. The following day was a national holiday, so as an honored guest he was invited to the presidium of the ceremonial committee where he delivered a thundering address on the beneficences of socialism and the greatness of the Party. The local people, overwhelmed by the dimensions of his devotion and high-mindedness, reached the sound conclusion that he must be a powerful and influential person, so in the days following the festivities the young man was lionized by the local notables, consumed the best drinks they had to offer, and loved all their daughters. In the beginning he refused to accept the little presents they offered him, but when they begged him almost on bended knees to help the working people, he decided to still the voice of idealistic conscience in himself and finally accepted an impressive amount of money for the purchase of fertilizers, for which the peasants had been fighting vainly for a number of years. Afterward, having taken leave tenderly of the local people, he simply disappeared. Sentimentalism ruined him, however. A few weeks later he wrote to his benefactors telling them how much he esteemed their spirit of solidarity with the have-nots since thanks to that spirit he himself had been transformed into a have. As for the fertilizers, which were as difficult to obtain in the city as in the provinces, he told them that he was sending instead a set of the complete works of Joseph Stalin. That was enough to bring

51

the police banging on the doors of his room (in an elegant hotel in one of the Black Sea resorts).

Not all contemporary Inspector-Generals, however, are guided by impulses of the heart, which guarantees them impunity and long-lasting success. Some of them bear the fancy title of Chairman of the Committee of the Defenders of Peace, and never have to flee the places where they swindle the naive of their money. They hold down official, state positions.

There is another consideration, as well. That is, that human ingenuity in the service of enterprise is inexhaustible, and a country where there is never enough of anything is a veritable Eldorado for the enterprising. It suffices, to appreciate the truth of this, to spend a morning waiting in line at the box office of a movie house running a currently popular film and buy ten tickets in order to sell them that same evening at a 500 percent profit.

The metaphysics and surrealism of a Communist economy open up unlimited possibilities for a person willing to expend a little energy. Improbable simplicity, as opposed to Western sophistication so well known especially from British films about operators, becomes the source of the most extravagant successes. The zenith in this sphere was reached once by a certain young Pole who read an announcement about an unusual campaign to collect bottles as the result of an insufficiency of the same in the economic plan and in the marketplace. He then repaired to the nearest grocery store, where he established that the price of a bottle containing a certain liquid designated as soup was lower than the price being paid for an empty bottle by the economic authorities. Unperturbed about the magnitude of his investment, he bought every bottle of the product he could find in stores throughout the entire city and surrounding areas, dumped the soup into the gutter, and sold all the bottles to the state at a handsome profit. In view of the fact that the soup itself was manufactured by a state enterprise, or in other words, that the bottles in question belonged to the state before their sale to the state, one has to admit that the young fellow displayed traits of genius. However, instead of being made Minister of Trade, he was arrested on completely noneconomic grounds.

The famous socio-moral principle, "Who doesn't work doesn't eat," on which Marxism bases its repudiation of capitalism, has undergone a strange transmogrification under communism. Now, as matters actually stand, who works eats *less* under communism, whereas the person who doesn't work has more time to pursue opportunities which will permit him to eat more and better. Nearly every young person leaving the school walls behind him knows this only too well. But not all of them are able to extract the appropriate conclusions from this knowledge. This intellectual limitation is what directs them most often to the groves of academe.

# 6 · How to go through a university without losing faith in life

THIS IS IMPOSSIBLE. After all, the university is just the place where one loses faith in life. There are those who swear that it is an institution predestined for this function in accord with the hidden directives of ideology. It is possible that the greatest theorists, reaching the deepest depths of human understanding, with their triumphant thought, determined to transform the university into a great academy of disenchantment in order to assist in the transformation of previous man into new man— Socialist Man. Official assurances concerning the humanistic goals of the university may be just a camouflage, indispensable in an era of transition, a kind of tactical concession to convictions consecrated for centuries. The university and the student's relationship to it are so constructed that the young idealist as well as the young conformist soon discover in it the uselessness of their respective attitudes.

The young idealist quickly learns that his way of thinking and reacting, as well as his ambitions, conflict with the sense of life transmitted to him by the knowledge of which the institution of higher learning is the distributor. The young conformist, who counts on the enlightened absolutism of communism and the possibility of dialogue within the limits of acceptance of its principles, learns the first bitterness of conformity. He quickly gets wise to the fact that a healthy and judicious opportunism as

54

well as intellectual cynicism (the bases of many successful civilizations) will never lead him anywhere under communism and that what is demanded is blind submission to dogma—since the stuff of which the best careers are made, even in scholarship, is often plain ordinary stupidity. Naive observers from beyond the pale of communism are doubtless shrugging their shoulders at this moment, considering it impossible that nonconformity, moral postulates, opportunism, and stupidity have any influence on attainments and success in mathematics, chemistry, or civil engineering. People who have lived under communism for many years have ample opportunity to observe how strange are the vicissitudes of the fates of mathematicians, chemists, technologists, and engineers, and how often the ignoramus and the charlatan have gotten the best of someone smarter and better qualified than they. Which does not mean that the ignoramus and the charlatan themselves are forever protected against a comedown; no, but if they do fall, it isn't because of their ignorance or charlatanism or their errors in the profession in which they were trained.

For the past fifty years the West has observed with astonishment the continuous exodus from countries ruled by communism. In the beginning, in the period of the Russian Revolution and immediately following it, people fled who were designated as class enemies: the wealthy, landowners, industrialists, military men, and high-ranking officials of the *ancien régime*. Many of the intelligentsia, representatives of that specific Central and Eastern European social class that derives its income from and devotes its high social status to culture, also sought refuge abroad, but they did not determine the character of the first wave of emigration. In those days the political left in the West had an easy job of explaining and assessing the phenomenon: it was said that a justifiable social upheaval was simply tossing parasitical social groups onto the junk heap of history. Lenin declared that a state of workers and peasants saw in that sector of the intelligentsia disposed to recognize the leadership and inviolable primacy of communism and the Party its dearest ally. From then on, such an intelligentsia had to become indispensable to the construction and final victory of socialism and had to call itself a *working* intelligentsia, as if the intelligentsia till then had never worked, had not created Marxism, had not brought about a revolution, and had not been the family cradle of Lenin himself. Proud of the precision of its terminology, Leninism has never been able to explain why an anti-Communist writer, who might have worked like an ant his whole life and produced two hundred tomes, is a *non*working member of the intelligentsia. Soon a paradoxical situation came into being: that sector of the intelligentsia that swallowed the holy communion of communism willingly and without displaying any symptoms of fainting began to prosper splendidly, incomparably better than the workers and peasants, the "owners" of the socialist state. The consequences of this phenomenon would amaze the classical Marxist theorists. It has turned out that in countries where Communist parties are in power they comprise an overwhelmingly greater percentage of bureaucrats and organizational workers than laborers and peasants, a fact sedulously concealed in official statistics. The main reason for this is that officials long have been esteemed in Eastern Europe and Russia as representatives of the intelligentsia, since in these countries even a middling education, the symbol of which is a gymnasium diploma, is *usually* enough to qualify one as a member of the intelligentsia.

And the paradoxes have continued to be compounded. Hand in hand with the growth of the social significance of the intelligentsia went its helplessness, its weakness, the ambiguity of its attitude toward the proletarian-Party authority. The position of the common laborer is straightforward, determined by the inviolable fact of work accomplished. The more complex position of the peasant in the structure of the new society was explicitly formulated by the classical theorists. The intelligentsia, however, was tagged with that clever yet contrary pair of epithets—"nonworking" and "working." Whether or not the individual representative of the class belongs to the so-called working intelligentsia is left up to the summary determination of the authorities, without the possibility of recourse to the holy principles of canon. The insubordinate physician, university professor, or schoolteacher can all of a sudden become a relic of capitalism who sucks the blood of the proletariat and gets fat on profiteering, even if he has fallen ill from overwork. Rendering such people impotent in the name of the best interests of the working masses, or throwing them out of work and depriving them of a livelihood, is treated as little more than a trifle. No moral consequences are occasioned and there are no possibilities for redressing the injustice; no means exist for "protest," even if the person involved is an Einstein.

This state of affairs gave rise to a new phenomenon, which the political left in the West views in perplexity, unable to understand or explain what is happening—namely, the exodus of the intelligentsia. For several decades now it is these people, above all, who have been fleeing communism—the engineers, architects, doctors, lawyers, economists, artists, professors in institutions of higher learning, intellectuals of one stamp or another. The imposition of communism on the countries of Eastern Europe, which are considerably more closely bound with the rest of Europe than is Russia, intensified the process to dramatic and shocking proportions unknown to the world previous to World War II. Until they put up the Berlin Wall, East Germany alone lost nearly 20 percent of her population as a result of individual flights, which were easier from that country because of its geographical situation than from other countries in the Communist bloc. It used to be that upon finishing a secondary school or university, a young East German, if he wanted to go on living and developing normally, had to run away to West Germany. Young East Germans, deprived of their right to vote in the places where they were born, voted with their legs, with the result that present-day East Germany is a kind of depopulated country, which any traveler can verify with his own eyes.

The relative improvement of socio-political conditions in Poland and Hungary after 1956, and a few years later in Czechoslovakia, which facilitated freer foreign travel for the nationals of these countries, brought with it an astonishing wave of almost mass flights. Among these who "chose freedom," asked for asylum, and refused repatriation to their Communist homelands, the overwhelming majority consisted of the so-called working intelligentsia. Can we infer from this that workers and peasants consider themselves better off under communism? Hardly. What it does mean is that members of the intelligentsia, distinguished *per definitio* by greater intellectual activity and decision-making ability, find it harder to reach an accord with their fate and strive more diligently to seek a way out, even if this involves risking their lives. But this phenomenon is chiefly an offshoot of the tragic and absurd life-and-death struggle into which the intelligentsia has been thrust by communism and which brings to mind an apocalyptic and grotesque *perpetuum mobile*. This struggle, which neither side has any real chance of winning, breeds feelings of imminent catastrophe among the intelligentsia, the conscious or unconscious fear of inevitable destruction of all intellectual and moral values, which are the chief concern of the intelligentsia as a social group and which determine the substance and essence of all of man's intellectual activity. Putting it somewhat more simply: It seems that the Communists ideally would like to have an intelligentsia which did not think. After all, anyone who lives under communism discovers in short order that communism regards as its most rabid foe not fascism, or the hydrogen bomb in the hands of the imperialists or the agents of the CIA, but human thought, and not only thought of the highest caliber, but the simple intellectual process of subjecting to criticism senseless assertions about the power of dogma. Since it is impossible not to think and at the same time go about pursuing a profession dependent on the labors of the brain, conflict is unavoidable and bound to be fatal. Communism understands this perfectly well, but the average young person discovers it only when he reaches the university.

While putting the finishing touches to what was left of the obstinate Russian intelligentsia by means of mass executions or condemnations to Siberian concentration camps, Lenin and Stalin stubbornly kept on insisting that they were creating and educating a new, socialist intelligentsia—the sons and daughters of orthodox proletarians and peasants. The Communist proconsuls, accepting rule over Eastern Europe from the hands of the generals of the Red Army and the NKVD, made hypocritical pacts with the intelligentsia of the countries involved, promising them privileges and respect. The Polish, Czech, and Hungarian intelligentsia had not passed through the hell of revolution and comprised at the time compact and formidable groups of considerable social influence. In countries, moreover, where the workers and peasants hated and dreaded new regimes and new rulers, the intelligentsia represented the sole reservoir of potential allies. Nevertheless, they were treated with distrust and the Communists didn't even bother to conceal their intention of immediately beginning to rear their own intelligentsia, and that as soon as it was brought up, the old one would be disposed of. The universities thus became open, above all, to the children of the Party elite and the Party apparatus, as well as certainly to the descendants of the so-called downtrodden social classes who would successfully be inculcated, it was believed, with "class consciousness" in secondary schools and political youth organizations. It was also believed that in accord with the Marxist concept of psychology, the inimicable (or, as it was officially termed, "unconscious") attitude of a worker's or peasant's family toward communism didn't matter since class consciousness is an organic element and the child of a worker, even though his consciousness is as yet unawakened, will always react correctly to the impulses of ideology, in keeping with his class association. This had about as much in common with psychology as the expulsion of the devil from a schizophrenic by means of exorcism. Despite the differences in method, the results in Russia were identical with those obtained in Eastern Europe. A new intelligentsia, the generation of the children of Communists at the centers of power and of the mythologically conceived Workers and Peasants, soon filled all the camps in Siberia, which had been deplenished for a while after Stalin's death, carried out an insurrection in Hungary, initiated far-reaching reforms in Czechoslovakia, and called forth the great war of Polish students against communism.

Quite recently the Polish Communists undertook the persecution and expulsion of Jews on a scale unknown since the time of

Hitler. The Jews made up a significant percentage of the intelligentsia of Poland and the campaign against them symbolizes, as it were, the aspirations and dreams of all those wielding power under communism: to cut off the intelligentsia, that eternal propagator of thought, aspirations, and ideas, from the live body of society, to bring it into conflict with society, to eradicate it through imprisonment, starvation, or expulsion from the country, at the same time destroying any sympathy for it among the broad masses—which was accomplished so easily in the case of Jews in an anti-Semitic environment. After this, the next step is to mold a new intelligentsia in place of the old one, an intelligentsia that will be obedient and useful in terms of the goals of doctrine, politics, and authority. This task must be accomplished, above all, by reorganized universities constantly staffed with new professors whose loyalty is researched more scrupulously than atomic reactors.

In this way, new generations of new intelligentsia are continually being produced, and each new intelligentsia, like the one it supersedes, invariably asks why things are the way they are—after which it turns against communism. And it will continue to be so as long as the Communists refuse to understand that no system of authority in the history of man ever carried off a victory over human thought, which will always turn *against* pseudo-truths that cannot stand the test of reason and so must be protected by the police.

Communism asserts that its ultimate goal is the transformation of human relations in the spirit of equality and justice, that its enemies are exploitation and injustice. These are attractive and far-reaching goals. And even though he may have his own opinion concerning their attainment, each student going on to higher learning is inclined to accept them and cooperate in their realization. He quickly learns, however, that the university does not embark on any crusades for the transformation of the world but instead limits itself to the effort to remake the student himself, and in a manner essentially different from all the principles of upbringing and education which lie at the foundation of civilization and culture. The student does not acquire the right to individual development and the intellectual transformation to which it necessarily gives rise. His professors do not interpret transmitted knowledge objectively, but enunciate formulas drawn up by others. Arguments of a contrary point of view are prohibited and conclusions are not subject to discussion. Unilaterality is regarded as the triumph of a *proper* outlook, philosophy, theory, and methodology. In the libraries there are no books dealing with the *complex* of human problems, and the absence of those which could nourish argumentation unfavorable to the official point of view is called the *routing* of false convictions.

The West knows little of the fact that each Communist Party, after assuming power, prepares a blacklist of prohibited books— as did the Holy Inquisition and Adolf Hitler. Books are prosecuted like criminals, outlawed from libraries and book stores, burned at stakes, annihilated. They are also jailed. Each university library has a special department of forbidden volumes that a student, or scholar, can obtain only with special permission. Who is detained in those book prisons? Many diversified felons, from Epicurus to Aquinas to Dostoevsky to Bakunin to Einstein—depending on the whims of the ideological watchdogs of the minds.

Thus the student begins to be transformed and remade along the lines of a theoretically conceived model of man. But this model has not been fully formulated, its logical and ethical foundations barely sketched and but perfunctorily outlined by the classical theorists. In its major structural and functional joints and connections it has been summarily assembled by the political exigencies of the ruling group. Thus, depending on the situation, the student is obliged to make a cardinal deprecation of biology as a science incompatible with a socialist world view and of psychology as the relic of medieval intellectual obscurantism, or he is asked to accept unquestioningly the assertion that Tito was an agent of the CIA. This is not to say, of course, that in a year's time such assertions won't be annulled and the student summoned to a serious study of biology, the marrow of philosophical materialism, and taught that the propaedeutics of psychology are contained in the works of Lenin and Stalin, whose ideas Freud falsified for the advantage of the capitalists, and that Tito is an old tried and true hero of the Revolution. The student, therefore, must agree to being remade many times in the course of his studies in conformity with mutually antagonistic standards of man and citizen. Moreover, he must agree to being shaped without the participation of his own power of judgment. This basic denial of the right to individual development, the cornerstone of European civilization from which arose all its glory, Marxism included, is deep-rooted, though difficult to observe at first. The repudiation of the privilege of personal intellectual experience represents a painful mutilation of the individual, but fatal effects are felt only when a natural reaction against it occurs.

Abstracting from concrete persecutions, such as dismissal from an institution of higher learning, deprivation of scholarships, forced conscription into the armed services for many years and the consequent shattering of hopes and plans for the future, disagreement with the vision of the world proposed by the Communists becomes inextricably bound up with a debilitating sense of forced alienation, isolation, and helplessness. One of the most effective of all tools for the construction of the new man is the rooting in him of the conviction that any form of opposition is bound to be ineffectual. The falsification of history may arouse anger or scoffing, but the belief that there is no way to rectify the falsification plunges the student into a mood of frustration which, multiplied by the number of students, becomes a generalized social malaise. It is a danger that tallies with the ultimate reckoning of the Communists themselves. The Communists are well aware of the strength of the instinctive and subconscious opposition against them, against their designs and practices, and so they work out elaborate countermeasures the main bases of which are the scrupulously planned confusion of concepts, the faultlessly conceived distortion, and a stock of such perverted, falsified, erroneous, and twisted facts that the struggle to bring about their rectification becomes impossible without a basic revolt against all criteria. The Communist strategy permits, then, the presentation of unconscious surrender as conscious choice, disorientation as the coherent synthesis of facts and convictions, the lack of knowledge as knowledge itself. Someone who has never lived under communism does not and cannot have any real idea of what it means *not to know* in such circumstances, of how extreme, far-reaching, and deep this is, of how much it resembles a gigantic apparatus working twenty-four hours a day at maximum capacity for the production of blackouts, smoke screens, and *ignorance*.

Even a very intelligent student hasn't the faintest idea generally of the historical period in which his parents grew up; every area of history, knowledge about society, and current culture is shrunk to immediate, temporary use and so squashed as to be in no way serviceable for the acquisition of truth. The uncanny transformer of truths invented by Lenin and masterfully perfected by Stalin works day and night in this process of excision, extirpation, "stain-removing," killing with silence—trampling people and facts sentenced to oblivion. The successes attained after fifty years are fantastic. The construction of a society in which knowledge of life and the world is truncated from the past and history begins with the beginning of the consciousness of every person is an accomplishment alongside of which Orwell seems like pulp science fiction. The achievements of opponents are always presented as manifestations of their downfall, even if this assaults the bases of common sense. It would be interesting to know what an American student would say if one of his professors attempted to convince him that George Washington was a Communist whom only distance in time prevented from enrolling in the Party. Probably he would want to discuss it, at least. The Czech or Polish student can only smile.

Infallibility is a suspect and repugnant property smacking of fideism for which there is no place in the contemporary university. In Western civilization learning and knowledge have scored outstanding triumphs precisely through the rectification of errors. The rule that the fairest conclusions and judgments are reached through argument with the unfairest assertions was accepted in antiquity. The right to err, unpunishable except by demonstrated proof of error, represents one of the most valuable instruments of human progress, inseparable from the basic principles of the search for truth. All philosophical systems and religions began to decline from the moment they proclaimed their personal infallibility and denied others the right of fallibility. Communism considers itself the most contemporary *scientific* worldview, yet falls into unheard of difficulties and loses itself in contradictions when it attempts to come to grips with the question of infallibility. As a totalitarian and monopolistic ideology, it must struggle on two fronts: it cannot admit its own mistakes, and it must punish the mistakes of others, even if these consist of no more than *perceiving* the mistakes of communism. Disbelief in communism is the greatest mistake and no one has a right to make it, even if it is the errors of communism itself that by and large are responsible for making it. But an error is an error only, as a certain Polish writer once observed, if it can be reproached *publicly;* if it can't, then there is no error, and that is the way the infallibility of communism is established— an error exists which everyone knows about but which no one has the right to speak of.

In such a climate the role and meaning of the university lead to the conviction that man breathes and the earth rotates, neither of which carries the danger of any error. In order not to fall into utter ludicrousness, communism conceals its infallibility behind the inviolability of the laws of history and the class struggle, of which it calls itself the sole binding discoverer and interpreter. This results in a paradoxical situation: history, absolutized by Marxism, records the errors of Party doctrine—such as the eruption of the first proletarian revolution in an agricultural country, instead of, as Marx predicted, in an industrialized society, and the countless economic catastrophes in the USSR— but in the understanding of the Party it becomes an inviolable instrument of infallible knowledge about the future, capable of charting the destinies of societies, individuals, intellectual and moral concepts, science and scholarship. Since history does not err now, but may sometime have in the past, the Party, its Great Plenipotentiary, never errs currently, presently, here and now, but does have the discreet right to innumerable and fatal mistakes in the past, although it is thereby freed of all consequences for its mistakes and recognizes no natural obligation to evince the modesty that would seem natural on the part of someone who erred so often, so abundantly, and so profoundly. The Party confers on itself absolution from all sin with the result that an error is an objective error, that is, one has the *right* to make an error, only when the Party recognizes it as such.

The ramifications of this state of affairs for learning, the universities, teachers, and students are appalling. It is very easy to trace them by means of the classic straight line. In the traditional cognitive sense a straight line serves to link two distant points in space. Its mathematical, social, economic, and civic utilitarianism proceed from this function. Under communism, however, a straight line serves, above all, the good of communism, and therefore the good of the Party and its leadership. Its next task is to demonstrate the superiority of the Communist system over all others. Then, service to the people, freed at last from their bonds, but not to their enemies. And finally, it also serves to link two points in space.

The higher principles have a universal power, but in no other sphere of life do they appear with such distinctness or create greater chaos than in the university. Their dialectical scheme, transferred to the study of pharmaceutics, literature, or theoretical physics, permits us to understand what a student thinks and feels under communism. One of them once pronounced words worthy of very serious attention: "I often ask myself the question: Was Karl Marx a philosopher or a scientist? It seems to me, though, that he was a philosopher. Had he been a scientist, he would have first tried out his system on animals."

65

# 7 • How to take advantage of the invention of the telephone

A CERTAIN CZECH said, "Only under communism is the telephone truly a *public* institution. Anyone who speaks over the phone can rest assured that the conversation doesn't belong just to him and the other party, but becomes in fact the property of society itself." His words contain more than a single wisdom. The most frightening of all is the one that points to the prodigious correlation between illusion and reality in the spiritual life of the theorists of later Marxism. They weave tender daydreams about society as a whole loving the political police and the other organs of security and regarding them as its most precious treasure. From the point of view of such daydreams, eavesdropping on private telephone conversations and then recording them on tape ultimately serves those who have been eavesdropped on and protects them from the temptations of intimacy, thereby augmenting the stock of society's achievements. The traditions of these daydreams are remote and go back as far as old Russian masochisms of the time of Ivan the Terrible, who taught his subjects that there was nothing more splendid than being smacked in the face by their own czar and who, one must confess, achieved certain results in ingraining such feelings in the souls of Russians. But the divergence of the interests of society and those of the Communists in Eastern Europe stares a newborn babe straight in the eyes as soon as he leaves his mother's womb, so that open conflict of the people with the police, whose chief job is to force them into submission on behalf of the Communists, becomes a sort of oxygen which everyone breathes all around him.

In America there is open discussion concerning the moral aspect of monitoring the conversations of delinquents and criminals whose antihuman and antisocial behavior is well known. A sizable segment of the American public considers that monitoring, even in a good cause, is ethically unacceptable and fights the practice. If during a trial an American prosecutor wants to present evidence obtained with the help of bugging devices, his motion is openly discussed and probed. It is more often rejected than accepted, and the reasons for rejection are publicly announced. A prosecutor in a Communist country does not waste his time with such trifles. He says, "On such and such day the accused said this and that"—and he submits tapes as proofs. And if the defendant protests that the proofs come from bugging, he faces an additional trial for slandering the prosecutor, the secret police, and the Communist state itself, where no such thing as bugging is possible.

Under communism, everyone is monitored about whom there is even the slightest suspicion that he is unfavorably disposed toward the system, or—in practice—nearly 90 percent of the people who have telephones, since as far as one can tell, that is the percentage of people who have something against communism. Nobody has been able to measure the number specifically, of course, due to the lack of free elections. To be just, those who are disposed favorably, even the most venerated persons, are monitored as well, and with considerable attentiveness, for no one can ever be sure whether they love communism with a proper amount of sincerity. Human feelings, as everyone knows, are fickle—one day one loves, another day one ceases to love. Only a well-installed tap will verify devotion and dispose of unnecessary doubts.

Obviously, any sort of public discussion on the matter of wiretapping is out of the question since the practice is of its very nature a clandestine operation and officially doesn't exist.

For that reason the slightest allusion to it in the press would be struck out by the censors, and public expressions of doubt on the issue would bring the unwary person a good few years behind bars. The orgy of bugging reaches the point of madness, especially in Russia where the mass production of electronic instruments of invigilation has taken on the proportions of a major industry. The government treats their manufacture as an article of the greatest need, more important than cereal for children. At the present time it is universally known that electronic devices are employed to monitor every step of every single person whose name has been entered in the files of the political police as "interesting," and considering the fact that the interests of the political police under communism are exceptionally broad, one has to conclude that the number of individuals monitored surpasses even the most pessimistic estimates.

Other Communist countries take a back seat to Russia when it comes to this dubious attainment, but even here the monitoring apparatus entwines all the more important political, social, and economic institutions as well as the countless number of individuals who count for something in the life of the nation— which means the most important Communists themselves. With their abiding inventiveness for overcoming the rottenness of life, people have even learned how to get along with this state of affairs, and what's more, have found ways of taking advantage of its unforeseen properties. A certain Polish engineer who for the longest time was unable to interest anyone in a project to bring about certain improvements began to divulge the particulars of his invention in telephone conversations. Since even a plan for the streamlining of a coffee mill is regarded as a state secret under communism, the fellow was immediately placed under arrest, and thanks to that reached the proper people, who took a serious interest in his ideas.

Since the open and exhaustive exchange of views is impossible because of censorship, certain dignitaries, monitored by other higher dignitaries, use telephone conversations with their aunts, let's say, as a means of conveying opinions which otherwise wouldn't stand a ghost of a chance of reaching the highest

68

placed people. It is enough to declare into the mouthpiece of a telephone that the first secretary of the Party or the premier of the government is an absolute idiot who neglects this or that problem to be taken into custody a few days later, or invited in for a serious talk from which it's possible to emerge with a promotion to a higher rank in the Party or administration. The risk is great, to be sure, since there does exist a third possibility, namely, that the person involved could be carted off to prison while the premier or secretary who had been insulted may decide to introduce the very ideas, solutions, and interpretations proposed over the telephone, taking credit himself for their originality. And this is what happens most of the time.

So common is the practice of telephone monitoring that if so-called technical difficulties and interruptions occur during a conversation, the parties conversing exchange such remarks about the functionary doing the monitoring as "He's not properly plugged in, we can't talk yet" or apostrophes addressed directly to the eavesdropper: "My dear fellow, won't you please hook up your monitor and give people a chance to talk?" Such a relationship proceeds from a correct appraisal of reality as well as from a certain inclination to anthropomorphize every phenomenon under communism. Generally speaking, every proper monitoring should be automated. But in a situation where man and his work are cheaper than even the most mass-produced magnetic tape, the function is assumed by a living being to whom the winter is cold, the summer hot, and who sometimes even belches on account of some digestive disorder. Instances of even quite audible yawning during unnecessarily long and dull conversations have been attested to, or the stifling of a cough during the flu season. Sometimes it even goes so far that the people being monitored share medical advice with their monitors, impelled, no doubt, by feelings of simple human solidarity. And so it is that socialism, whose most loftily enunciated idea is solidarity among all peoples, attains still another apogee in telephone monitoring.

The role of such widespread telephone bugging in the formation of the human psyche is enormous and in keeping with the inherent precepts of communism as an all-embracing and cohesive world view. The main thrust of present-day communism is no longer the liquidation of the private means of production, but the infinitely more important battle with privacy as a concept. The annihilation of the right to privacy and separateness is the next logical step after the limitation of the right of material ownership. At the end of the road is the elimination of people's personal lives in the name of a theoretically conceived life. The eradication of the element of intimacy from a telephone conversation leads to an atrophied sense of intimacy in the human consciousness. And this tallies with the ideal of the Communist rulers, who strive toward the realization of this goal in a manner that is clear to any impartial observer, although it is camouflaged by a pyramid of slogans collectively known as the new morality. It would indeed be naive to maintain that the basic purpose of telephone monitoring is the collection of information —its explicit and directly utilitarian function. The true purpose of monitoring is the dissemination of the conviction that a person does not belong to himself. The more widely and deeply the conviction penetrates the masses of society, the closer is communism to its ideal—the absolute rule over the human psyche, the rule over souls.

So many religions, philosophies, and social movements have strived to attain the same goal in history to no avail that the prospects of communism in this area are none too rosy. An additional comfort is the productive inefficiency of communism. Even today the telephone is an object of uncommon luxury in Communist countries. Several years may go by from the time when an application for the installation of a telephone is submitted to the telephone company until the moment of the appearance in someone's apartment of the little black box connecting its proud possessor with the rest of the world. The telephone is a sign of privilege, good connections, or uncommon means. The official allocation of a telephone does not mean much. It's only the skillful financial dealing with people involved in physical labor (bribes to the men who do the installing—who otherwise never seem to have enough wire to do the job) that finally permits one to enjoy the trappings of civilization. For well-to-do representatives of private enterprise who live at some distance from a city and who are in a position to express their gratitude by means of ready cash, sometimes arrangements (and resources) resembling those of military operations are found. How this happens will forever remain a mystery among the working people, who also must somehow exist under communism.

# 8 · How to use the mails

I F SOMEONE has written a letter and decides to entrust it to the postal system, he generally leaves his house and heads for the street in search of a mailbox. Under communism this works differently. A person with a letter in his hand indifferently passes by the first mailbox he meets, and continues past the second, third, and even fourth without bothering to pause. What is he looking for? He's looking for a post office. Perhaps he even will pass a post office and with a sigh wander farther. Where is he going? To the *main* post office, the center and source of postal authority and machinery in a given city. This hypnotic quest ends in a situation foreigners generally have a hard time understanding. The main post offices in all Communist cities are always inhumanly crowded with human beings positioned in intricately twisted lines where they wait for hours on end to reach a little window for the *possible* settling of their business.

This is an insignificant detail of existence of significant cognitive-explicatory power.

In democratic countries the eternal complaint that the postal system doesn't function as it should, that it holds packages too long, and that it doesn't take pains over their *terminal* delivery, belongs to the oldest traditions of social grievances. In Communist societies, on the other hand, every citizen simply *assumes* that the postal system doesn't function at all, that it operates on the principle of some sort of undetected necessities materializing from time to time in a series of indeterminate accidents. This means that postal offices, buildings, and boxes, as well as the uniforms of letter carriers, are symbols of something which may exist but cannot be checked by means of general social criteria. The fact of receiving a letter, package, or newspaper through a post office still doesn't prove anything, since it's the rule rather than the exception that twice as many packages, letters, and newspapers are expected than actually come through, though the real number of lost or missing items can never be ascertained. It's only a sign that some undetermined power, not subservient to the control of reason or experience, did in fact deposit a given letter in someone's mailbox—which most assuredly does not mean that the reply to the letter will meet with the same fate and find itself in the mailbox of the addressee. Political necessity—for how can a state exist today without a postal system?—the sole rational element of probable functioning, rests on the hard fact of the existence of the political police which is always in a position to intervene in cases of exaggerated dereliction of duty and arrest and imprison sizable numbers of post office employees; not so much those who are guilty of neglect and delays, but those who are the easiest to indict and can be most conspicuously chastised before the public as sacrificial lambs. In view of the fact that the main centers or central organisms of handling and distribution are the most visible and lend themselves the easiest to punitive operations, their activity tends to be somewhat more expeditious than that of the rest of the institution. Thus it is that the wisdom of life under communism teaches that if we wish to give a letter a greater chance to become a letter, that is, a writing heading for a certain destination, we have to mail it from the most central post office there is.

The mailbox represents the lowest level of the postal system. Generally speaking, the lowest levels of anything in a Communist society are barely alive, and if they are, they are in a state of complete lethargy and impotency. In the consciousness of the person living under communism, the profound irrational conviction has taken root that a letter deposited in a mailbox

73

never leaves it. Irrational I say, because every day everyone sees a variety of functionaries emptying the mailboxes all over the city or town. Despite this, people simply refuse to *believe* that *their* letters were extracted from the mailbox and entered into the normal circulation of the postal system. Precisely because the mailbox stands on a street corner for the express purpose of receiving letters and dispatching them on their way, and is, moreover, adorned with the seals and inscriptions of state and postal authority alike, everyone knows only too well that something must be wrong. It all seems too simple. Each step offers proof that everything is in fact extraordinarily complicated, and the complexity is no guarantee that anything will be done, except better explain why nothing can be facilitated, attained, or accomplished. Life teaches the citizen every step of the way that the state does not want to give him anything, that it wants on the contrary to take everything away from him, beginning with taxes and ending with his time and sympathies. That being the case, why, then, should it want to help him by transferring a letter of his from one place to another? The notion of social contract simply does not exist and the fundamental principle of coexistence with one's fellow men under communism—"You grease my palm, I grease yours"—is powerless in this instance, since how can you pay off the whole postal system? To whom do you give a tip so that your letter will reach its destination?

The universal crisis of confidence in everything from a product in a store, which if it is bread contains more artificial admixtures than flour, down to a word in the newspaper, which informs the citizen that he is living in the most fortunate of all societies, results in an exclusive reliance on one's own powers. The feeling of belonging to some sort of functioning social mechanism evaporates. Since a letter has to be transported by a postal employee from a mailbox to a post office and from there to the main post office for central sorting, and since it is known that the postal employee only makes so much, doesn't give a hoot about his job, and isn't afraid of losing it, then it has to be accepted that he doesn't give a hoot either about expediting anyone's letters, an indifference it is difficult to hold against him.

74

Only the letter carrier's good will, good mood, whim, or some other fortuitous circumstance determines whether or not a letter will ever reach its destination. Wouldn't it be better, then, to eliminate some of the element of chance by taking one's letter as far as possible before relinquishing control of it? It is this kind of reasoning that leads people to send every trifle, even greetings to a brother, by registered letter. In Poland the post office once had to appeal to the public through the press not to send so many registered letters because of the organizational problems this was causing, as though the Polish postal system could experience any further disorganization. Naturally, such a request resulted in a vast increase in the number of registered letters, and the circulation of a rumor that ordinary letters were being thrown into wastepaper baskets.

If the postal service under communism is a symbol of social impotence, then the letter is a symbol of the impotence of the individual. It is a universally accepted truth in Communist countries that there is no such thing as a secret in correspondence— which hardly arouses any special wonderment among people for whom the concept of privacy is succumbing to gradual atrophy. The consequence is that people learn to write a second time in their lives. The first time they learn is in elementary school; the second time, in maturity, when they instinctively take shelter in ambiguity. The fact that all letters "controlled" by the authorities (and this includes virtually all letters coming from abroad) are brutally torn open and later pasted together with Scotch tape and provided with a messy stamp indicating "Damaged En Route" arouses feelings of embarrassment.

Intimacy and privacy belong to the most sharply combated elements of civilization under communism. There exist a rich exegesis and a still richer system of rationalization affirming their antisocialist and antisocial nature. All thoughts, reactions, feelings, and especially conversations and correspondence, should, theoretically, belong to the state and to the collective; their disclosure is a sign of loyalty, their sincerity a synonym of love for the Party, the system, the fatherland. Where the most deeply perceived concern of every individual must be equatable with the concern of the community, there is no room for vacillation, embarrassment, tact, and the idea that something shouldn't be said because it's not proper. The unceremonious tearing open of someone's letter is painful precisely because of the unceremoniousness. The true art of force is alien to communism, which has not yet come to the realization that a little politeness and discretion sometimes remove the hateful character of force. How many women in the history of mankind have felt some uncertainty as to whether or not they were violated when their violators courteously assured them that they had just been carried away by their own powerful emotions? Who knows, perhaps if communism could master this finesse it might be able to strengthen its authority to the extent that it could be strong without feeling the need to use force.

All this may be viewed still differently, as is evident from the words of a certain Czech film producer who once said, "When you come right down to it, we've got the most human postal system in the whole world. In the final analysis, every person, even the most lonely, may be certain that sooner or later someone is reading his mail."

# 9 • How to be a woman

CONSIDERING ITSELF a world view which most accurately mirrors the contemporary spirit, socialism has made woman the equal of man in rights and responsibilities. As its adherents maintain, for the first time in history it has given women full equality with men. The assertion is fair and nothing can alter it.

Problems arise, however, from the uncompromising emphasis on the adjective "full." The twentieth century, with its moral and emotional displacements, its new mosaic of male-female interrelationships, and the general tendency to transvalue all values, has placed before mankind the problem of equality of rights in a radical way, without any restraints or equivocation. There is no doubt that on the scale of contemporary problematics the position and role of nineteenth-century woman are insupportable. The limitations imposed by society, custom, and economics by which the situation of woman was circumscribed for centuries collapsed after World War II. From then on, both the status and nature of a woman's life have undergone still more profound changes. World War II was followed by the invasion of women into all spheres of society and the economy. The basic and apparently irrevocable changes in the collective psyche, which have been shaped in large measure by the mass media, the transforming dimensions of human life, the demographic explosion and its consequences for individual human relations, the dislocation of the frontiers of youth and old age resulting in the designation of new borders of participation in life, the revolution in sexual attitudes and mores, the technology at the disposal of the human body—all of these things have led to the erosion of previously held ideals, ideas, concepts, and norms. The institution of marriage, the goal of a woman's life in the course of the last ten thousand years of civilization, has been forced to adjust to completely new arrangements and transformations and probably will never regain its former sense and character. In the light of all this, equal rights with men seems a desirable and irrefutable necessity.

But *full* equality with men? Enforced with absolute consistency to logical conclusions?

In countries where the left has not attained totalitarian power in the course of revolution, but has acted upon public opinion in one way or another, or has actually constituted governments within the framework of the parliamentary system, its influence on the fate of women has been positive. This influence has generally been equated with progress or the struggle against prejudice. It has unyieldingly opposed the disgrace of prostitution as well as the various indirect disgraces fostered by so-called marriages of convenience, which some of its more ardent critics such as G. B. Shaw have characterized as "legal traffic in human bodies." It has opposed hypocrisy, prudery, and bigotry in sexual mores, taken the side of women injured by the manifold insensitivities and traps of life, and destroyed the aberrations of social propriety which have been the cause of so many individual misfortunes. The extremist theories of "free love" or the collective "community of women" in a projected Communist society of the future had their supporters (both male and female), but did not come to grips too decisively with the dangers inherent in complete equalization of rights. Nevertheless, the post-revolutionary period in Russia wholeheartedly embraced these theories. "Free love" became the slogan of the moment and a young girl who objected to bestowing her charms on more than one revolutionary ran the risk of being accused of counter-revolution. This state of affairs didn't last very long, however, since the instinct of self-preservation of society as well as edicts of the government, which quite early perceived anarchic elements in these practices, restored more traditional values. In a way, it was like the first and last ideological defeat of romantic communism. The family, an institution embodying the most conservative model of human relationships, and condemned as reactionary by the extremist theorists of Marxism for its preservation of the instinct of ownership in a form most difficult to combat, seemed, ironically, to be the social nucleus indispensable to the construction of a new, more progressive society. The effort was now undertaken to oppose the proletarian family to the bourgeois family.

It was asserted, for example, that the bourgeois family is a microcosm of reactionary society; it is torn apart by the conflict of interests, and corroded by putridity, hypocrisy, and mutual hatred concealed behind the masks of deceptive conventions. The proletarian family, on the other hand, represents a model of idyllic simplicity, noble feelings, and tranquil happiness. There was a problem, though: the lack of any proof to support the thesis. The continued murdering of their own families with axes by proletarians drunk with joy and no longer conditioned by the bestiality of life under capitalism seemed to conflict with the theory. The result was that the belief was propagated in the press, literature, and everyday life that every bad and unworthy family bears the stamp of reaction, while opposition to it holds the promise of medals reserved for Heroes of the Revolution. What this amounted to was a kind of correct honoring of the actual labors and traps of marriage, which are pretty much the same in all social systems where people walk on two legs and awake every morning in bed with the same person.

The controversy over the politico-ideological qualification of marriage, even though in itself a concession to repudiated concepts, did not negate the full equalization of women and men. Exaggerated egalitarianism always leads to unforeseen tyrannies. In the area we're talking about, marriage and the extension of full rights to women, it led to puzzling disasters. The differences between a man and a woman are, from the very nature of things, considerable. This is something that even the uninitiated have no trouble recognizing even with the naked eye. It is therefore more than doubtful that they'll ever be *fully* overcome. But communism has resolved this dilemma in a simple way: *full* equality of rights has taken the form of granting to women the possibility of taking any job, even the most physically exhausting.

One must confess that in present-day socialist societies you see women in more prominent and responsible positions in political, administrative, and economic life. But at the same time, there has appeared in the streets of Communist cities a strange creature whom people speak of as a "working woman." You can see her on cranes, in railroad yards, at the heaviest construction sites, in mines, on highway building jobs, etc. She lives for the most part in special buildings reminiscent of army barracks but referred to in the idiom of communism as "workers' hotels" —always plentiful in all cities requiring a supply of labor. Our working woman gradually loses all attributes of femininity, but at least not on the same basis as motivates those creators of fashion in the West who proclaim the obliteration of the distinctions between man and woman in dress as well as in sexual custom. Losing her feminine attributes, the Communist working woman somehow also loses her human attributes and becomes a physical entity whose predestination is the fulfillment of a specific quantity of work in a specific time. Her femininity does not relate to any sexual concept, homo or hetero.

What inclines a woman to accept this process of degradation? In the first place, want. Under communism there is no welfare system for the poor, while the income of a substantial segment of the population is always a good deal lower than the most modest costs of subsistence. Heavy physical labor, on the other hand, is always well paid—when one can find it. In every society there is always a large number of women who have been injured by life, abandoned, unwanted by anyone, with illegitimate children—and it is precisely to such women that communism offers a concrete way out. The reduction of the proportions of life's goals under the impact of propaganda occurs easily; the physically strong woman takes on heavy work, doesn't make a bad living, and—if one is to believe the literature of socialist realism —acquires a new dignity and a previously unknown happiness. The only trouble is that after a certain time she ceases to be a woman, physically as well as spiritually, but it's precisely this aspect of the problem that no longer arrests the attention of literature, sociology, or psychology. The Communist press, that tireless and stupefied apologist for the Communist way of life, regards this new psycho-physiological state of woman as an extraordinary and praiseworthy achievement. Its beloved, widely advertised and photographed theme is the (true) fulfillment of several women who have assumed the functions of captains of merchant vessels on the high seas. As we know, the lives of seamen deprived for long weeks of the companionship of women assume a very special character, which has been dealt with extensively in literature. Hence the position in such circumstances of the woman who is single yet invested with authority is distinguished by certain specifics which are difficult to analyze in categories of scholarly coolness and objectivity. Looking at the matter logically, a woman who wishes to pursue such a career should reckon among her highest qualifications a repelling physical unattractiveness or, to put it somewhat differently, she must be antiwoman. For only in this way can she guarantee a kind of honesty concerning her ambitions and possibly confirm her single-mindedness of intention as regards a choice of profession. Any other attitude would suggest no more than inhumane malice and hypocrisy, or just plain ordinary stupidity. Thus, setting before a woman her own ugliness as a prerequisite to attainment of her goal in life gives rise to the suspicion that all is not in order here with the fundamental laws of nature.

It has to be stated definitively, however, that the great majority of women living under communism desperately strive to defend their femininity. I should also add that we would be equally unfair were we to assume that in theory and practice socialism consciously sought the production of antiwomen. Yet it is obvious that in its efforts to counteract the experiences of thousands of years, it falls into an unforeseen and embarrassing shallowness of thought. This is characterized by a lack of theoretical analysis and a summary and superficial perfunctoriness in the treatment of a problem which in its very essence is so complex that no religion, no philosophy in the history of mankind has known precisely how to deal with it.

*Full* equality of women with men is basically a vulgar platitude, a cheap hackneyed phrase that means nothing, resolves nothing, facilitates nothing. Despite all the changes and innovations in civilization and culture, even under the crudest coating of transformations and socio-cultural *sophistications,* we still continue to encounter the unchanging, rudimentary teleological model: a man wants many things in life, while a woman wants only one—a man as a life companion. Again, despite its pompous and pious declarations to the contrary, socialism has brought little change to this arrangement, although by limiting human possibilities in general, it has struck man more grievously than woman.

Our age can truly be called *antimarital* without any serious reservations, yet it is clear from the evidence that marriage seems more and more to be the most desired form of union between two people, especially between a man and a woman. And the woman who lives under communism, despite all the roads now open to her, universally and emphatically wishes to pursue that of marriage.

Now we come to a subtle issue, in general rarely and only at best sparsely discussed in Communist literature and sociology. Under communism marriage for a woman is a more burdensome undertaking than in a democracy. The chronically low level of the material sphere of life usually necessitates employment by both parties to the marriage, but the woman still has to care for her home and children. In such circumstances, the woman's life becomes in effect a kind of penal servitude of early rising, working in an office or factory from nine to five, standing in line for groceries whenever she has a free moment, doing the housecleaning when she's the most tired—that is, after work—preparing meals for her husband and children in moments of paralyzing exhaustion. How she finds time under such conditions for other marital functions as well as for maintaining her appearance remains a mystery. On the other hand, the premature fatigue, aging, illnesses, and indifference to beauty of women living in Communist societies is no mystery to anyone. Everyone admits in such a state of affairs that contrary to the wisdom of the ages, the best guarantee of marital success is a healthy and strong mother-in-law. The only problem is where the mother-in-law can be kept, since the average family consisting of four people usually lives in two small rooms.

Yet despite the trials and tribulations of marriage, the institution has taken on a kind of new lustre and significance under communism. It has become something of a spiritual refuge for people surrounded on all sides by the absolute harshness, indifference, and cruelty of social conditions and human relationships. In a world that suppresses all intimacy and privacy, that holds man as an individual in contempt—that, indeed, in principle is directed against the individuality of a person's life, that dialectically and bureaucratically crushes the individual's right to a personal destiny—marriage presents the only socially accepted option in behalf of these values, the only chance for permissible privacy, the only possibility for unselfish personal relationships. It is, likewise, the only accessible, authentic luxury in a way of life in which everything is shabby, tawdry and of poor quality, beginning with mutual loyalties and ending with clothing. The quality of marriage always remains a matter of individual good fortune and individual effort. It is perhaps the last preserve of man's better, uncommon, ennobling feelings, of a sense of sublimity and dedication, of the tormenting need for submission to and solidarity with another person, of all the impulses for good in man from which the vital tissue of communism has been utterly washed out, although there is hardly a place for these feelings in a system that assumes the prerogatives of universal Mother and universal Wife. Marriage is one of the last elements forging a link with the world of tradition and other better existences subconsciously and instinctively preserved in the collective memory.

But there is another side to the question: Under communism marriage is more susceptible more frequently than elsewhere to repelling vulgarization. It becomes a ground for unbearably humiliating, downright debasing experiences which people living in different social systems can't even begin to imagine. In a panorama of social interdependencies where one room with a kitchen represents a worldly fortune and achievement tantamount to a millionaire's wealth, an unsuccessful marriage becomes transformed into a disturbing spectacle of triviality, shameless insipidness, and wretched meanness. The struggle for an apartment in a Communist society still awaits its Balzac; its dire consequences for *one* human life, the assortment of passions arising from it and determining it, the moral consequences and downfalls resulting from it can be shown to the world in all their complexity and depth only by a literary genius. Dedication, spiritual torture, deception, prostitution, and all shades of degradation make up the subject matter of these common daily tragedies, although it never occurs to anyone to regard them as tragedies under the oppressive burden of everyday reality. Under communism a man succumbs to mental disorders because of an apartment, commits suicide because of an apartment, so it should be obvious that he will also marry for an apartment and ruin his life for an apartment.

When you think about it, there *is* room here for an authentic tragedy along classical lines. But the tragedy does not proceed from the destructive force of love or from a criminal act of treason or from the hell of envy—the eternal leaven and content of marital tragedies which seem to have evaporated from the lifestyle of twentieth-century people. As everywhere else, adultery, perfidiousness, and the trampling of virtues and bonds in Communist societies serve only as the pretext for pseudo-philosophical discussions over a glass of whiskey. Nobody shoots anyone or strangles anyone because of them anymore. Their limitless vexations now occasion only the difficulties of getting a divorce. But even without them there are enough gloomy, moving tragedies which spring from the very nature of communism itself.

84

Communism recognizes the right of collective responsibility, the same as Hitlerism and caveman. If someone is accused of animosity toward communism, then his wife is automatically accused of the same crime, even if she has dedicated her life to the Party and its ideals. How many times in the course of the past fifty years have loving wives been forced to sign the falsest accusations against their own husbands by the threat of blackmail or physical torture, or in order to save at least their children from being sent to a concentration camp from which there is no return? How many times has a wrongly imprisoned husband learned from a judge that his wife has applied for a divorce on patriotic and ideological grounds, no longer wishing to live under the same roof with a fascist betrayer of the working people? Regardless of whether a letter with such an accusation, written in his wife's hand, was the result of mystification or factual apostasy, its effect was always shattering and often gave complete victory to the political police—the mistreated man confessed to a crime he didn't commit or broke in spirit and went mad. Moreover, the wife forced into sleeping with her superior in the factory where she works, or with an omnipotent Party secretary, in order to redeem minor transgressions caused most often by simple want or by the necessity of securing a hospital bed for a sick child is no less significant a component in the Communist melodrama than she was in that of servile feudalism and beastly capitalism.

One of the valuable aspects of a woman's life was and still is what I like to think of as self-creation by means of a complicated, tradition-rich organization of her own appearance, her own exterior. Because of the impoverishment of Communist economics, practically speaking there is nothing under communism that a woman needs, and what there is, is of such poor quality and taste that it arouses only feelings of joylessness, distaste, and frustration. However, to blame economic woes entirely for this lack of everything would be an unreasonable oversimplification. In the 1930s Stalin occasioned far-reaching ramifications with his all-embracing principle of industrialization at any cost, or at the cost of the utter ruination of the life of several generations in the name of the construction of socialist heavy industry. What resulted were new norms of life and custom whose principal task was to relieve the romantic spartanism and orthodox abjuration of the first post-revolutionary period, giving society nothing in return. The military camp and the mystique of electrification had to yield to a stabilized society in the name of the catechism of work and obedience. It is difficult, however, to stabilize a society without paying attention to the element of consumption, in the light of which what Stalin introduced could correctly be termed neopuritanism. All the charm of life was condemned to exile; demanding anything of life was recognized as an ideological crime; happiness, sensuality, and the most circumspect premises of humanism were condemned as bourgeois rot, corruption, and degeneration. Lipstick and silk stockings became instruments of Satan, now portrayed in the press as an unctuous capitalist in tails and top hat, predatory and obscene. Sex became exclusively an element in the provision of children to the ideal society of the future; feelings of love were reserved, above all, for Stalin and the Party, and only a well-defined portion of them had the right to devolve on a husband or children. A woman who was rumored to have committed adultery was called before the court of her Party cell whose judgments in no way differed from the practices known as witch-hunting in the tradition of old New England. A girl who was accused of breaking the customs in a factory, for example, was transported to a concentration camp in Siberia for the rest of her life. Any woman guilty of looking after her femininity—and thus, above all, her appearance—was an ideological enemy.

There were cases where if during innocent joking in a group of people, a woman declared that she loved some Ivan or Grisha more than anything else on earth, that woman was soon arrested and sentenced to years of imprisonment. Her words, of course, had been reported by some casual agent of the political police, which in turn declared them inimical to Stalin and the Party. At the same time, the Ivan or Grisha in question was also arrested so as to eliminate a potential rival of Stalin.

Neopuritanism never took hold in Eastern Europe, apart from bureaucratic and political methods of pressure. In Russia, moreover, it has undergone a fair degree of relaxation in the past ten years. It would be a mistake to assume that it has disappeared from Communist reality completely, since the lack of basic commodities constantly has to be concealed beneath slogans, and to this end a neopuritanism modified to current demands can still render useful service. Communist sloganeering portrays life as a collective *struggle for something* organized by the Party: a struggle for an economic plan, for peace, for this year's harvesting of corn, for the cleaning up of a dirty street. Mobilization is a concept equal to a good state of being. The words "Are we mobilized?," visible on every page of a newspaper, possess the same meaning in the dream fantasies of Communist leaders about the societies ruled by them as "How are you?" in democracies. The ideal of mobilization by its very nature is antifeminine, for it places woman exclusively alongside a machine, in a kitchen, or with a weapon in her hand, strengthening her unshakable feeling of weariness, helplessness, neglect. The sense of a woman's life under communism rests on the overcoming of these feelings and the acceptance of the struggle for herself, for her own identity with the world surrounding her. She can go along with much, do without many things, and give up a great deal, even to the point where her entire life becomes a dedication to something or someone—but the one thing she cannot do is stop being a woman. Only demobilization permits her to feel like a woman again.

In the face of this, conditions accommodate her to themselves, existence determines consciousness, new attributes and competences are born in woman. Predatoriness and aggressiveness for centuries constituted woman's principal weaponry in the struggle with life; under communism these attributes acquire a new lustre as they are effectively transformed into enterprise, ingenuity, endurance, and inventiveness. Where stores don't have any good cleaning powders, or shampoo, or face cream, everything has to be acquired or replaced with a product of one's own making. All these commodities, as well as all fashion accessories, can be found in special shops which import them from capitalist countries (Kleenex is accessible only to the most wealthy, who obtain it in special packages from the West), but their cost prohibits their acquisition to some 99 percent of the population. In such a situation, when the Italians launched the style of simple black pumps on flat heels (called "ballerinas" at the time) in the early 1950s, girls in Warsaw used to buy inexpensive tennis shoes, cut out the tops to conform to the Italian pattern, and then color them black. That they weren't the chic Italian "ballerinas" everyone could ascertain for himself at first glance, but they gave Warsaw girls the feeling that they were fighting for something rather than just passively submitting to a drab existence. Their victory was a splendid reward for their labors. In the streets of New York or Paris it is hard to take notice of a nicely dressed woman, radiant in her feminine apparel; since virtually all are well groomed and dressed, someone has to be really exceptional in order to attract attention. In the gray streets of Moscow, Bucharest, and Sofia, filled with drab crowds, a woman who is struggling with communism for her own identity blossoms like a cheerful gay-colored flower that refreshes the heart and eye with its invincible humanity. She stands out from the general context of life. And what could be a more wonderful reward for a woman than the assurance that she is unique, exceptional—which she can read in the glances of other people?

# 10 • Why toothpaste does not clean

U NDER CAPITALISM, when someone who has bought toothpaste squeezes it out of the tube in the morning and
cleans his teeth with it, the thought doesn't enter his head that
he is the agent and witness of something singular. The fact that
toothpaste foams in the mouth and cleans the teeth without doing them any harm—actually helps them by protecting them
from decay—doesn't seem worthy of special attention. But if
something like this happens to a person living in a Communist
state, someone who has bought Communist toothpaste in a
Communist store, he feels as though he's come face to face with
a miracle. His joy and fascination know no limits. His day flows
under the spell of the phenomenon; he informs his co-work-
ers and even distant acquaintances about it, and spends long
moments discussing the strange and wonderful occurrence. This
is because to the person who lives under communism and
wishes to endure within the proper proportions of existence
shaped by intelligence and experience, it is obvious that toothpaste does not clean teeth, and precisely for that reason is called
"toothpaste." By the same token, the same paste, used accidentally to clean spoons or a washbasin, proves unusually effective. The Communist term for such a state of affairs and
the resultant consequence is "correctness." For a long time now
nobody has been amazed by this and everyone knows that every-

thing is in perfect accord with the obligatory order of things and ideas. Once a person has familiarized himself with the peculiarities of its mechanism, he can live in it even without the feeling of constant danger.

When a new or improved product—let's stay with our example of toothpaste—appears in the West, the representatives of Communist industry overseas obtain a tube of it in a drugstore and take it back to their country for duplication and manufacture, operating on the principle that the Communist countries recognize and honor no patent regulations. Patents are honored only in those exceptional cases where a product—a machine or drug—is dependent on the constant supply of exchangeable parts or ingredients from the West. In other cases, for the good of their own working people, it is considered permissible to rob people in the West of their inventions and improvements. Thus French, Italian, or Dutch toothpaste travels to a Communist laboratory where it is subjected to analysis. The lack of appropriate instructions, which are essential in every contemporary technological process, accounts for the fact that even working diligently, the Communist specialists always lack information about something or other and are unable to determine a crucial component of a formula or prescription. They cannot, however, share their anxieties and failures with their superiors, complain about their bad luck, or even discuss the problem from a professional point of view. Their superiors, after all, are neither professionals nor specialists, but Party *bonzes* who the day before may have been running a municipal transportation enterprise or a plant seed store, or who simply may have been transferred, because of financial mismanagement, from the political police, in which they reached the rank of lieutenant, to the position of director of a toothpaste factory. Bear in mind that a faithful member of the Party is its most precious treasure, no matter what offense he may commit in life, or what he may steal, or whose rights and whom he may violate. It should be obvious, then, that such people usually haven't got the faintest understanding of chemistry and cosmetics. Yet they do understand that for the concealment of their own ignorance the best method is to accuse the specialists and technicians of incompetence or sabotage or the waste of materials obtained with invaluable foreign credits. Since the technicians themselves are equally well aware of all this, they prefer to lie that they have correctly analyzed and deciphered a formula and understand perfectly how to duplicate it. They also know that in return for their competent lies, a bonus will be added to their monthly salary—which in some way absolves every lie and invests it with the attributes of a delicious joke. A social system which punishes the truth while rewarding falsehood can't ask to be taken too seriously, can it? This state of affairs irrevocably predetermines the quality of the future product; moreover, probable failures and difficulties can be blamed on the countless ambushes and dangers that lie in wait for the product before it appears in its final form. In this way, a faulty concoction heads toward the production process, with no heed paid to the truth recognized as far back as the ancient Greeks, that nobody ever succeeded in extracting a correct conclusion from a faulty premise and doubtless no one ever will.

In the production process it often happens that the ingredient with which the Dutch or Italians were able to make an exceptional toothpaste is unobtainable on the local market and that the substitute suggested by the technicians is absolutely worthless. The technicians know that it is useless. Yet they have to pretend otherwise so as not to interrupt so successful a cycle of unending mystification. To be sure, the wisest course would be the cessation of production of the product in question, but that step is the one that is never considered. The new type of toothpaste already figures in the total, all-state economic plan, in the countless statistics of production and consumption, in the reports about already attained achievements of the great chemical industry combines to which the given factory belongs, in the sales receipts of the stores which will sell the toothpaste (and know in advance how much they will sell), in newspaper articles praising to the heavens the concern of the leaders of the proletariat for the teeth of the proletariat, in the speeches of economic planners and Party activists extolling the toothpaste as an unusual accomplishment of local industry and the Party direction of industry. Two solutions to the problem remain.

The first: To produce the toothpaste without the particular ingredient, asserting, of course, that the paste contains it. This is a generally simple and effective solution demanding no special measures and holding no threat of protests or complaints from the consumer. After all, no consumer in his right mind believes that the toothpaste recalls its Western model even in the slightest degree and will treat it the same as every other toothpaste previously produced in his country—that is, as not really fit for use and purchased simply because there isn't any other available. The danger of this solution lies on a completely different level. One has to suppose that every director of a factory has faithful, devoted enemies anxiously awaiting his downfall, lying in ambush for years on end for his slightest slip, error, or carelessness. Thus no sooner does the toothpaste appear on the market, than at a meeting of the local Party organization, or the Communist cell directing the factory, the director's assistant arises and in a lengthy address sprinkled with quotations from the writings of Marx and Engels accuses the director of the deception of the working people and irreparable harm to the hygienic well-being of the broad masses of the population. (This same assistant may be the comrade who a half a year earlier had proposed the production of the toothpaste without the key ingredient, a decision confirmed in plenary session by the Party organization. The Party organization justified its action, let it be noted, on the grounds that production without the ingredient represented a financial saving, an argument of universal persuasive force throughout industry.) The director, in turn, will try to shift the blame onto the technicians and actually may succeed in having them fired, but this doesn't help him very much since he himself will be punitively removed to another position and sometimes even dismissed from the Party. In such a case, his place will be taken by the assistant director, with nobody on the scene seeing anything at all unusual in the action, since this is a universally accepted method of advancement under communism.

The second solution: The director of the factory may consider the manufacture of the given toothpaste an unusually prestigious undertaking, and if he possesses sufficient courage, zeal, and dedication to the matter to wander into the maze of bureaucratic procedure, he may even try to have the missing ingredient imported from abroad. An operation of this sort has some chance of success only when, in addition to the aforementioned attributes, the director has the right kind of relations with and protection against the monstrous banking institutions that decide on the expenditure of each and every sum spent abroad. The fruits of these efforts and labors are scanty at best, however. Let's assume that after countless obstacles the missing ingredient finally makes its appearance at the factory; what then? It either shows up in the finished product in a ridiculously small amount or, and this is the greater likelihood, not at all. Why? No sooner does it reach the factory, when the bulk of it is stolen. Where rare parts and ingredients that are very hard to come by are concerned, the workers in a Communist state seem to command the same knowledge as the best-trained technicians. In such cases, their sluggish apathy and disinclination to work are transformed almost with the speed of lightning into a feverish efficiency. When even the slightest possibility of a little extra income appears on the horizon, the worker undergoes a marvelous metamorphosis from a proud proletarian into a sophisticated tradesman. And so it is that the prized ingredient soon turns up on the black market. Its appearance on the official market comes somewhat later, and in the modest packaging of a cosmetics cooperative (the term is explained in the following chapter) bearing the name of Lenin's grandmother. In this form, the product will be distinguished by a slightly higher price than the state equivalent and will faintly recall a good toothpaste. When the state factory releases its product, it will proudly call it the newest of its sort, improved according to special models, and in a certain space of time the toothpaste will be hailed as a success and begin rapidly disappearing from the market because it has, quite unexpectedly, become the favorite snack of domestic fowl and is being bought up in huge quantities by chicken farmers who use it as a fattener. The factory director, whether

93

the old one, if he has managed to hang on, or someone new, will receive the Order of the Revolution for distinguished achievement in the field of toothpaste production, the newspapers will carry lengthy articles about catching up to and even surpassing the West in the science of chemistry, with special mention, of course, of the socialist regard for the health of the laboring masses, and nobody will find this at all unusual since everyone knows that journalists also have to live.

# 11 • What is a work cooperative?

IT IS HARD to find "work cooperative" in classical Marxist literature. It is a form created, instead, by life. Creations of life are born in a simple dependence on the conditions of life, something the classical Marxist theorists did not foresee despite the fact that the concept of conditioning plays such a great role in their philosophy.

The cooperative arose out of a combination of need and disgust. Its origin is like the procreation of offspring which nobody has any real desire for between partners who feel no strong attraction for each other. Communism knew what to do with cultivable land and with factories after the Revolution; it was all settled in no small detail by the founding fathers of the order. But life isn't made up exclusively of factory products and soil; someone has to make baskets and gloves, fit new keys for locks in place of lost ones, resole shoes, repair broken windowpanes, clean and repair sanitary facilities—even in the most classless and just society. Before the victory of socialism, these things used to be done by craftsmen, but the social status of the craftsman was always doctrinally suspect. The classical theorists of Marxism judged that he represented a relic of the Middle Ages condemned to liquidation by the history of industrialization. Those who were responsible for the practical implementation of the ideas of the theorists regarded the craftsman with obvious detestation. To them he was little more than the embodiment of petit bourgeois culture—with his eagerness for profit, narrow-mindedness, and superstitiousness—and they considered him as the potential source of all sorts of nagging problems. In the twinkling of an eye, the self-reliant, thrifty, industrious, and insufficiently repressed craftsman became a rotten small-time capitalist. The very fact that he preferred to work alone, far from the loyal effort of the collectives, seemed shocking and threatening. That his individualism was the generator of various loathsome efficiencies—meeting deadlines, solidness of the finished product, low production costs—invited the charge of provocation. On the other hand, although the development of industrialization beyond the borders of communism reached proportions never foreseen even by the most apocalyptic imagination of the Marxist theorists, not only was the craftsman not liquidated in the West, but he was endowed with a new role in economic progress. He was transformed in large measure into the service trades, which have had a resounding success in democratic capitalism, garnishing a dominant share of the income of society and extending their prerogatives to entirely new, rapidly developing areas of the economy such as television maintenance and repair, travel agencies, movie theater operation, photography, and garages, in which the mechanic appears the natural spiritual heir of the Nüremberg Meistersinger or the Shakespearean artisans of *A Midsummer Night's Dream*.

To communism, the position and nature of the craftsman is a slap in the face, a blow below the belt. Not only did the socioeconomic element for whom the classical theorists of Marxism foretold extermination at the hands of bloodthirsty monopolies survive and blossom under capitalism, thereby casting a shadow on the predictive powers of Marxist theorists, but he also appeared as a so-called problem in the post-revolutionary order in which he was authoritatively *unforeseen* and where he was *not supposed to even exist*. The frustrated managers of the Revolution soon discovered for themselves how much easier it is to build metallurgical combines than consent to the production of coverlets, suspenders, and electric bells by small manufacturing plants or determine who has to press pants. But since someone finally had to concern himself with things like stopped-up drains, there arose the concept of the work cooperatives or unions of small manufacturers working as happily for the greater glory of socialism as their brother laborers, only in small shops rather than in large factory plants. In this way, the work cooperative became a concession on the part of lofty doctrine to the practical demands of life on earth and everything that can't be accommodated by theory alone.

Like a child who is hunchbacked, squint-eyed, unloved, and hurt from its earliest years, the cooperative pays back its parents with a shrewdly concealed hatred and a deep inclination for the nastiest wrongdoing when nobody is looking. At first, the profits taken in by the cooperatives were thought of as the property of the members of the cooperatives, but when the socialist state and the Communist Party came to realize that cooperative members working only for themselves are capable of producing with their bare knuckles and the simplest hammer a hundred times more than a state worker who has at his disposal the most sophisticated machine tools and automation, ideology redressed the inequality and by means of the tax screw began to squeeze the last drop of juice out of them, allowing no possibility for growth.

The cooperatives had to then mount a counteroffensive and defend their right to some sort of existence. It began with lip-service. The importance of names is very conspicuous in the whole economic life of communism, but it was the cooperatives that first demonstrated what it is possible to accomplish in this sphere. Shops manufacturing Ping-Pong balls in the name of Karl Marx or ointment for corns in the name of the October Revolution or tomato stands in the name of the Paris Commune no longer surprise anyone. In the half-century since communism achieved power, the members of cooperatives have perfected their techniques and more and more frequently devise names designed to express their affirmation of life and the system they live under by means of the most subtle allusions, such as "The Happiness of the People Cooperative for the Sanforizing of Fabrics," or the "Happy Future Workshop of Wooden Buttons."

Some ooze with a favorably viewed patriotism, such as the "Baking Cooperative in the Name of the Battle of Stalingrad," or the "Plastic Shaving Mugs in the Name of the Destroyers of Fascism." Once, in Rumania, a cooperative devoted to the manufacture of prophylactics, which are as important from the viewpoint of the interests of society as oil, decided to call itself the "Rosa Luxemburg Contraceptives Cooperative," but the appropriate authorities reacted rather negatively to the proposal and the cooperative had to be satisfied with the title "Workers' Solidarity."

Every Communist enterprise has a director. The cooperative has a chairman. The income possibilities of a director are rather rigid and determined from above; loosening them requires special deliberations. In comparison with the director, the chairman of a cooperative enjoys a much wider field of maneuver, which is why the number of chairmen behind bars is considerably greater than the number of directors. Let's take, for example, the manufacture of some measuring apparatus consisting of a dozen or so precision parts. It suffices for affiliated cooperatives to form a sort of small illegal trust for the mutual supply of necessary components in order to create a fertile field for bribes, irregularities, and double bookkeeping. Splendid earnings in a market chronically short of a great variety of commodities allows the cooperatives to acquire considerable capital, something the Communists wage a life-and-death struggle against for ideological reasons. To the extent that a cooperative chairman and all those under him skillfully do *not* steal, the government collects its revenue by means of taxes. Too forceful a collection gives rise to apathy and a disinclination to work among the members of the cooperative. There is no way out of the situation, therefore, and so the classical Marxist theorists have to yield (even the most powerful Party dignitary must, from time to time, have a coat dry-cleaned). Once again, the manifest freedom in interpretation of the classics appears inestimable, and after a certain time nobody really knows whether Marx and Lenin did or did not teach that a damaged steam iron should be repaired collectively or individually.

## 12 · On private initiative

A TRAVELER in Poland, Hungary, or East Germany sees a store here and there, or a tailor's shop, less often a small bakery, and very rarely a small restaurant adorned with a plaque bearing the proprietor's name. These are relics of the time when the Communists, after taking power as a consequence of the conquests of the Red Army, found themselves face to face with the rabid hatred of subjugated peoples and took refuge in coquettish pseudoconcessions and declarations. The slogan of the immediate postwar years was the so-called people's democracy, or a system in which the Communists promised to preserve all the political and economic freedoms of the usual democracy providing that the people consented to the use of their name in the official designation of the Communist-run state. The political fashion of the period demanded, furthermore, that no Communist Party should call itself "Communist" but rather the "Workers' Party" or the "Party of the Laboring Masses"; the word *communism,* with reference to the new regimes, was subject to confiscation whenever some naive journalist wanted to call things by their right names. Nationalization affected only heavy industry; agricultural reforms gave land to the peasants, which it did not claim back, even after the imposition of collectivization; merchants and craftsmen had the right to open their own businesses, which was called "private initiatives" in the politico-

99

economic jargon. In the private plants of small industries it was permitted to employ up to fifty workers.

In the beginning of Communist rule, then, Polish, Hungarian, and East German cities had streets full of private stores. Later, the stores began to be concentrated in special streets in special districts. The impression of ghettoes would have been created were it not for the unusually effervescent and pulsating mercantile activity of these neighborhoods. A strange phenomenon came into existence: these stores, which collectively represented a real hatchery of trashy goods catering to the worst petit bourgeois tastes in clothing, fake jewelry, small furniture accessories, and other common everyday items, became a veritable Mecca for the liberated proletariat and lower-echelon Party officials, who regarded the commodities in these stores as the acmes of consumer culture and material ambition and also as the best proof of *their* social advance and success in life.

This obvious *boom* had its other side, however. For many years the owners of these stores led the life of the first Christian martyrs: every quarter-year they were thrown into an arena of revenue offices full of wild animals disguised as tax officials. The Communists never thought seriously of honoring the promises they made in the honeymoon period of the peoples' democracies and quickly decided to liquidate proprietors' signboards, in keeping with the dictates of an ideology freed from the constraints of tactics. At the same time as this decision was taken, Communist economists and planners, worried about chronic inflation and the chaotic excess of paper money on the market as a result of a senseless employment and wage policy, quickly grasped the splendid service that a skillfully harassed private initiative could render in draining the market. As they pushed forward to socialism, the Communists began more fiercely to eliminate those political and social institutions which the classical theorists had promised to preserve and develop. At the same time, they set about preserving what the classical theorists had cursed in the beginning and promised to uproot mercilessly. Hence, private merchants had the right to increase their turnover while the tax squeeze raked in practically everything they made. The so-called surtax system was invented; this is based on the ability of every tax office, acting completely arbitrarily and without any legislative authority, to set the amount that has to be paid by the proprietor of a store or shop. Since the proprietor of a store or workshop is a vestigial relic from the era of vanquished capitalism and morally deserving only of hatred and derision, according to the theory and dialectics of Marxism, he is politically and ideologically a potential enemy and a living contradiction to the obligatory social system. As such, he cannot count on any legal defense and no court will accept his case, even if the tax office scalps him, his wife, and his children in its collection of irrationally assigned tax rates.

At first, the role of the small private workshops and manufacturing plants in the overall economic scheme, as, for example, in Poland, was considerable. They provided society with many commodities, especially those which demanded careful professional finishing. In the early days of communism in the country, Polish hospitals equipped themselves with surgical instruments almost exclusively from private initiative. For the state to manufacture soda water at a time when it was considered imperative to construct gigantic metallurgical combines seemed unthinkable, which is why in the beginning nobody had anything against this manufacture being assumed by private initiative. Soon, however, it appeared that while the metallurgical combines continuously remained on the drawing boards of state construction commissions, the private entrepreneur was in a position to expand his enterprise in a geometrical progression—to increase the production of soda water and begin the production of syphons, for example, and, if he were permitted, to organize plants to manufacture trucks to transport *his* syphons filled with *his* soda water. In the light of this, it became necessary from the state's point of view to crush him as a danger threatening both doctrine and class interests, although nobody doubted his use to a society forever squabbling about soda water, syphons, and cars.

In the sixties private initiative under communism was breathing its last, although the process of taking its last breath has characterized its existence from the very beginning. It is holding out more strongly, speaking in relative terms, in the private cultivation of fruit and vegetable gardens near enough to cities to provide urban dwellers with fresh produce. Doctrinal dispensation for such gardening has been given even in Russia, where the members of a *kolkhoz* have the right to maintain private kitchen gardens and to sell their products in the city. In Eastern Europe private fruit and vegetable growers are millionaires. This fact can be explained only by the metaphysics which dictate that socialism is in a position to produce any number of tanks and submarines, but is organically unable to produce lettuce and make it available to grocery shops.

The question remains: Why haven't the proprietors of stores and workshops given them up and sought other outlets for their talents, instead of hanging on for twenty-five years, continually harassed by the state? The answer is at once very simple and very complicated. First of all, they do make out rather well financially, despite the harassment. And, as a well-known Polish dramatist once said, "Nobody ever invented capitalism, it was begotten by life, which some have called the history of man on earth. Socialism, on the other hand, was created at a desk. It is no surprise, therefore, that it falls into constant conflicts with life." Unable to explain its difficulties, socialism refers to them collectively as the unextinguished "class struggle." But though the existence of classes is easily observed, class conflict itself is rather doubtful. Classes do not struggle with one another; they only envy and imitate one another. The tax official who plays the role of a bloodthirsty tiger in the life of a merchant or fruit and vegetable grower earns on the average 1000 *zlotys* a month in an economic system in which a pair of shoes costs 500. Only the laws of life itself can effectively oppose inhuman concepts and laws. Why does his son have to go to school barefoot? The rest is silence—a silence that explains why private enterprise does not die although it cannot live.

# 13 · How to read signs in public places

I F YOU ARE at a big bus station looking for the bus which is
supposed to go in a certain direction, the best course is not
to read any signs. Communist bus stations, like bus stations the
world over, are provided with a certain number of signs whose
theoretical purpose is to give information. The difference between signs in a Greyhound bus station, however, and those in
a Communist station is simple: in the first, the signs mean something; in the second, they mean absolutely nothing at all. Or, in
many cases, they mean something exactly the opposite of what
they say.

Such a state of affairs is rooted in doctrine. Lenin and his col-
laborators very soon came to the conclusion that it was completely immaterial, if not an outright threat to the group wielding power for the sake of realizing communism, whether the
written word conformed to the truth or not, or even whether the
contents of a document could be verified. As Lenin understood
very well, no one ever derived any real benefit from credibility
in politics. Consequently, this marked the beginning of what is
today called "propaganda," and in communism replaces knowledge, science, literature, and all the communication media together. When thousands of marchers in a May Day parade carry
banners saying "Long live the people's government!" no one
around, including the dignitaries on the reviewing stand, reads

these words, or derives either inspiration or information from them. No one, in fact, even notices them. Everyone knows quite well that in communism the people do not have any government, so the only sensible attitude to take toward the content of the banner is to benevolently ignore it. There is no harm in asking the person carrying the banner if it is heavy, expressing joy when he says he can hold out. But the words on the banner and their meaning simply do not exist for anyone. If the banner says, "Let's all fight for the fulfillment of the economic plan!" everyone knows that such a recommendation should be politely ignored. The plan is sheer nonsense, for which its authors will be sent to jail in a few years; it will never be fulfilled; it has no connection with the economy, and everyone will do his utmost to avoid having anything to do with it, for which the Communists will cruelly persecute them. Thus it is logical and self-evident to anyone who has lived under communism for even a few days, and is capable of drawing conclusions from his experiences, that what is written and on public view, including the signs at a bus station, has the same value as the political slogan on a banner. This principle has never yet let anyone down, and its relevance even extends to street signs. Whereas in all of New York there is only one street whose official designation differs from the name in popular use, there are dozens of such streets in every Communist city. The only thing to do in such a case is to ask people for information at every step. Hence the most nearly reliable information in a Communist country is, despite all the shortcomings of human nature, information that is passed from mouth to mouth—a rather ancient method whose accuracy was questioned as far back as in the Athenian marketplace.

Therefore if we are wandering around a Polish bus station in search of, say, the bus to Warsaw, and after various false leads finally stumble across a bus with a sign saying "To Warsaw," instinct tells us not to get aboard. Previous experience has taught us that such information may or may not correspond to the truth and that the chances are perfectly even for either outcome. We must, therefore, ask not once, but several times, enunciating our words very clearly. We must ask as many different people as possible, carefully avoiding people who look like bus drivers, conductors, or are wearing a transportation service uniform. It is pointless to ask people we suspect of having any official connection with buses, because by the very nature of things they don't know anything, can't know anything, and don't want to know anything. Even if they are friendly and overcome by the desire to help, their good will is cancelled out by their total disorientation—the natural mental state of everyone employed in a Communist institution. However, an even worse eventuality may arise: the person asking questions may be given completely wrong information. This could happen for one of four possible reasons:

1. *Stupidity. Because of the mystique surrounding the uniform in uniformed countries, a man wearing a uniform considers himself far superior to everyone in civilian clothes. Thus he prefers giving totally false information to admitting that he does not know something, which would, he thinks, belittle himself and the uniform.*

2. *Fatigue. People who work without a break under difficult conditions are wrong over and over again. They bear no responsibility for their ignorance and it is hard to blame them for it.*

3. *Bitterness. Servile work without the right to protest fills people with a desperate desire to get back at other people and to find relief in the senseless torment of their fellow men.*

4. *Lack of time. Because of the ridiculously low wages which do not cover basic needs, people who are charged with even unusually responsible functions are constantly involved in quite different activities, such as selling vodka, weaving baskets, or stealing parts which can be sold on the free market. So they cannot stand being bothered by stupid questions.*

Thus if you should happen to ask the wrong person, you may very easily find yourself on a bus going in the completely opposite direction, and discover this only after traveling two hundred miles. But a question which is supported by some demonstration of humanity—the presentation of a pack of cigarettes, for example, or a scarf spontaneously removed from your neck and offered as a heartfelt gesture signifying the universal solidarity of the proletariat—may yield quite positive results, even if it is asked of a functionary in uniform who is being torn away from his work. He will immediately leave his post regardless of the importance of his functions (checking tickets, overhauling the engine, etc.) to go somewhere known only to himself in order to talk with certain people only he knows, and then he will return with precise information. Nonetheless, even then you should insistently and emphatically repeat several times, "But are you absolutely sure that this is the bus which is going to Warsaw?" And only when the official pathetically strikes himself on the breast and cries in a tearful voice, "My dear man! Would a patently honest man like myself deceive such a decent man as you? I give you my personal word of honor that this bus is going to Warsaw! The word of honor of an honest man, not of some state institution"—and you see no signs of drunkenness in him—can you board the bus with confidence.

The question remains as to why a bus has a sign saying "To Warsaw" when it isn't going there at all. The simplest answer is that it is due to the carelessness of the employees, and there are an infinite number of reasons for this carelessness. But there exist other, more deep-seated causes. For reasons known only to himself, the head of the station or the director of transportation thinks the bus with the sign "To Warsaw" should remain in the designated place despite the fact that it is not going to Warsaw at all. So the bus remains there. None of his subordinates will ask why, much less dispute the director's decision, because they are all long accustomed to senseless instructions. Even the most surrealistic order is accepted with resignation and surprises no one. So the bus stays. In the meantime, the reasons for the director's decision have long lost all significance, or he himself has forgotten about them. But the bus stays there, because the higher up and more important the director of a Communist enterprise is, the less idea he has of what is going on in his enterprise. And the less idea he has of this, the more his activity is based on the authority of the Party and the political police, which makes everyone mortally afraid of him and even less inclined to question his decisions. He, in turn, is afraid of everyone, sits in his office totally isolated from his colleagues, and would never dream of making an inspection of the terrain entrusted to him. In this way, a bus which is not going anywhere, but has been provided with a sign giving a destination, is somehow institutionalized. It serves no useful purpose, but neither does it bother anyone, so it is of no concern to anyone. Sometimes the director or head who issued the order was thrown out a long time ago or is now in prison, but the completely irrational situation he created continues and lives its own life.

Signs have a die-hard existence, especially among people who generally pay no attention to them. The fact that a sign saying "Writing Materials" hangs over some store does not in the least mean that things to write with are sold there. Because Communist countries exist in a state of permanent economic crisis and there is always a shortage of everything, such a sign simply denotes a place where there is no paper, ink, pens, pencils, envelopes, etc. The question then arises: What does it have? Sometimes you may get electric light bulbs here, because someone in the planning commission came to the conclusion that since you cannot write in the dark, a light bulb is a writing material. Of course, by the same token, it is hard to find light bulbs in electrical supply stores. Instead, you may find burning ointment there, for, as everyone knows, you can get a shock from an electric current. Ultimately, there is a certain powerful antilogic in all this, which a man learns to make use of and grace with little niceties. As in the story about a slightly nearsighted old lady in Prague who went into a meat store and asked whether they had any butter. "Here we have no meat, madame," the salesclerk replied with studied politeness, and then added, pointing to the other side of the street, "In *that* store they don't have butter."

# 14 · How to oppose

## In Youth

Youth is a wonderful time for opposing everything. Then the intoxication and delights of resistance arise from the heartfelt conviction that the world can, even must, be changed. In communism, true enough, a young man soon comes to realize how arduous and dangerous it is to set out to change the world. But the charms of revolt continue to beckon. From the first time he consciously formulates the idea and his desire to express it is awakened, a youth in communism is confronted with an agonizing dilemma, one horn of which is the imperative of resistance, the other, his awareness of its futility. Childhood, school, the first years of maturity teach that there is no sense in opposing, because all resistance is condemned in advance to failure. Traditions of resistance do not exist; historical science makes not the slightest mention of them, and the press, literature, and the cinema are equally silent on this score. Sometimes they are mentioned in the midst of one's family or friends, but only as personal catastrophes, existences wasted in prison or in extreme poverty. Generations have been cut off from other generations, even from those directly preceding them. Looking backward is useless. No one has any notion of how the stylishness of just bygone epochs and generations are differentiated. The twenties, thirties, and fifties seem an obscure maze of sameness—neither popular songs nor fashion nor architecture bear any proof of change. If there was a revolt in the preceding generation, the generation following knows nothing about it. Not a trace of the events is to be found anywhere. Printed information about them does not exist and public reference to them is forbidden. Literature cannot convey signs of revolt or memories of rebellion, since the deadly efficiency of Communist censorship eliminates the remotest allusion. The only sign of resistance recorded in the most profound and most courageous books written under communism is the psychological-moral opposition of the individual within his own soul. The most honest and independent writers, even when they are writing without hope of publication, are so fascinated by the impossibility of opposition that even when they examine the fate of a man or observe the evil in the simplest human experience under communism, they carefully eliminate any record of tremors of resistance in the reality surrounding them.

The countries of Eastern Europe have a rich tradition of rebellions against force, which is regarded as a magnificent historical achievement. Thus at the beginning of the Communist era, when the lying and misery of communism were revealed to East Europeans in all their horror, the lack of any concrete, continuous resistance in Russia seemed incomprehensible to these people. Recent memories of the bitter struggle against Nazi tyranny when none of the invaders' atrocities could eradicate the ever-growing resistance seemed to show the way. However, just a few years were enough for East European societies to realize that power in the hands of the Communists represented an even more formidable danger than fascism, and that the goals and practices of communism were even more genocidal than the exterminating madness of the Nazis. Despite this—or perhaps just because of this—there arose no resistance movement which was even remotely reminiscent of the concentration of collective effort directed against Hitler.

As the Russians extended their rule over Eastern Europe, they liquidated every center of the struggle against Hitler with a cold fury, accusing people who had heroically fought the Germans for six years or had rotted in concentration camps of being, at bottom, German agents assigned to the fight against communism. It was a crude trick, based on the brutal dialectical principle by which every armed non-Communist must by the nature of things be an anti-Communist, while every anti-Communist *eo ipso* is a fascist bandit. It soon became apparent that when a functionary of the same political police that watched and arrested people sat in the courts and on the editorial boards of newspapers, the administration of justice was degenerating into a tragic parody. Astonished societies followed the strange trials of people who throughout the war had given proof of unprecedented heroism and self-sacrifice and who now suddenly sat cringing with fear on the prisoners' benches, confessing to the most senseless charges, reciting grotesque and ridiculous litanies of their faults and crimes, and listening to the ludicrous justifications of their sentences without a word of protest. People read in the papers about priests who had spent irreproachable lives in the service of God who now, on the prisoners' bench, were confessing to the murder of female foundling children. They heard on the radio the voices of famous physics professors in Warsaw, Prague, and Budapest accusing themselves of having been life-long agents for the Honduras military intelligence. After their confessions, these people would disappear; their bodies were carried out of the cellars of the Polish, Czech, or Hungarian political police headquarters in the middle of the night and no one, apart from their families, thought of them again. Then these societies instinctively understood why for twenty years no news had come from Russia about socio-political resistance, despite the fact that psychological resistance to communism represented the same oxygen of existence there as everywhere else where communism ruled. A paralyzing recognition of the Communist technology of power penetrated the consciousness of these societies. This technology had developed and used *such* inhuman catalysts for dissolving the human will, had discovered *such* new methods for drugging entire nations with fear and a sense of the futility of existence and the pointlessness of life, that slowly, as if with the aid of some monstrous antihuman chemistry, it paralyzed resistance, and finally, even the intention of resistance in the human soul, thereby nipping an eventual act of resistance in the bud. This boundless contempt for truth and verisimilitude bore fruit: the absurd, which had been ruthlessly driven out of literature and art, became the most effective instrument of rule over compliant, overpowered minds in the hands of philosophical monists who were absolutely convinced of the teleological values of the world constructed by them. East Europeans understood why the extreme left, which had seized power and was using terror to preserve it, was so terrifyingly superior to the extreme right, which uses *only* mass murder to stay in power. The slow, methodical destruction of human dignity by the victorious left led to a paralysis of heroism in the opposition to ideas, political morality, and ruling systems such as humanity until then had never known.

And yet, we are always reading in the newspapers that someone *is* opposing. We are continually coming across proofs that resistance exists. Now and then, isolated groups of intellectuals and students protest and resist. These demonstrations must not be confused with the spontaneous explosions of open revolt which have broken out in Berlin, Poznan, and Budapest over the past twenty-five years. The latter made the world realize that societies do not willingly accept communism. But though they had an important significance, their effects varied and were not so important. In Poland revolt brought two years of a milder political climate. In Berlin a considerable amount of consumer goods was put on the market. In Hungary a bloody hecatomb was followed by relative economic stabilization without any political concessions. Communism is not afraid of armed revolts or insurrections because it knows it can always deal with them. Open revolt is impossible against modern technology in the service of modern totalitarianism, and the democratic West will forget the bloodiest repressions in a few months. Communism really fears only writers, students, and isolated, doomed liberals. It knows that they are that deposit of independent thought it cannot reach, and that thought is the field on which the final battle will be fought. Thought can be kept deeply hidden and preserved for a long time. It is a territory which cannot be brought under control, and lack of complete control means the downfall of communism. Hence the target of the fiercest attacks planned by the most ruthless staffs is man's thought. Communism will never abandon its bitter and cruel violation, rape, and assault on thought. It will use every means to bring thought under its control, even if this requires the criminal sterilization, pulverization, and absurd dehumanization of thought. Communism fears not only well-formulated thought, but also more rudimentary forms such as impulses, inclinations, or whims. A Polish art historian once said, "When I showed a reproduction of a Braque painting to some children who had never in their lives seen anything but plaster-of-Paris busts of Lenin, portraits of Stalin, or paintings by socialist realist artists, only one little boy said, '*That*'s pretty,' although he could not explain why he liked it. But *one* like him was there." Communism has got itself into a moral-ideological situation whose logic teaches it that to stay in power it must either extirpate from the boy what he has barely taken a liking to, or kill him, because otherwise the boy will be a disseminator of anticommunism. So communism chooses the second solution. Because, however, it cannot murder all its subjects—indeed, there is no way it can find out the impulses and likings of *all* its subjects—it subjects them to psychological pressures of an intensity and scope unknown in history. In this way, it tries to kill their thought. Or their human nature.

But it is a vain effort, because although you can physically smash the thinking apparatus, you cannot kill thought. From this we can draw the optimistic conclusion that, from a historical perspective, communism is doomed to inevitable defeat.

A man living in the democratic West cannot imagine an environment in which you cannot say something, assert something in public, or publish something. In the meantime, right next to him, in a world which has shrunk so that the distance between Washington and Moscow is but several hours by plane, live people who are as remote from him in time and space as the people of the early Middle Ages. Not only can the citizens of a Communist nation not say what they think is right to say, they are not even allowed to think in a different way from that pre-scribed by the political canon that runs their lives. At this point a free man living in the democratic West, cleansed of the excres-cence of centuries of restrictions, burdens, and conventions, will say, "That's nonsense! How can you create conditions in which a man cannot think what he wants? After all, thinking is not a social process, but a psychological one. A man thinks what he wants, and says what he considers appropriate in a given situa-tion. If he doesn't want to say something, then he doesn't say it." Western man thus assumes the free choice to say what one wants as an inviolable axiom. He rules out the existence of an environment in which such a free choice does not exist. None-theless, such an environment is a fact, as is his inability to under-stand it.

If a word is the natural consequence of a thought, then in communism there ensues a fundamental breakdown in this rela-tionship, which determines both thought and word in an obvious and entirely new way. This phenomenon was perhaps best put into words by a famous Russian writer after his escape to the West. He wrote:

> The most normal, most natural, and most essential of all desires—to speak the truth, or what is thought—is a for-gotten and unreal dream in Soviet Russia. Throughout his entire waking life, man in communism lives in fear of saying something which should not be said aloud.

The enslavement of thought is determined to a greater degree by the fact that there are things which *should not* be said aloud than by the fact that there are things which you are *forbidden* to say aloud. Fear before oneself is transformed into an inner self-control which dehumanizes man to a far greater degree than a political ban against stating forbidden views. Freedom of thought may be a psychological problem, but as a social principle, it assumes the possibility, even the necessity, of free expression. When the first Americans proclaimed freedom of conscience the major value for which they left their native lands, and which they intended to make the cornerstone of life in the New World, they meant the possibility of openly admitting that they were Puritans, Quakers, and Nonconformists. Communism has turned the clock back four hundred years: freedom of conscience is *ex officio* represented as psychological leprosy. A man's conscience is not his own, but belongs to his social class before the Revolution. And after the Revolution it has to be artificially prefabricated into something which is loftily called "social membership" and actually represents a prescription for man which has been conceived by theoreticians, politicians, and administrators. It is natural, then, for a man's thoughts, as well as his behavior, his rights, his duties, his past, present, and future, to undergo strict codification and continual refashioning. Man in communism does not develop by himself; he is not formed by life or defined by his friends and the people close to him. He is created by prescription, by recipe, by a sheet of paper written daily by specially appointed planners who have no idea of the shape of the actual man's nose, the color of his eyes, or of his stomachaches, besetting worries, and sorrows. For this knowledge is not part of their duties, and facts do not concern them in the least. But still they reserve for themselves absolute power to regulate everything concerning a man, even, if they see fit, the shape of his nose.

Rebellious younger generations always hide behind something which they do not get from life, cannot obtain at a given moment, or something which is forbidden them. To them, a prohibition represents a shield which they hold in front of them as they march forth to revolt. If there were no prohibition, there would be no need to rebel; hence the prohibition is just as important and valuable as the rebellion itself. In democracies a prohibition is usually partial and weak and can be overcome. There are institutionally established channels for challenging the prohibition. Because of this, the revolt of young people in the West is characterized by a great deal of moral worth as well as by some rather cheap tricks, or the usual abuse of existing freedoms and license presented as virtue. If, for example, some social group has legal and constructive opportunities for advancing and realizing its goals, but its individual members do not get what in their opinion are appropriate gains, usually because of their own individual defects, these individuals combine to form a movement. This broader alliance, in turn, proclaims that something has been denied the whole group, and depicts individual, often private, deficits and failures as faults of the socio-political system, or else puts the blame on other social groups whom it accuses of often imaginary persecutions. Nonetheless, in correctly functioning democracies such trumped-up claims get enough attention, advertisement, and publicity so that they are transformed into a so-called social problem, which is investigated and solved within the framework of general social needs and priorities. In this way, social movements—be they large, small, or quite small; right, wrong, or absolutely farcical —arise in democracies by virtue of an indestructible *perpetuum mobile* and determine the imperfect perfection of democracy, its eternal youth, and its dynamism, which is not always rational, but generally always moves the world forward.

This state of affairs is unthinkable under communism. If in democracies freedom of expression is not synonomous with the attainment of a political or social goal, and does not automatically mean that a demand will be met, it nonetheless always acts as the concrete starting point for change. Under democratic conditions, then, opposition is a clearly defined concept. Where there is no freedom to express one's convictions, a prohibition encroaches on metaphysics and opposition acquires an infinite range of unclear, ambiguous meanings. Where there exists in the mind of the rulers an unshakable principle about what people are and are not allowed to do, and the power that controls the human mind usurps for itself even the privilege to draw up the prescription for opposing that power, true resistance is often overshadowed by false resistance, the number of shades of resistance cannot be counted, and the very act of resistance is hopelessly corrupted and decomposed. During the Stalinist era a boy who wore a crew cut instead of having his hair combed straight back, or a girl who wore a pony tail, were regarded as heroic nonconformists at their universities regardless of their

115

beliefs and stated opinions. Wearing a certain hair style was an act of opposition, but this act could be interpreted in various ways. It could be seen as an act of resistance against certain principles and criteria. It could also be construed as camouflage for the propagation of communism in a more attractive form. An infinite number of possible interpretations lay between these two hypotheses, for in communism dogma can be replaced as easily as the filter in a car—when one is worn out, you throw it away and replace it with a new one. Thus if communism needs to show signs of resistance in certain political and historical situations, it organizes resistance for itself under tight control. There can be two reasons for making a show of resistance: either there is a need to demonstrate tolerance to resistance in front of the non-Communist world, or there is a need for provocation, that is, the artificial creation of a center of resistance in order to begin harsh repressions for pedagogical or didactic purposes. These schemes suggest a question as fundamental as it is incomprehensible to the Western democratic mentality: namely, what is allowed and what is forbidden to the young people who resist and oppose under communism?

The answer is simple: They are allowed nothing; or rather, they are allowed *not* to threaten the existing order. Their resistance, should the need for it arise, has to be worked out in detail by the control organs created for this purpose, such as the Party apparatus and the security police. The slightest transgression of the limits laid down leads to repressions whose perfidy, cynicism, and ruthlessness can neither be imagined nor understood in the West. The scum of society, pimps and criminals recruited under the watchful eye of the political police as "workers," push their way into university auditoriums where students are allegedly discussing forbidden problems, and beat up everyone present, students and professors alike, until they are unconscious or in some cases crippled for life. This is called the spontaneous anger of the people in defense of their Party and its ideals. In March, 1968, when Polish students protested the illegal arrest of their colleagues, these "workers" killed a pregnant student by trampling her to death in the gutter. The Warsaw newspapers unanimously described the incident as the "disarming of a CIA agent by workers indignant at the provocation." Long prison terms and deportation to concentration camps are communism's usual response to students who want to question the political regime and the ideology it represents. The mildest punishment is expulsion from school, which means that the student's life ambitions are wiped out for good, since all universities belong to the state, that is, to the government, and dismissal from one automatically means that the "guilty" person will not be accepted by the others. An equally popular punishment is forced conscription into the army for an undetermined length of time. In practice, this lasts up to five or seven years, because only the army, not the laws or regulations, decides when a soldier thus recruited can be discharged.

The young rebel in the West who opposes capitalist democracy feels himself outside the system the moment he takes the communion of his rebellion. Yet he can live *within* his society, fighting it with his every thought, his every word, his every deed. He sees himself as someone storming a mighty fortress, a fortress whose internal moral and rational laws are not binding on him. The amazing thing about democracy is that you can live within it while opposing it and rejecting everything it stands for—and still prosper and enjoy its privileges without feeling threatened as a person or a citizen. It is remarkable how democracies guarantee the force and the effectiveness of the hatred of people who hate them and want to destroy them. These are states and feelings unknown to someone opposing communism from within. While such a person may be desperately aware of his opposition and his hatred toward communism, he still always feels surrounded, overpowered, and swallowed up by the system. He soon comes to the conclusion that if he should ever succeed in changing something, it would be a change within the framework of the system, and he begins to regard this eventuality as the maximum possible attainment. Such a conclusion leads him to the position of a revisionist. What revisionism is, however, demands separate discussion.

An interesting role in such a system is assigned to the youth

117

organizations. If an American student managed to sneak into a meeting of a Party organ making decisions about the activity of the youth organizations in communism, he would get the shock of his life. If he tried to tell his colleagues on an American campus about it, they would laugh at him, or ship him off to a mental hospital. There is only one school, or student, organization in a Communist country and it has a complete monopoly in all schools and universities. Attempts to organize other organizations are forbidden, illegal, and punished by long prison terms. In Poland and Hungary fifteen-year-old boys have been condemned to ten years in prison for meeting in private homes and listening to American jazz records. (In Stalinist times this was defined as a subversive activity by the political police.) In turn, the independence, or even autonomy, of the official youth organization is a complete fiction, though it is proclaimed in every line of official declarations. Such an organization is not created by youth; on the contrary, it is the work of older people, often people who are quite old. It is these older people who conceive and plan the student organization, supply its ideology, goals, aims, policies, tactics, even its ideals of daily life and models of behavior. It does not belong to youth, but youth belongs to it. Concepts such as the generation gap or the idea that youth has its own special interests, so familiar in democracies, here are denied; it is forbidden to activists to even discuss them in public under the threat of severe penalties. The Communist Party considers itself the sole representative of everyone without exception, including young people and children, right down to newborn babes. Thus, to their way of thinking, the generation gap is an invention and a trick of bourgeois ideologists who are trying to disrupt class solidarity in the name of imaginary counterrevolutionary divisions. According to the Party, a perfect convergence of interests exists between a first-year biology student and the resident of an old people's home, inasmuch as both boundlessly love the Party. So the student youth organization is ruled in dictatorial fashion by the local Party committee which a given school is under. Its meetings are led by adults, often by elderly instructors who come wearing the organization's uniforms, red ties, etc. These are paid employees of the Party apparatus, so-called agitators assigned to "youth work." Their dullness, bald heads, the pseudoliveliness of their manner, which is modeled on the values and rules of army barracks and held up as an ideal, and their lifelessly recited political formulas grotesquely harmonize with the atmosphere of pseudoenthusiasm and false devotion to the cause which is obligatory at such meetings. The blind obedience of the activists finally takes on the character of flawlessly organized imbecilism. Judging from what is said and propounded at these meetings, young people believe and accept the convictions and principles of seventy-year-old Party leaders who see the present-day world in terms of the problems and possibilities of fifty years ago. Party secretaries with sclerosis and rheumatism decide what today's teen-agers should shout at demonstrations and what music they should listen to. We might add that the job of youth activist is very well paid and that everyone who agrees to be a so-called youth leader and to deliver speeches at public meetings and congresses of the "representatives" of Polish, Czech, or Russian youth receives special bonuses for every outcry raised against American "imperialism."

The young American rebel may envy his young Communist counterpart only one thing. The latter longs for concrete freedom and can only imagine its taste. The former possesses it, and the result is satiation, the loss of the ability to truly taste it, and the deprivation of the painful delights of winning freedom. In the West young people now have only sex and politics. In the East they are still fighting for the bread of freedom, beside which sex and politics are like a cake which does not satisfy anyone. Hence that despairing cry of a Columbia University student during one of the radical-revolutionary meetings: "We'll never have a revolution in this country! Too many people are too happy!" There will never be a shortage of unhappiness, despair, and injustice as ammunition for revolutions in Communist nations. Indeed, these things are in such abundance and people are so boundlessly and absolutely miserable that they are incapable of the thought of resistance, of fighting and freeing themselves

119

from communism. But will things always be this way? The words of the "Internationale"—"This battle will be the last"—sound most false in the countries ruled by communism. Even if today opposition there is an irrational, even a surrealistic, spiritual position, still everyone there knows that the Book of Genesis has not yet been closed and what battles there are yet to come.

## In Maturity

If a Communist who is correctly oriented in his own system of beliefs is asked about the protocause and crux of all things, he will reply: History. Marxism borrowed from Hegel the concept of the spirit of history, and supposedly gave it a scientific basis. Certain opponents of Hegel have contended that the conception of the spirit of history is only evidence of a shameful flaw in the character of the German idealist philosopher; namely, his overwhelming laziness. Being himself pathologically incapable of spreading marmalade on his bread for himself, Wilhelm Friedrich Hegel saddled history with an enormous job which had to be performed. A century and a half later, in the communism practiced daily over vast expanses from the Pacific to Berlin, this principle is the main cause of the dissolution of the societies built by Marxists. If history regulates itself automatically, like the latest Swiss self-winding watch, then everything is determined by an irreversible process, and concepts such as moral responsibility—individual or social—are good for scrap metal. Free will of the individual can be thrown on the junk heap. Energy and diligence in carrying out one's assignments and the eventual personal advantages arising from this have a suspicious odor about them and are a kind of petit bourgeois deformation which must be fought. It was because such conclusions were correctly drawn from Hegel that, after fifty years, Communist governments are completely unable to produce the necessary quantity of meat per capita, or to organize city traffic.

Communist societies are tightly shrouded in an all-pervading mood of abnegation. The Communist mass media make feverish efforts to dispel it with cheaply cooked-up pseudoenthusiasm or pseudodynamism, but the hopelessness and futility of this effort strike even the most stupid, but most well-disposed, observer. In Poland this atmosphere has given birth to a neologism to describe a certain existential posture: an obscene metaphor for helpless drooping which defines the only correct attitude to take toward an all-enveloping reality. It is natural, then, that the opposition to communism on the part of mature people, caught up in the routine of everyday life, is subjected to the same conditioning as the rest of existence. This gives communism a completely unexpected advantage because the only reasonable answer to the question: How do you oppose in maturity? is: But is it worth it? Does it make any sense?

One of the fundamental differences between youth and maturity in any regime is the sense of what is impossible. But whereas in democracies the problem of the absolute and the awareness of the unattainability of ideals are philosophical problems that usually lead to various interpretations of compromise, in communism these problems end up in the sphere of individual and social pathology. Thus the process of maturing, which in democratic humanized societies is primarily a development in the direction of more moderate judgments and hopes, in communism becomes the development of a dulling resignation. Communism does not admit the idea of compromising with anything or anyone, neither with an idea, nor with society, nor with an individual, because reason, the heart of compromise, represents a mortal threat to doctrine. Therefore people living under communism are offered only the possibility of capitulation.

Resignation and capitulation are forced on people in a brutal manner, to the accompaniment of degrading mockeries of common sense. Every day a man living under communism reads in the papers that he is living in the freest political and social system in the world, knowing only too well that he doesn't have the right to freely elect his leaders or even the right to write letters to the editor about it. A man loses his dignity when he is forced to accept lies which are in glaring contradiction to his normal perception of reality. And it is this which gives rise to a hatred that is even more choking and desperate than the anger of youth, which comes in blinding flashes. Young people, even the most embittered of them, do not lose hope. A middle-aged man questions hope, and this destroys him psychologically, since it is difficult to live fully without hope. An old man lives without hope and nothing is left for him except hatred. Thus no one hates communism as terribly as old people. If their children and grandchildren have swallowed the Communist wafer, or merely want to exist within the framework of their time without feeding only on negation, they accuse them of having forgotten too easily about the torments of the past era, of idealizing it in their memories, and of not understanding the new era. This is an obvious oversimplification of something older people do not know how to explain, and this inability to explain only intensifies their ingrained hostility. Because they know something that young people cannot know, they have a perspective on lies and abuses which is so difficult to formulate and communicate to younger people, and, like every insight gained from the experiences of an entire lifetime, defies description. They know the pain of comparison and the agony of a correct conclusion that cannot be put into words because it is so rich in experience; that is, a truth which is given and revealed by the very hardship of existence, and therefore impossible to name.

The only available form of effective opposition remains simple honesty. By remaining true to himself, a man in communism saves himself in an uncomplicated manner that brings psychological relief. This is, however, the most difficult thing of all in an environment whose mightiest forces are unleashed for the express purpose of deforming man. These forces can be fought only by accepting one's own destruction, and this requires either stupidity or heroism. And not many middle-aged or old people are ready for suicidal heroism in their daily lives, without special circumstances. You cannot escape from these forces, but you can deceive them and lead them on a wild goose chase. And this is what the vast majority of people in communism try to do.

This is done most effectively by giving in, or, as it is popularly called, selling yourself. But the act of selling yourself and your conscience opens up completely unforeseen eventualities of resistance. In this manner, something that can be regarded in a simple way as iniquity often becomes the starting point for simple human decency.

You can sell yourself sincerely, renouncing your inner life, your faculties of judgment, your own thought, and your dignity. This leads to spiritual death and the deprivation of your humanity, but it also guarantees the peace of psychological deadness and the comfort of an insensitive conscience. But it does not at all guarantee that your interests will be safeguarded, for there is no loyalty the Party would not depict as criminal disloyalty, should the need arise, hurling the delinquent down from the summits of success to the depths of failure. You can, however, sell yourself on the surface; that is, take the sacrament like the Jewish Marranos and remain true to the old faith, in this case, to yourself. Then something unexpected happens: the element of struggle and opposition which you sold yourself to avoid suddenly appears in a fascinating new light. The unceasing obsession with sabotage which never leaves the pages of the Communist press is essentially a propaganda device for terrorizing the masses. However, cases of an apparently dedicated manager, scholar, army officer, or engineer waiting whole years for an opportunity to give vent to his pent-up, deeply buried hatred are not rare.

Things do not, of course, always occur with such Machiavellian sophistication. The enormous number of Party secretaries in an East European province who secretly or half openly have church weddings, christen their children, and observe religious holidays represents an essential part of the opposition process, though with a rather grotesque hue. You can sell yourself openly, loudly proclaiming your loyalty and devotion to the Party, and in your heart wish the worst defeats upon it and passionately curse it. You can sell yourself secretly, declaring at every step and to everyone you meet your distrust of the regime, while at the same time you inform your superiors about how others spit at the regime—and thereby make yourself a career as an informer. You can, in a word, do many things, including not getting mixed up in anything and simply remaining an honest man. Though, as I said, this is the hardest course of all.

Some people are helped by religion, which is enjoying a renaissance under communism. But this is not an unequivocal revival or the eruption of new forces, as the following story best illustrates. During a mass in one of the Warsaw churches, when the worshippers were devoutly kneeling, only one man remained standing. "Excuse me," whispered someone next to him, "why aren't you kneeling?" "Because I'm not a believer," was the reply. "I'm against the government."

Opposition in maturity is most effectively reduced by one of the Communists' more brilliant ideas, a quite exceptional achievement of the Communist technique of ruling which is invisible to outside observers. It is the delicate and complex mechanism of satisfying society by displays of pseudoindependence, and even a kind of pseudo-opposition.

In official political terminology Communist society is composed of Communists and non-Party members. In the strange undertaking which Communists call elections to autonomous legislative bodies, the list of names which everyone *must* vote for usually bears the name of National Front, or Electoral Bloc, or Coalition of Communists and Non-Party Members. This creates the desired impression of unity and solidarity of the *whole* of society behind the Communist program. Thus if non-Party members are to be nominally accepted as candidates for deputy or social activist, they should come from that section of society which is not Communist in order to represent it. This, however, would be too simple, too much in keeping with logic and a common sense of decency toward the simple truth. To avoid this, non-Party activists are named exclusively by the Party. These are for the most part convinced Communists devoted to the cause, or common careerists, ready to commit any filthy act, or submissive terrified creatures forced to servility and blind obedience by the political police. These people would gladly join the Party and meekly do whatever the Party demanded or ordered. However, the Party itself has ordered them *not* to join but to spread its gospel and accept every filthy thing it does, while obtrusively demonstrating to all and sundry their *lack* of Party membership. Such people are called professional non-Communists in Eastern Europe. They can be divided into two categories: professional non-Party members and professional oppositionists.

The principle behind their existence is as simple as it is brilliantly utilitarian. In countries where 90 percent of society lives in sharp opposition to, if not in deep hatred of, its rulers, the rulers must try to provide a little psychological relaxation for such a huge mass of people. Because the masses cannot be given what they want—this is an ideological assumption, since communism is based on *not* giving people what they want—they must be given the illusion that they are getting it. But no one, neither Communists nor their subjects, is so stupid that he does not soon realize that the giving is all for show and the illusion is only just that. Still, when existence is so awful and people have been brutally deprived of everything else, even a recognized illusion begins to acquire a certain value, and the Communists thereby create for themselves the aura of people who give *something*. Then the convention is accepted by both sides, and the fact that *nothing is given* no longer counts, while the *fact of giving nothing* remains. Thus people who are supposed to be the same as other people and do not belong to the ruling elite allegedly get the right to vote in order to say what the governed want said. All this is the illusory play of the reflections of artfully placed mirrors, which give such a false image of reality that they relieve anger and provide an inexhaustible supply of jokes. But this doesn't bother the Communists at all, for, having made some fellow the spokesman of the non-Party masses forever, they no longer care whether anyone believes or questions his representativeness. Doubts cannot be voiced publicly, and there is no place to publish one's contempt and exposures. Hence the illusion is institutionalized, or even sanctified, and all the Communist countries are full of "honorable," "irreproachable," and "independent" scientists, writers, and social activists who go to the appropriate office of the political police or Party apparatus every morning for instructions on what they should say today on radio, television, or in a press interview. And all their listeners and readers know this perfectly well. But appearances are kept up, and this is all that concerns the Communists.

The technology of producing professional non-Party people is just as refined as the idea itself. As in every action, the deciding factor is the profitability of an undertaking. In a country where 90 percent of the population is anti-Communist, a person can live quite well off his role as a non-Communist. He need only to get a license for it, and the Communists will give this franchise. But the Communists must be given something in return. This can be an old aristocratic name, the personal reputation of a prominent individual, or talent. Clergymen of all faiths are very welcome. So are former members of the far right, even outright fascists who underwent miraculous transformations after the Communists took over and traded in their old celebrity for comfortable apartments and the new celebrity of a convert. The professional non-Communist then makes appropriate declarations in the press, on radio and television, as well as in person on special occasions such as at elections, international congresses, academic ceremonies on state and national holidays, and protest meetings against American invasions and aggressions. Backed by his historical aristocratic name, his priest's garb and theological education, his achievements in the field of molecular physics, or his glory as a poet, the professional non-Communist resolutely declares that the Party knows better than the Pope what is good for the Catholic Church; that lies are truth and the truth stupidity; and that two plus two equals five if the Party thinks so, since there is no objective arithmetic but only arithmetic that serves workers and arithmetic that serves capitalists. He will declare that the sun moves around the earth, that little children die of hunger on Wall Street, and that Stalin was a more brilliant physicist than Einstein, as long as it is of benefit to the Party and the proletariat. In return for this service, he receives cash bonuses, passports to travel abroad, the right to be treated in luxurious clinics, as well as a false sense of his own importance. False, because this importance is assigned and determined exclusively by the Party, and it is only its whim which decides if and when the career of the professional non-Party man will continue, what dimensions it will take, and what public image is in store for a given professional non-Party man.

The classic example of this type of career is that of a certain president of the Union of Polish Writers. This man, who has a noble name and the talent of a lyric poet in love with the charms of sensuality, married into an extremely wealthy family before the war and received a country estate as his dowry. When the Communists took over Poland, the poet determined to avoid poverty and expropriation regardless of the price he would eventually have to pay. Thus ten years later he had won the highest state decoration from the Communists and the permanent position of non-Party representative of Polish literature. In the meantime, his duties included publicly repeating that whatever the Communists did in Poland and the world, it was wise, correct, valuable, and a blessing for the Polish nation and the rest of humanity. Moreover, he, a poet, a nobleman, and a good Pole, gave his word of honor as an honest man that he had no connection with the Party. He thereby signed his name to every crime and every lie of the Communists. And because he was a powerfully built man with the profile of an ancient Greek Zeus on a tourist souvenir, the Communists began to send him to international conferences and congresses devoted to problems of peace, where the president fervently swore that the Russian delegates were the instrument of peace and the American ones, of war. These appearances won him no end of respect and friendship from American and West European intellectuals, who went into raptures over the fact that such an un-Communist-looking gentleman and aesthete was getting along so marvelously with the Communists, who ask him to speak on their behalf even though he does not belong to the Party. They began to visit him in his home, which had been saved from expropriation, and to enjoy meals served by efficient servants in the heart of a Communist country. And their enthusiasm for communism grew in proportion to what they didn't know about it. One of the

127

things they didn't know was that every day the poet-president reported every detail of their stay to the security police and received precise instructions on what he should say to induce his non-Communist, liberal, progressive guests to make statements which could be used in propaganda campaigns. This was part of his duties as a licensed non-Party man.

Besides the professional non-Communists, there exist in communism the professional oppositionists. This is generally a very small, carefully selected, and well-matched group of unusually reliable people whose loyalty to the Party has been closely scrutinized and is beyond suspicion, but who, from time to time, lapse into disobedience and nonconformist follies. The Party is perfectly well aware what advantages can accrue from these harmless outbursts of rebellion and lets them make them. The professional oppositionist counts on the fact that nothing will happen to him whatever his conflicts with the Party and his monstrous heresies. Even if he is mildly persecuted for a while and denied honors and positions, the opportunity to publish if he is a writer or a publicist, or a chair at a university if he is a professor, he is persecuted in a manner which is ultimately to his advantage, if only in that he gets the reputation, spread by word of mouth, of being the victim of persecution, which automatically assures him sympathy and popularity in society. The phenomenon of the professional oppositionist is far more delicate, complicated, and ambiguous than that of the professional non-Party members. Its substance is the staggeringly complicated net of interdependencies between the Party, its ruthlessly exacted *raison d'état,* and the professional oppositionist himself. It's a bit reminiscent of the structure of popular spy novels with their never-ending game of "You know that I know that you know what I know." The professional oppositionist acquires his status after a rigorous security check by the political police, which issues him a special security clearance. Not to him personally, of course, but rather for use by the mysterious manipulators in the depths of the dark police and party cabinets. Henceforth someone says somewhere that even if he commits some act of disobedience or apostasy, he should be punished, but not too harshly, castigated but not destroyed. Thus the professional oppositionist often does not know that he has been named one, or that he has been given a green light for various escapades. At first, he thinks he is acting in good faith and is prepared to suffer the consequences. Unless, however, he is a very stupid man, which is not infrequently the case, he soon realizes that he is acting under special conditions. If, as is most often the case, he is a calculating and shrewd man who is only pretending to be impulsive and nobly indignant, he begins to weigh his words very carefully so as not to cause the Party any embarrassment and thus force it to react harshly. He knows how much he is permitted in order to retain his license for opposition and knows that the Party knows he knows. Consequently it will not deal him any real blows but will only pretend to strike him in order to maintain his reputation for intractability. Basically, he does not want to hurt the Party, which is his surest and ultimate support. Likewise, the Party pretends to be angry and shocked by his words or actions, but at the same time it turns away its face to hide its smile of satisfaction that everything is running as it should—that the professional oppositionist is ostentatiously shaking his fist at the Party, but advancing no very real opposition. He then receives cheers from the crowd for his licensed courage, and bonuses from the Party for not overstepping certain limits and thus forcing it to take repressive measures. When he is publicly rebuked by the Party (though not too harshly), the crowd sympathizes with him, praises his honesty and independence, and even declares that perhaps the Party isn't quite so bad if it can show such indulgence and forbearance. And this is the effect the Party counted on. It has displayed a false tolerance while in fact it tolerated nothing it did not want to and has opened a safety valve for people, having allowed an impulse of protest or resistance, knowing full well that it would not be dangerous. This enables it to ruthlessly and brutally suppress the resistance of true, uncompromised ideological oppositionists, drowning them in a flood of hypocrisy and the pharasiacal proofs of its liberalism in dealing with the professional oppositionists.

There is a third side to this pageant, namely, the democratic

West, which cannot conceive that even opposition can be planned, and at the sight of the rampaging professional nonconformist goes into ecstacies over his courage and the extraordinary evolution of communism to better forms, better times, and true freedom. The naiveté of the West is then a carefully calculated factor in the planning of resistance as a concession to opposition. This naiveté is a major incitement to the development of even more ingenious and cynical versions of pseudoresistance, and if it did not exist, the Communists would be forced to liquidate an entire branch of the Party devoted to fabricating lies about their own reality. The gullibility of the West has contributed to the creation of the position and status of two of the most notorious professional noncomformists in the history of Communism: Ehrenburg and Yevtushenko.

A man living under communism who has reached middle age knows these subtle connections between morality, both individual and social, and opposition to communism. In this knowledge lies the source of his terrible frustration, apathy, inertia, and alienation, which have been discussed so many times by scholars and writers who managed to escape from communism. When he reflects on the nightmares accumulated in the course of just a single lifetime, he is inevitably overwhelmed by the bitter reflection: Is it worth it?

# 15 • What is the plan?

IN COMMUNISM the plan is neither a word nor an idea, but a magic formula. According to the founders of Marxism, the idea of the plan was that it would become the source of socialism's victories and successes, the open sesame to the universal happiness of mankind, the key to a utopia which was supposed to change into paradise on earth with the help of the plan. Love for the plan is a nineteenth-century sentiment originating in times when the bourgeois capitalist world—as Marx and his followers saw it—was sunk in the hideous sin of planlessness and laissez-faireism, thereby creating chaos, indeterminism, criminal profit, and universal poverty on this planet. The early apologists of Marxism tended to see only the socio-economic element in the plan, for at the time they still believed that economics was the soul of Marxism. Thus in the orthodox Marxist's worldview, the word "plan" activated a spiritual state comparable only with the state of grace in the soul of a Christian. The plan's goal, as he understood it, was to become the supreme regulator of the entire life of society, from production and distribution to demographic growth and the instincts determining it. It was to introduce order into chaos and, in the final analysis, to be a moral agency. The loftiest consequence of the plan was that it would make people happy, individually and en masse.

Like every splendid incarnation of Faith, Hope, and Charity, the plan was fated to become a mangy, miserable flop in a reality dreamed up by prophets and realized by professional revolutionaries. In the twentieth century it turned out that the apocalyptic development of the means of production and the multiplication of all social functions brought the plan and planning into every political and economic system higher than a hunting and fishing community. From what was supposed to be the triumph of Marxist thought, the plan became a secondary element of everyday life, even in Paraguay and Borneo. In the second half of our century democratic capitalism deprived the plan of its charisma, but in return applied it in every field, popularized it, simplified it, and developed it within the framework of maximum social utility. The openness of public life in democracies, the flourishing of statistics and the social sciences, investigations free from the conditioning of political mystification, market research, and community planning—all this ushered the idea of the plan into daily life without ideological hysteria. It was only under communism that the plan was put on a pedestal of inviolable values which made its extreme and ultimate failure a foregone conclusion. It became the source of a chaos the likes of which mankind had never known. It led to a confusion that was insurmountable because it was planned. In the name of harmony, common sense, and efficiency, it created disharmony, nonsense, and indolence on a scale unknown in history. Like every attempt to take control over the whole of life, it resulted in a parody of life.

Communism made a central, mysterious, and unshakable value out of the plan. It subsequently had to be the work of a single agency. This means that only this agency knows everything about it and, consequently, that no one outside the agency can question the plan theoretically, much less practically. Thus the simple idea of first thinking through what has to be done acquires the prerogative of planning the entire wealth of existence. And this, as philosophers know, no mortal man has yet managed to do. But because the abysmal failures of Communist plans are never disclosed, there is no indication that the idolization and sacrosanctity of the plan will ever come to an end. Likewise, the

chances are poor of ever attaining the social and economic progress for the sake of which the fathers of Marxism conceived the
idea of the plan.

Instead of navigating the treacherous reefs of theoretical arguments and analyses, let us take an example from life. A bridge
was needed over a certain river in Communist Poland. If every
screw and every toy has to be centrally planned in advance, you
can easily imagine how much planning must go into an entire
bridge. And since Communist states plan the production of both
screws and toys five or six years ahead of time, the central economic plan is officially called the Five or Six Year Plan for
Development or Progress. The bridge, then, existed in the central plan, based on maps of the terrain which turned out to be
not very accurate. Because central planning always and on principle is a theoretical business, in a few years everything concerning the bridge contained not only the seeds of error, but also the
seeds of fatalism; that is, a solution of matters which was condemned in advance to be wrong. So years went by in prepara-
tions, planning, sketching, and ordering materials from firms
and factories. These, of course, were also subordinated to the
central plan and their production planned in the same place as
the bridge. When the builders finally arrived at the building site,
they found that, according to the plan, the bridge would join the
two banks of the river at a sharp obtuse angle, not at a right
angle, as is usually the case. This deviation from tried and tested
methods came as a complete revelation, inasmuch as the bridge,
when close to completion, did not join the two banks orthog-
onally, but seemed to stretch out into the distance along with
the river, making the crossing a kind of neverending winding
path which followed the course of the river. This attraction began to draw crowds of local peasants, who tried to explain to the
builders that they must have gone crazy. The chief engineer responsible for the construction replied that he had two choices:
either he could finish the ridiculous bridge according to plan, receiving his salary and perhaps even a bonus for conscientious-
ness, or he could ignore the plan, build the bridge correctly, and
go to prison. If the river did not conform to the plan, that was

133

the business of the central planning agency in the capital, not his, and he would not argue about it with anyone. The peasants went somewhere else to complain, and subsequently a commission of the planning agency came to the construction site. However, as always happens with commissions, by the time it arrived, the bridge had been completed according to the plan. The commission loyally declared it an unheard of scandal. The security authorities arrested the engineers and, while they were at it, a few peasants from the local council who were accused of allowing maniacs or saboteurs to build an absurd bridge over a national river, dear to the heart of every patriot. The commission also recommended that the bridge be corrected and the plans revised. Shortly thereafter, a new construction team arrived, which on the basis of the new plans managed to give the rebuilt bridge the shape of a paragraph sign, making it a spectacle on an international scale.

To make matters worse, unforeseen complications arose with the strangely shaped bridge because the raw materials supplied according to the plan had been incorrectly used. Among other things, the electric wiring got tangled up so that the bridge is "live" and everyone who walks on it gets a shock. The simplest solution would have been to tear the bridge down—bomb it, destroy it—but this was out of the question. The bridge was in the plan, the sacred and inviolable plan, the ultimate tabernacle of the Communist idea of success, achievement, accomplishment, and the improvement of the world. The careers, jobs, even the personal freedom, of too many people—from the lowest strata of that region to the highest-ranking posts in the Polish economy—depended on the continued existence of the bridge. Thus the bridge stands to this day. A solution was even found for the unforeseen problem of electric shock. It turned out that the plan for that region provided for special medical aid in buildings located near a dangerous electrical current. Thus an ambulance was put on duty twenty-four hours a day near the bridge. Anyone who steps on the bridge and gets a shock is immediately taken to the hospital. This, of course, represents the patent and natural triumph of the plan over man.

# 16 · How to go shopping

RULE NUMBER ONE when shopping is that you do not buy what you need or what you want, but what is for sale here, now, and at the moment.

A traveler from lands far from communism would stop with amazement at the sight of the following scene: Through the streets of a large city, in the midst of beautiful churches and buildings, each of them a masterpiece of the European Baroque style and a testimony to the magnificent traditions of Christian civilization, a bunch of people run. Their faces are filled with happiness and excitement and they are loaded down with armfuls of toilet paper. Major social differences can easily be detected within the group. An old professor, scholar and intellectual, carries a dozen or so rolls in both hands. He is having trouble, but there is a smile of pride on his face. A brawny worker with bulging muscles stoops under the weight of a huge pack. Evidently he has been thinking not only of his family, but also of his neighbors, his friends, and maybe his superiors at the factory, for whom there is no better present imaginable. An officer in the tank corps, forgetting the strict dignity of his uniform, marches forth with rolls of toilet paper hanging from him like medals won on the field of battle. A housewife with an elaborate garland around her neck looks like she has just returned from a trip to Hawaii. She is followed by schoolboys and office workers who have evidently abandoned their desks and offices on hearing the news that toilet paper has appeared in a local shop. The traveler, intrigued by the crowd's excitement, eagerly seeks an explanation for the scene and enquires what it means. Were some new properties of toilet paper discovered during his journey away from home, the TV news, and newspapers, which he does not yet know about? Did the morning news on the radio reveal a new use for it? Was some previously unknown and important vitamin discovered in it? No, the answer lies elsewhere. These running people were singled out for an unusual distinction. By an accident of fate, they found themselves in the vicinity of a store just as it was receiving a shipment of toilet paper. They waited patiently, perhaps even for hours, while it was unpacked and a good part of it was put aside for the private needs of the salesclerks. They waited as the salesclerks, tired from the extra work, stopped to eat lunch, drink coffee, or engage in the interminable conversations of people who do not hurry for anything. And they waited until the regular sale began. Then they bought as much as they were able to carry by themselves. Those who lived nearby ran for help, communicating the joyful tidings to everyone they met on the way. Good fortune descends on people without warning, hence the enthusiasm in their glances. And getting toilet paper is considered one of the most fortunate events of life under communism.

Why Communist countries capable of producing atomic power plants and spaceships cannot produce enough toilet paper for their citizens remains a riddle which the boldest and most brilliant minds of the epoch have given up trying to solve. So there isn't much chance that my commentary on the subject will throw any light on the darkness. I am inclined to look for an eventual explanation in metaphysics, though this is an instrument which has been too fashionable of late to be of use in clearing up the mysteries of existence. The commonly accepted and relatively simplest explanation is that a planned Communist economy is ruled by the principle of importance, not need. People need toilet paper, but it is not important enough in terms of economic theories. Theory always establishes a hierarchy of importance; it

is hardly surprising that many of the attributes of basic humanity are not assigned their proper place in it.

Someone arriving in the capitalist West from a Communist
country first goes through a state of spiritual exultation which
takes the form of an obsession with hot dogs. The strange and
inexplicable fact that a warm hot dog can be obtained on many
street corners for a small payment seems to him a phenomenon
bordering on black magic, or an achievement on the scale of
building the pyramids. Does this mean that the epoch-making
discovery of the hot dog is unknown to communism? No, hot
dogs are known to communism, only you can never get them
anywhere, especially when you feel like having one. But when
you don't feel like eating one or have utterly forgotten about
their existence, their shape suddenly appears in the window of
some shop, which you enter only to find a long line leading to the
counter. This means hours of waiting before you can get a hot
dog. Occasionally hot dog stands appear on the streets of Communist cities like sparks in a swamp, but their existence is the
exception rather than the rule. Their operators get a fixed salary from their state enterprise, not dependent on the sale of their
product. Their profit incentives are minimal and they have little
interest in selling. This last statement isn't completely true, because they *are* interested in selling their wares—only not to the
legitimate customer at the official price. Instead, they prefer
selling their entire daily supply at once to illegal black-market
entrepreneurs, a dangerous business which, however, pays lav-
ishly. Then they spend the prescribed eight hours comfortably
leaning on their wagons with folded arms, informing the hungry
that all their wares have been sold, which, of course, is true. The
hot dog lover may receive such a response immediately following the wagon's appearance at its location early in the morning.
The tender-hearted or naturally courteous vendor is sometimes
willing to inform the disappointed hot dog lover where he can get
his hot dog. But this is usually somewhere very far away and at a
price much higher than the official one. However, such displays
of human feeling are rare, for unless the vendor is a complete
idiot, he knows that the world is swarming with provocateurs,

137

agents of the secret police, and inspectors from the enterprise that considers him its pride and joy and gives him bonuses for the efficient and speedy sale of his wares.

Still, there are some uncorrupted vendors who are true Party members, mindful of its appeals, or who are merely inspired by their mission to bring hot dogs to those who need them. These people's efforts are thwarted by planning.

Suppose the planners of the enterprise distributing hot dogs may responsibly decide on a selling location in the neighborhood of a big building where thousands of people work, or near a bus stop where thousands of workers get off. In communism, however, there always exists a glaring discrepancy between the initial plan and its realization, which are sometimes many years apart. Thus when the hot dog seller arrives with his wagon, he finds that the building was built a long time ago and is already falling down, or that the bus stop was long ago moved somewhere else. Now the location is surrounded by empty fields and the nearest pedestrian can just about be seen on the horizon. The Communist vendor is not allowed to leave his post, however, so he stands there for the full eight hours without selling a single hot dog. His suggestions to change the location are favorably received by his immediate superiors, but the decision to make a change has to go through so many channels, plans, adjustments, and be approved by his superiors' superiors, that long months go by during which the vendor comes back every day with unsold hot dogs. Because of the shortage of refrigerators, the hot dogs are thrown into the garbage dump, where the overfed neighborhood dogs fastidiously pick at them. The other solution of the problem, i.e., so-called resourceful initiative, does not enter the picture at all, since under communism trade is not run on the profit principle or on the principle of feeding the hungry with surplus food, but according to so-called socialist norms of work. These preclude the degradation of human dignity by philanthropy and make sure that not the slightest trace of enterprising spirit, officially called "corruption," gets into the proletariat's souls. Thus unless corrupt colleagues and cheats inform the idealistic vendor that it is better to sell his hot dogs on the black market for a fat profit, people eager for hot dogs will have no chance of getting them. And only if the vendor takes the road of evil, crime, and risk will he prosper and his need to serve society be fulfilled. Admittedly, the Communist state will regard him as a speculator, but people *will* have hot dogs.

Against the background of such facts it is not difficult to understand why a new arrival from a Communist society who can see a hot dog stand on the street corner from the window of his New York hotel room—a hotel whose manager is eager to supply him with hot dogs at any hour of the day or night—regards the phenomenon as a *fata morgana,* an illusion of the senses which reason cannot explain. Only an intelligent Communist, true to his ideology which explains everything, knows that these wagons were deliberately placed near his window for propaganda purposes, in order to give him a false picture of America, and that the vendors are CIA agents.

The line is just as much a symbol of communism as the hammer and sickle. But unlike the hammer and the sickle, it is also its most inherent characteristic, defining human existence within it. Under communism men spend their lives on line. We can analyze the tragicality of the line by taking the example of ham. Someone—let's say the Communist Everyman—is wandering through a food store one day when he sees that ham is being sold at one of the counters—lovely ham, lean and pink, the kind of ham people in Communist countries dream of at nights. Everyman sighs deeply, for he knows that such a ham implies a line, which will mean a very long wait. But the ham smells, calls, tempts, beckons. Everyman's family has not known the taste of ham for many weeks, perhaps months. So wasting time, neglecting work, or missing an important meeting do not seem too high a price to pay for the delights of ham. Thus Everyman gets on line and slowly, very slowly, moves forward. As he moves up, his consciousness, which had been filled with the image of the ham and the desire to get it, begins to take in certain elements of the situation he had not considered earlier, and the situation, as everything else undergoes a metamorphosis in the human *esse* according to Heraclitus' law. First of all, the ham is disappearing at a frightening rate, and a quick assessment of the distance between the ham and himself, calculated according to the quantity of ham and the number of people ahead of him, seems to indicate that it will be gone by the time he gets there. Such an occurrence will seem absurd to anyone used to shopping in capitalist stores, since stores in capitalism are rarely unable to satisfy their customers' *quantitative* needs. And a shortage of ham in peacetime, in the absence of an earthquake in the immediate vicinity, seems pure surrealism. Moreover, even if for unknown and absurd reasons such a shortage did occur, the customer would simply return the following day to wallow in monstrous piles of ham which had been ordered immediately by the store after discovering a sudden and unexpected demand for ham among its customers. But under communism, as Everyman knows, the store receives a consignment of a product not according to demand, but according to the plan, and when this consignment is exhausted, no force on earth can meet the demand. And since the victory of the Revolution, consignments of ham have been microscopic and in inverse proportion to the claims made in the Communist press about the towering superiority of the Communist agricultural economy to the decaying capitalist one.

But the existential troubles of Everyman do not end here. As he gets nearer to the ham, he begins to worry about the problem of quality. The wonderful meaty pink ham is changing with every second and every yard of distance covered into a fatty, unappetizing, veiny ham, quite different from its picture a half hour ago when Everyman decided to take his place in the line. Of course, existentialism now has Everyman in its clutches, and by way of free choice, he can leave the line. But it is this choice of his own fate which is the most complicated matter. Everyman is under the influence of external stimuli and forces, such as the continual discussion by other people in the line about various problems connected with ham from a historical standpoint and at the current moment. Someone sent from the middle of the line to reconnoiter has brought back the news that next to the salesgirl is lying a fresh, uncut slab of meat from the supply to be sold today. This information makes a big difference in Everyman's calculations. Now there's a chance that the people in front of him will buy up the ugly fatty ham, and the freshly cut juicy one will come to him. So it's worth waiting another half hour, although his calculations may backfire, since the people up front are rebelling, refusing to buy and arguing with the salesgirl, voicing the bitterness and disappointment of frustrated and cheated people. Indeed, in a capitalist country any customer would laugh at a salesgirl who tried to sell him something like *that* as ham. But communism is based on discipline and decree, so that what has been officially recognized as ham by a state-owned store cannot be questioned by the customer. The salesgirl, therefore, treats the customers with profound contempt, cuts the horrible ham with the indifference of a Greek Moira, and dispenses it as a way of getting back at those protesting. Nonetheless, this time Everyman's optimistic calculations seem to be correct. A lucky star is shining on his feverish computations and he reaches the counter just as the last of the bad ham has been sold and the salesgirl is removing the scraps from the machine. Everyman waits, confident that she will bring out the new one and start to cut it. But this is not what happens. The salesgirl announces that there is no more ham, that the ham is finished for today. Excited Everyman and the crowd behind him point to the enormous untouched slab of fresh ham. But the salesgirl says coldly that it is the supply for tomorrow and puts it away under the counter. Then the trouble starts. People shout at the salesgirl. She calls them names, refers to the regulations, and fights back bitterly, but contemptuously, certain that no harm can come to her. She is a state employee, backed by political reason, the authority of the people's government, the power of communism, Marx, Lenin, and the sales plan. Everyman and the people behind him hold a position which is lost in advance. They must argue about their right to the ham with the state-owned store, that is, with the state, that is, with official social doctrine, or with Marx and Lenin themselves. Moreover, the salesgirl has her own serious vested interests in the new ham. She must take the best layer home for herself, and also some for her relatives who have already paid her for it. She must save some for the store manager (since one must be on good terms with one's superiors) and some for her colleagues in other departments, who in return will give her the best butter and imported fruits which are unavailable to the masses. Immersed in defeat, Everyman leaves with bowed head and aching feet. As he passes the cheese counter, he notices that an enormous piece of cheese, something rare in this store, this city, this country, is just being cut into for the first time. A long line is already forming. Everyman feverishly vacillates with new existential unrest. Should he get in line or not? He is overwhelmed by despair. His family at home wants to eat. . . . So he probably will end up in line.

In a capitalist economy, when a new product appears on the market, its fortunes are generally easy to predict. If it is a good product and scores a success, it will be put on the market in sufficient quantities to meet the demand for it, it will be available to everyone who can afford it. If it scores a great success, its producers will soon flood the stores with new, improved versions, raising the quality to increase interest in it and raise profits. The better a product is, the more you can be sure that the market will be supplied with ever-increasing quantities of it. No one need rush to buy it; there will be enough for everyone. When a product is not successful and the need to sell it off quickly arises, it is put on sale where it may be quickly bought because of its low price.

In a Communist state the mechanics are diametrically the opposite. When a new, sought-after product appears on the market and the interested customer learns of this fact in some supernatural way—a prophetic dream, a lucky foreboding, a telephone call in the middle of the night (since advertising in the information sense does not exist, or else, like classical literature, informs the reader of an event several centuries after it has sunk into historical oblivion)—then he must drop everything and run to where it is being sold. The immediateness of the action is the condition for its success, and we mean this literally. Students run from their schools with their excited teachers at their head, policemen stop directing traffic, engineers abandon their trains, surgeons tear off their aprons during an operation, and women in labor stop screaming and ask in a sober voice whether something can't be done to enable them to get in line at once. Obviously a product which arouses such expectations will disappear from stores the moment after it appears there (sometimes even before, having been stolen by the store personnel for speculative purposes before it can go on sale to the public). Whatever is left is thrown at the rampaging crowd, which is full of speculators who are buying the product to sell it later illegally at inflated prices. The latter were informed about the product earlier than anyone else by the store employees, for a suitable compensation. Clearly the product will soon turn up on the black market, where only a very few people will be able to obtain it. For a fanatic of legality who was unable to get the product at once in the legal way, it has stopped existing for good. This is due to one of two reasons: (1) either the factory which produced it no longer does so; or (2) if the factory does continue to produce it, the product will keep deteriorating in inverse proportion to its success.

This amazing and sudden deterioration of something—an object, a social institution, a service—which had scored a deserved success represents an inscrutable enigma of the Communist economy. Its explanation must be sought in the precipices of an ideology which defines every fact in rational categories invented by the staff of the Russian Bolshevik Revolution more than fifty years ago, categories still regarded by Communists as the most correct way of communicating with the ruled masses. Under capitalism a new product looking for sales advertises its novelty, its uniqueness, or its superiority to what is already on the market; it stresses its usefulness in making life easier or else appeals to intimate needs and snobbery. Under communism, with its remarkable semantics, a simple floor wax, a new laxative, or the most ordinary projection equipment in a newly built theatre are described in the media as a brilliant victory for socialism, a giant step forward for the world revolution, or a fatal blow to the imperialist plot against the people's government. This is what the newspapers write, passionately stressing that these goods were produced by the Party, thanks to the Party, with the help of the Party, and for the Party. Over the past fifteen years the Communist regimes in Eastern Europe have toned down this terminology a little and have permitted a few notes of sobering self-criticism. This means that toilet bowls are no longer referred to as a triumph for the proletariat, though the construction of an apartment house taller than others, the manufacture of express elevators, or the launching of a new fishing trawler are still vaunted as the impressive victory of something over something else. And you can still go into a store, say, a button store, where not a single button will be sold, though the walls will be covered with statistical charts showing a tenfold increase in button production over the pre-Communist level. The sources of this bombast lie in the enthusiasm and revolutionary frenzy of economically backward countries. But its continuation for fifty years not only makes a caricature of life, but also provides the basis for the catastrophes and psychological tor tures of people who are only trying to buy a little ham or toilet paper. If the marketing of a half-decent refrigerator is a brilliant victory for ideology, then, as everyone knows, brilliant victories do not occur every day; they happen rarely and must last for a long time. So the impossibility of repeating the victory becomes understandable, justifiable, and forgivable. A factory which has carried off victory with its product enjoys the fruits of its success and rests on its laurels; in other words, it does not improve, or even, sometimes, continue to produce, the product. Ideology has got a good mark for itself; it has triumphed in refrigerators and now is marching on to new victories in the battles for shaving cream, tractors, zippers, bicycles, and canned beans. Communist Cuba calls an ordinary harvest of sugarcane a victory. However, its leaders complain that they cannot collect a big enough harvest to meet their needs. Before communism no one in Cuba spoke of victory in the fight with sugarcane, but the harvests far surpassed their needs.

The styling of an economic advance or a production achievement as a "victory" may have far-reaching and profound perspectives. Victories are won over something, in the name of something, with the help of something, or despite something. If

144

we ignore communism's idiotic babble about "revolution" and "imperialism" in connection with ham and toilet paper, as well as its idiotic claims of superiority over everything else, it becomes fully apparent in their terminology how futile the Marxists' dialectic endeavor is. What do they really want? What are they trying to do? Are they not at times trying to break and transform human nature, but on the basis of false moral and psychological premises? Their experiment is corroding the existence of entire societies, destroying the lives and fates of millions of individuals, and the longer it lasts, the more failures and disappointments it brings, despite all the trumpeting about triumphs and victories. The founders of Marxism postulated that when social conditions had been changed by history, idealism and altruism would flourish and human nature would be transformed into an instrument of virtue and justice. Conditions were changed, but human nature has not changed in the direction expected and planned, and what is worse, nothing indicates that it is about to do so in the near future. Never in the history of the human race have social conditions brought out so many of the worst features of human nature, so much mutual hatred, organized crime, intensified coercion, and cutthroat indifference of man toward man. Never before has the principle *homo homini lupus* permeated a human community so deeply, to the point where even the relationship of the person selling ham to the person wanting to buy it is affected. In utterly materialistic, anti-idealistic, and dehumanized (according to the Communists) American capitalism, famous for its contemptuous disregard (according to the Communists) of the working man, human labor has become the most expensive socio-economic good. The result is that everyone who wants to buy ham can get it in any amount, while the salesgirl smiles politely on; toilet paper is a detail of daily life unworthy of notice, and the construction of enormous houses, bridges, and ships is called ordinary economic activity.

Under communism, which has erected a gigantic monument to the idea of work in its philosophy and its literature and canonized it as the highest value, human labor has become the cheapest, least profitable, and most frustrating aspect of human existence. Under communism work is not remunerated, it is motivated, and motivations come from the cheap, dehumanized, trashy, completely superfluous political pseudogospel. Under communism, work does not have a lasting, concrete, and inspiring value; it has only justifications that interest no one and irritate everyone. The Cuban Communist leader tries to pay Cubans for their work with speeches about "victory," and here the special split in the meaning of the word becomes apparent. To the Cuban agricultural worker, the word is a swindle pure and simple, and his healthy human nature resents selling his sweat for the miserable pennies of political propaganda. To the Cuban leader, the word signifies that triumph over man's nature predicted by the founders and prophets of Marxism, a nature which one day will finally be forced to work in exchange for words alone.

However, so far nothing points to this victory; there is not the slightest augury of it in communism as we know it. On the contrary, a sober and unprejudiced look tells us that human nature has not changed under communism and is not changing, or, if it is, then only for the worse. Throughout the entire non-Communist world young utopian leftists believe that when they come to power and free their societies from the capitalist law of profit —in other words, change economic and social conditions—people will begin to produce out of the sheer love of production, and will get safer cars, better painting, and more hygienic sausages. How many generations before them believed the same thing! In the fifty years of its existence, communism has shown that just the opposite happens.

The act of buying and selling, or the act of exchange, is as old as mankind. Its meaning is based on the mutual coordination of the exchange value of the goods offered. This fundamental principle undergoes complete disintegration under communism. The price of a product has nothing to do with its value, but is only a symbol used in balancing the general economic plans. In this way, the act of exchange loses its economic legitimacy and is moved into another category: it becomes a moral act. We can best investigate this transmutation by using the exam-

ple of buying pants. Let us assume that Everyman now finds him
self in need of pants and goes to the store to purchase some. As
he enters, he notices some pants on the shelves and racks. But
drawing closer, he finds that all the pants within sight are exactly
the same color, style, and size—ten sizes too big (or small) for
him. He does the sensible thing and turns to the salesman, who
is standing indifferently against the wall or having a carefree
chat with a fellow employee, and asks for information and suggestions. Most likely the salesman will not answer him at all; if
he does, it is only to rudely inform Everyman that there are no
other kinds of pants and the customer can take what they have
or go to the devil. This time it happens that Everyman, fed up
with all his setbacks, opposes the salesman in an equally rude
manner. But this is just what the salesman has been waiting for.
With undisguised satisfaction, he heaps a torrent of insults upon
Everyman, revenging himself on him for all *his* setbacks. For
whom can he blow off steam at and get back at for the miseries
of his hard and poorly paid job if not his wife and his customers?
He is not interested in selling anything, since he receives his
miserable salary whether or not he sells any pants, and doesn't
worry much about his commission, the so-called "economic in-
centive," because it is so small. Besides, he is the employee of a
state-owned store which will never be liquidated even if it does
not sell a single pair of pants during the entire Five Year Plan.
Moreover, and this is perhaps most important of all, he is
completely right: there are no other pants besides those on the
racks, and even if there were, the current stock would have to be
sold before they would be put on display so that the customers
would not be confused by what, in depraved capitalism, is
called choice.

Naturally, Everyman leaves without the pants. But something else could have happened.

The salesman feels a wave of idealism, the desire to serve his
people awakens in him, or he might feel a spark of personal
sympathy for Everyman, or simple human compassion at the
sight of his despair. He goes to the back of the store and brings
out an interesting pair of pants which meet Everyman's modest

demands. The fact that one leg is shorter and narrower than the other is no longer important; obligated by such a display of humanity, Everyman will not turn up his nose at them. He pays and receives the pants, which are practically unwearable, but his soul is filled with bliss. He got pants and came into contact with a man who understood him and extended his hand to help him in his hour of distress. A man can endure even communism, Communist stores and trade, and the Communist torture of shopping, if now and then he can see a tiny flame of humanity flickering in the midst of the gloom.

# 17 · How to be cheated by the state

T HE TITLE of this chapter is not very precisely formulated.
Cheating of citizens by the state is as old as the very institution of the state. There is nothing new about it, and the Communist state by no means has a monopoly on this type of activity.
The fact is that cheating has played a major role in the tradition
of statehood. Citizens are lied to, and it is officially called "informing the people." Other states are misled, and this goes by
the name of "foreign policy" or "diplomacy." When weaker
nations are brutally forced to buy or sell at fraudulent prices, it is
called "free trade" or freedom of the seas.

A Communist state, provided the necessary conditions exist,
applies exactly the same methods to accumulate and preserve its
power, only increasing their brutality by the totalitarian system
of ideological principles underlying its activities. What is new in
its practices is its notorious talent for robbing its citizens, even
the poorest of them, of tiny sums a decent pickpocket would be
ashamed to take. Although we can more or less correctly imagine
a powerful Western democracy plundering some country of its
rich oil deposits, even the American Internal Revenue Service,
known for its petty greediness, furnishes no examples of taking
money from citizens which it cannot legally claim in taxes. Indeed, as a matter of course, it returns money paid to it in error.
If you tell a citizen in a Communist country that in America you

can argue with the income tax authorities over the amount to be paid, and also prove to these authorities that they are wrong about something, he will call an ambulance to take you to the madhouse. For he knows that if the Communist income tax authorities demand and collect twice as much from him as he actually owes, and he protests, he will be forced to pay the correct amount later and will be fined for misleading the authorities besides, while he will never see the money he paid the first time. If he insists on going to court to prove he is in the right, he will go to prison for spreading slanderous propaganda against the people's government and its agencies.

These fraudulent tax manipulations against its own citizens look like large-scale operations, however, in comparison with the other sources of the Communist state's income. Everyone living under communism knows that the highest standard of services can only be obtained immediately following the mobilization or opening of a new business, and is strictly limited in time. This means, for example, that you can get good meals in a newly opened restaurant only during the first few days of its existence. The opening was, of course, depicted in the press as an unprecedented victory for socialism, and the restaurant's soups and cutlets were held up as a triumph for Marxism, considering their size in relation to their low price. This state of affairs lasts for a week; then the cutlet you order turns out to be a third smaller, at the same price. How did this happen? It's quite simple. The management of the restaurant sees that it is not taking in the planned revenue, something that can have a disastrous effect on the manager's future career. So he turns to his superiors in the state concern to which the restaurant belongs with the proposal that the amount of meat in an individual serving be cut down. As a rule, the answer is positive, since the concern is having trouble getting enough meat from the eternally deficient ministry of agriculture. No mention is made of a change in price. This would be a *faux pas* with respect to the national economic plan, which is fixed once and for all. So the customer is gently robbed of a few ounces and a few cents. Moreover, the state has accomplices with

150

whom it must share. First, there is the cook, who cannot live on his salary and must cut something off the cutlet for himself. But he cannot do this effectively enough unless he slips something to the director. So the state, in order to rob the customer of one third of the cutlet, must let its two accomplices take another third. And so after a month the customer is paying the same price for a third of the same cutlet that a short while ago was the glory of the restaurant and socialism.

The Communist state's ingenuity in picking its subjects' pockets of their last pennies is amazing. In one of the outlying suburbs of Budapest, a bus line came to an end. The trip downtown was long and tiring, so it is not surprising that the people living in the suburb were delighted one morning to find a bus with the sign "Express" standing beside the regular bus. The new bus was decked out with banners saying that the state transportation concern was introducing this epoch-making innovation to celebrate the anniversary of the October Revolution and as proof of their concern for the citizens' health. The express bus was supposed to provide a direct link between the suburb and downtown Budapest without making a single stop in between, cutting the journey's time in half. The cost of the trip would be four times higher, but the equipment was also better than in an ordinary bus, the floor cleaner, and the seats more comfortable. Many people welcomed this improvement with enthusiasm, but many, those who were poorer, who knew that the only thing which cannot be planned in a planned economy is the budget of a poor family, continued to use the cheaper and inferior bus. After a while they noticed that the number of cheaper buses was decreasing and that they were leaving the terminal less frequently, while the more expensive buses were increasing in number. This made their lives to some extent more difficult, but their real troubles began one morning when they read an announcement at the bus stop saying that the cheaper bus had been liquidated while the number of more expensive ones would be increased so that it could meet the needs of society. When this happened, the only way the poorer passengers could avoid the high fare was to walk to a far-off streetcar stop. For a few weeks the express bus ran according to its schedule, until one day its users read a new announcement saying that in view of the growing demand, one stop had been introduced on its route between the suburb and downtown. After a while more stops were introduced, and before long, the bus was stopping at every place the cheaper bus had stopped at previously, in keeping with the demands of the working people on the route. Soon its seats began to rip, its floor became dirtier and dirtier, and the sign "Express" disappeared. The only thing that didn't return to its former state was the fare. Someone wrote a letter to the editor of a local paper on this matter. An answer was given in the lead article, which accused the writer of petit bourgeois selfishness and love of luxury as well as a lack of class solidarity with all those who wanted to go to work for the glory of communism. No mention was made of the fare.

The patriarchs who devised socialism and communism in the name of the most splendid ethical principles would have been very amazed, and perhaps even deeply grieved, if they found out that the most powerful lever of interpersonal relations in the society they conceived was the ancient, primitive principle, "You for me, me for you." In Russia, right after the Revolution, an attempt to sell two eggs on the free market was punishable by death. Despite this, the institution of the bazaar continued and neither concentration camps nor the shortage of goods for trade could destroy it. During the abysmal poverty of the first Five Year Plan in the Soviet Union, a single pair of shoes passed through dozens of hands. The exchange was always made in shabby little yards outside the city where people yielded to their innate instinct and need for reciprocal trade despite all persecutions. After a while the Communists came to the conclusion that they could not eradicate this instinct from human souls and decided to learn from it. Their success surpassed all expectations and soon the Communist state became a giant swindler on a scale unknown in the history of cheating, skulduggery, trickery, and fraud. It was the only state in history you could not argue with or bargain with, or where you could not call upon the police for help when being robbed, cheated, or plundered. In the countries of Eastern Europe the institution of "Komis" flourishes. This is a state-owned business that buys from citizens who receive them from relatives abroad, luxury articles, jewelry, and gifts, which are so much in demand in underfed and underclothed societies, and sells them on a supposedly free market—organized and controlled by the same state which ruthlessly suppresses the free market. Of course, these businesses suck the last drop of blood, the last penny, out of both the seller and the purchaser of these goods. Both are exploited to the utmost, and the usury of state agencies reaches proportions which would make Shylock blush with shame. And where can you complain? When someone moves into a new apartment building, which was built by the state and is state property, and its hydraulic installation does not work, any protest must be carefully worded. Defective plumbing in the toilet is a matter between him, the government, and the theories of Marxism.

The "You for me, me for you" principle extends far and wide. A citizen in a Communist nation stands in dumbfounded amazement before such an incomprehensible phenomenon as the "Welfare State" in democratic capitalism, where people are given various things in exchange for nothing, where scholarships, grants, and donations are offered to professors, writers, and students who openly proclaim their desire to destroy those who have given them this money. When someone living under communism wants something from the state, he must in return give at least boundless adoration and blind obedience.

A certain Polish premier comes relatively the nearest to capitalism: he sells cars. It may sound somewhat unlikely that the premier of a large Communist state is involved in the sale of cars, but such is the case. Every year prestigious international exhibitions are held in Poland on the understanding that the exhibits will remain at the disposal of the Polish government after the exhibition is over. Thus every year a few cars of good Western make are left in Poland. In a Communist country such cars represent the pinnacle of the dreams of the highest-placed personages—luminaries of science, giants of literature and art. In view of this the premier sells them the cars. Of course, his prices are speculatively higher than official prices and the cars have defects which are hard to repair. But who will haggle with a premier, or complain?

# 18 · What civic labor is

COMMUNISTS CALL by the name civic labor, or civic action, everything that should be done around and for people in return for the money they have paid to the state in taxes—*but isn't done and needs doing.* This means that if a recently built residential district begins to go to pieces—walls crack, the plumbing doesn't work, the pavement is splitting, garbage is piling up everywhere, water doesn't reach upstairs—the residents of this district, who paid for their apartments in advance and are paying taxes to maintain the streets and public utilities, are called upon to remedy the catastrophe through civic labor. We must point out that civic labor is completely voluntary and unpaid. No one is forced to do it, but not showing up at the appointed place at the appointed time entails a lot of unpleasant consequences and gives a person the bad reputation of being antisocial. Civic labor is never called for to fix, adjust, or streamline something, but is always done in honor of Lenin's birthday or the anniversary of his death, on behalf of world peace, or for solidarity with the Viet Cong fighters. Thus work which elsewhere is done by a modestly paid craftsman in a matter-of-fact and businesslike manner is performed by people who don't have the slightest knowledge of the work involved, are tired from working all day in their own professions, and hate each other for their undeserved humiliation and wasted moments of their lives.

The only consolation is that every civic action has within it elements of unintentional suicide. The following story is telling in this respect. A large team of Communist dignitaries arrived in Poland for the opening of a new airline. They boarded a brand new, beautifully painted plane and took off. After a few minutes, the doors to the pilot's cabin opened and a beaming teen-ager, wearing the shirt of the Communist Youth League, appeared. He declared with emotion, "Comrades! This flight is a great day for our state airlines. We are inaugurating a new line which will join cities and proudly raise the banner of socialism in the airways! Our young brigade of Communist fliers is enjoying an additional triumph in the fact that the airplane we are flying in was marked for the scrap heap. For years it was unusable, but we young Communists decided to repair it in our spare time as a civic action. Our leaders expressed doubts about our chances for success, but our ardent will overcame all difficulties and our leaders' hesitation."

The young Communist did not finish his speech. Panic reigned in the cabin. Various ministers, in the midst of wailing and cries of terror, demanded that the plane land at once. The line was not inaugurated on *that* airplane. Afterward it was said many of the dignitaries had ruined their careers by their unaccountable coolness toward the idea of civic labor.

# 19 • Ethics and metaphysics for every day

W HY DOES evil exist in the world? Innumerable philosophers as well as ordinary people have asked themselves
and others this question. The apologists and exegesists of many religions have always given evasive answers. One of the more popular of these was the thesis that without evil, there would be no
good. We come to know good through evil, and an excess of
good generally turns into evil. A few people also claim that an
excess of evil ultimately turns into good, but there are fewer
proofs for this and no one is too sure on this score.

Communism has illuminated much of the darkness in this region and introduced a little solid truth and some inviolable
axioms where the shakiness of relativism formerly prevailed.
Of one thing we are certain in communism: regardless of how
much evil communism produces, this evil never turns into good.
A Czech journalist once expressed this philosophical abstraction
in concrete terms when he said, "Sometimes I have the impression that our government exists *only* to make our lives difficult."
This simple observation conceals awesome depths.

The lack of freedom and justice, the most striking elements
of life under communism, are nonetheless not the main factors
that determine a man's fate there. This fate is determined by the
lack of opportunities for a person to develop as an individual
in society and to develop his humanity within himself. Without

157

these two components of his fate, *homo* will never be able to create or advance either himself or his society, to say nothing of industry, literature, and education. Is it possible to somehow get around the inhumanity of this system? The history of the human race shows that man has managed to free himself from all fetters and has even outsmarted the worst oppressors. Communism, the most modern of the tyrannies, has assimilated the experiences of centuries and is ready for this. Individual development eventually becomes a privilege allowed the individual under the strictest control. And at a terrible price, at the price of servility, humiliations, and degradations that make Byzantine-feudal models of government sadism look like the comic expressiveness of a silent film. Subservience to a doctrine which is represented by the director of a state agency or a party dignitary hides despair and failures more damaging than physical humiliations before force. Having one's human dignity trampled on is not the same thing as the *complete* eradication of this dignity, which is the price one pays in submitting to an ideology in order to get the right to develop oneself. A Western Communist or revolutionary is in no position to understand that when revolutionary enthusiasm is channeled into the daily grind, it can only lead to a tyranny whose sole instrument of power is the breaking of characters. This absolutely contradicts his picture of the post-revolutionary world he is fighting for. But this is not the place for a discussion of the difference between dreams and their realization. The meaning of human degradation in communism is inseparable from the abyss of lawlessness represented as law which permeates every aspect of life from the center of power down to a pickle store. Oriental despotisms, feudalism, and the old aristocracies ignored the law in special cases of great importance, but usually scrupulously insisted on observing the law in small matters. Therefore, despite their crimes and atrocities, one could live within these systems and even develop as an individual who shapes his own humanity. By opposing them, a man enriched himself. But a man who fights communism is reduced to acts of madness and despair.

Thus life under communism is hell—but not for everyone. It is hell for people of good will. For the honest. For the reasonable. For those who want to do something in a better and more efficient way. For those who want to develop, enrich, increase. For the sensitive. For the straightforward and the modest. It is the stupid people, unaware of how mean and ludicrous they are, who prosper under communism. Toadies, opportunists, and conformists get along famously, especially since they are able to do *nothing* with a clear conscience, because they do not think they should do something in exchange for their servility. They feel relieved of all responsibility, which increases their feelings of self-importance. The absence of a sense of responsibility is, generally speaking, a condition of success in communism. The more irresponsible someone is and the more he is able to manipulate his irresponsibility, the farther he will go. Cowards and lazy people get along marvelously; by not doing anything, they run no risk of making mistakes, and receive awards for their inertia. But communism is a real paradise for cheats, swindlers, crooks, and adventurers. Less effort is needed than in the capitalist system to make a pile. One need only declare oneself a loyal and dedicated Communist at a proper moment and to proper people to obtain wealth and honors.

That there are close to four billion people on earth makes us see many things in a different light than in the past. Under such a burden, our ideas of good and evil change. Government interference in the life of the individual, social and economic planning, and the priority of the interests of the collective look different when seen in this perspective. Communism has been proposing these things for a long time and it is hard not to go along with it in this respect. But it does not know how to cleanse them of force and corruption. It is almost as if its very touch changed them into lies and injustice. Those who point to the economic and organizational incompetence of communism as proof of its inferiority are making a mistake. I believe that for all its failures and all its obscurantism, communism will, in the final outcome, fill all its citizens' plates and even give everyone a little house with a garden, shabby as it may be. This will be due to the budding of a modern technology and means of production, even

159

though they will be gagged and messed up by doctrine. Poverty and prosperity are no longer the red and the black in the roulette game played by the modern world. But what of it? Prosperity will not liquidate the metaphysics of injustice in communism, ensure individual and social justice, or open up prospects for the development of the individual, except at the price of moral concessions; in other words, it will not liquidate the immanent evil of the system. The brutalized lies with which communism has filled its own world and infected ours violate all the rules of common sense. No one who is ready to fight for his own dignity and wants to remain true to his own conscience will agree to call day night, ignorance culture, crime decency, a lack of goods affluence, or slavery freedom, on the strength of the Communist leaders' decrees. It is through the lie that communism becomes omnipresent, and transforms itself into a property of being, a partner of existence, a pantheistic element which is even concerned with cutting nails. The terror lurking in this state of affairs is inconceivable to people in the democratic West.

Can, then, a person living under communism ever attain spiritual equilibrium, the goal of every reasonable man of good will? Probably, but only at the price of moral capitulation. For example, by accepting evil and injustice as immanent elements of existence. Communists solve this problem with suspicious ease. If injustice exists at present, they say, it is to serve future justice, whose coming is inevitable and guaranteed by our correct and unimpeachable theory. A Polish philosopher has remarked, "The horror and corruption which are the fruits of a doctrine claiming to possess complete and infallible knowledge about the future surpasses the boldest forecasts. For the conclusion drawn from this doctrine is that the moral problem of the individual does not at all mean applying your own standard of justice to historical events, but rather adapting your own sense of justice to the dictates of historical necessity, embodied in practice by the Party, its leadership, its current acts." A Communist's faith in future justice may be a sign of honesty and idealism, but how do you explain this to an old-age pensioner who has received a parcel of old clothes from his relatives in the capitalist West and is taxed by the state as a speculator and an enemy of the people? How do you explain this to a craftsman who specializes in a rare type of artificial limb which would mean salvation to many invalids, when the state does not produce such artificial limbs and therefore forbids their manufacture and sale, accusing the artisan of wanting to restore capitalism? And how do you explain it to the invalids waiting for artificial limbs which the Communist state cannot supply?

Much has been written on the theme of communism as a religion of hate. This accusation is well founded, but it is often oversimplified. A proclamation of hate is not in itself a qualification of morality: a good Christian also hated sin, and all sorts of ethical equations are possible on this score. The point is that communism makes hate as important as love. It does not distinguish between these two feelings; it identifies their value for man's moral health, and only differentiates their color, direction, and symbolism. A good Communist who loves the proletariat and the Party is obliged to hate all those who do not love the proletariat and the Party. Such is the ultimate logic of his moral guidelines and the feelings that control them. Ultimately, anyone who is *different* becomes an enemy who deserves to be hated and must be destroyed in order to secure one's own existence. In terms of the development of the human race, this is a regression to the most primitive codes of ethics. In everyday practice, it has a comical effect and becomes lurid and grotesque. The Communists make their most convulsive effort trying to convince the world as well as themselves that the interests of the Party, the state, and society are identical, while life reveals the abysmal divergence of these three interests at every step. Anyone living under communism is aware of the agony that accompanies every attempt to reconcile or coordinate what he himself wants or proposes with what the Party and the state demand of him. The result is that everything is eternally divided and a man can never be in harmony with his environment. Under democratic capitalism, as long as an individual's interests do not collide with those of society or other individuals, he is left alone and allowed to do what he sees fit. Under communism, an artist who wants to paint a picture must take into consideration what this picture will mean to the Party, the government, the trade unions, schoolchildren, the approaching anniversary of Lenin's birthday, the ministry of industry if he wants to paint a steel mill, or the ministry of agriculture if he intends to paint a strawberry.

Everyone is instinctively convinced that if anything changed in communism, or if today's totalitarian communism were replaced by humanitarian socialism "with a human face," this characteristic of actualized Marxism would remain the determining factor of life under it. Communism always strives for and demands the same mandate. It will brand any attempt at resistance hostility and call upon its adherents to hate it. Thus the philosophy of power in communism is simple. It assumes that everyone in the state has something to hide and the first principle of ruling is to discover what it is. When the general public is raised to the absolute, it means that as the highest value it has the right to do everything. And because the general public is the law of history as represented by the Party, it is difficult to avoid the suspicion that the twentieth-century Communist leader believes he has full power over every shred of his subjects' thoughts, feelings, and biological existence.

Studies on alienation under communism are made difficult by a certain imprecision which is universally regarded as the apogee of theoretical Marxist thought and generally respected everywhere as a magnificent achievement of the spirit of the explorations of European civilization. For someone who has experienced communism and looks at it from the standpoint of the 1970s, Marx's basic thesis about the class struggle seems to be a kind of mistake. There is nothing like a class struggle in our picture of the world, only the struggle of individuals speaking in the name of classes. Social classes themselves have a capacity for living together, for infiltrating and imitating each other, for acquiring each other's worst features, which has not been sufficiently investigated. A person who is alienated under communism is a man who has at the same time been sucked in and completely bound by the functions and servitudes which, paradoxically, determine his alienation. He has been putrified by an excess of socialization and keeps waiting for the Kafka who would show him exactly *how* the relation between man and society *kills* in communism, not the intangibility of relation. Trapping a man in the cogs of a machine does not automatically bestow power over his soul. A Western observer cannot understand why a man caught in the steel grip of such powerful dependencies and social ties displays so little interest in them. But people living under communism are concerned with nothing outside their immediate range of feeling and acting, because nothing short of a cataclysm on the historical scale can change or improve their lot. They have become desensitized to all aggravations; their only weapon is resignation. The vast majority of them wish harm upon their own country and society, secretly rejoice over its failures and defeats, and long for catastrophes such as wars, economic breakdowns, or natural disasters, professing the principle that *the worse things are, the better it is,* in this way alleviating their own bitterness and despair. In the West inflation, a flood, a crop failure, an airplane disaster, or, conversely, a sensational new product or a medical advance, in one way or another concern everyone. In Communist societies a national disaster strikes many people, but it does not concern anyone, and no success, however spectacular, is to anyone's advantage.

Communism came to men with the proposal that if they gave communism power over themselves, communism would give them a better life. In the countries where it received this power, the people are worse off than at any time in these countries' histories. The feeling that life is worse is so acute there that it is the main cause of suicide. The West cannot comprehend this type of polarization, and is at a loss to deal with its manifestations. The problem of ethical deterioration, so apparent to people living in these countries, becomes hopelessly muddled in the eyes of the West and leads it to make judgments that only induce melancholy despair in these people. If two poets strike a note of criticism in their poems, but only one is in jail for it, it means that only one is a decent man, while the other is a common scoundrel. To the West, both are fighters for creative freedom—and this simple misunderstanding determines the painful weakness of the West with respect to communism.

# 20 • Communism and Nazism: a short comparative study

RUMINATING ON this topic is generally regarded as vulgar, as something too unbecoming to be done. But why? No one really knows for sure. It is the terror of a convention. Too many people who later became respectable declared themselves Communists at some time in their lives. Those, however, who survived both Nazism and communism, without consenting to participate in either, are not versed in such subtleties. In Eastern Europe there are millions of such people, and the rule consecrated by intellectuals that communism and Hitlerism are *not* the same does not hold water with them. Because if one thinks about it unsqueamishly, pitilessly, and to the end, it is all too easy to establish their grisly similarity.

Communism, as we know it, is the inventor, theoretician, practicer, engineer, and technologist of crimes which Nazism, as we came to know it intimately, may also have dreamed of, but lacked the strength to perpetrate. The criminality of Hitlerism lay in the planned murder of people in horrifying numbers, in horrifying ways, and with a horrifying rapidity. But in the final analysis it was *only* murder. The adverb *only* in this case is the quintessence of cruelty, but there is an explanation for it. The unforgivable sin of murdering amidst tortures, with the victim's lips sealed with plaster or in the agony of suffocation by cyclone gas, will remain with Hitlerism and those who murdered in its name forever. Our century's curse will never be lifted from Nazism, and the symbols and names connected with it, until those who survived breathe their last and curse those criminals and their crimes once more. Nazism murdered stupidly, bloodily, wallowing in torn guts, or antiseptically, thoughtlessly, in the modern way, always with the maniacal smile of a sadist, but also of a cretin, a brutal oaf, and a boor disguising himself in the impeccable garb of a dress uniform and the surgical accessories of modern civilization. But these things, extraordinary as they may be, do not replace a genius for evil and cannot create it out of nothing where it does not exist. Even in the most seductive scenarios of its mythologies, Nazism always remained nothing more than a precisely thought-out, well-organized, and well-equipped slaughterhouse. It destroyed in the name of criteria which were vile but patently simple: because someone was a Jew, a Pole, or a partisan. But while Hitlerism murdered and trampled to death entire nations and millions of individuals, it did not deprive them of that which is perhaps not most important, but was all that was left in that eschatological moment: it did not deprive them of the dignity of death, the lucidity of their sacrifice of their own lives, which were taken from them by history, by someone's grim power, by the brutality of other, evil people. Under Nazism a man could die with dignity, even with pride, without denying himself, without destroying his soul, without losing that last particle of humanity whose spark smoulders at the bottom of even the most terrible despair. Hitlerism crushed the body and paralyzed the heart with mortal fear. It plunged the weak into the muck of their own weakness and tore out their honesty and honor with tortures. But when someone had enough strength to defend his humanity, Nazism became brutishly helpless in the presence of what in a man was stronger than biology. It could only keep crushing until matter disappeared; it could not and did not know how to destroy ideas and moral positions. Those who were shot, beaten, hung, suffocated, or buried alive died horrible deaths, but many of them surely retained up to the very last twitch some awareness that they had saved something, that they were dying and knew why,

166

that they had not lost, and that their now impotent rage, curses, and hatred had some pure and dazzling meaning.

Violent death at the hands of another man is probably always and everywhere the same in its horrible psychological and physical essence. However, it seems to me that the death of a Jewish Communist handed over to the Gestapo by the Soviet NKVD was the most terrible of all deaths. It cut a man off from his own existence without leaving him a shred of awareness of the meaning of that existence. The Nazis called people who opposed them bandits and killed them, but they could not extirpate them from the feelings of those who remained alive. The Communists managed to do even this; they knew how to deprive people of everything their identity, even their shadow (as in the old German legend), their past, and their future. Hitlerism was able to turn life into a jungle in which you could not trust streets, houses, and above all, another human being. Communism went a step further in many directions: by fertilizing the soil of life with the thoughts of Lenin and Stalin, a thicket grew up around man in which he could not trust even himself, or shapes, colors, odors, and the air. Communism made life itself its instrument of oppression and the product of its system, that is, of itself. It managed to join the executioner and the victim in a relationship of such abysmal mutual degradations that everything dissolved into an unspeakable goo, while man sailed onto a nightmarish reef on which he had to perish like a man and could be reborn only as something else. As what, I don't know. Perhaps as a subwheel in a phantasmagorical super-machine, perhaps as a buckle on the shoe of a super-sovereign of subexistence, which is what some wormlike, many-legged Politburo finally becomes. If communism and fascism are the fatal blights of twentieth-century humanity, they differ only in their technique of eating away the living tissue of organisms, and their methods of ulcerating and festering the matter of life. Nazism did a lot to stamp out a human being, but it cannot boast of the achievements described in the books of those who escaped communism, or at least managed to communicate their knowledge of it to the world. Nazism murdered for the shape of a nose, and this created a compulsion to fight to the very end, without any possibility of coming to terms until evil was eradicated at any price humanity would have to pay. Communism creates the *impression* that a man can come to terms with it, and afterward destroys the man who believed and is now defenseless, destroys him for what is good in him, for his independence of thought, for his sense of dignity, for his opposition to lies. Helping your neighbor in communism represents the same moral choice as it did under Hitler, and punishment for an impulse of human solidarity is inevitable. Only in communism do you sometimes wait for it for years, long enough for the world not to notice.

# 21 • What it means to "mean well"

THIS IS a moral category which was created not by communism but by life under communism. Used in the past tense—"He meant well"—it becomes a norm for morally evaluating a man, his life, and his actions.

Life in a Communist state is based on a never-ending struggle with someone more stupid and inferior who has the power to decide on everything a man wants to do and be. Everyone knows that the outcome of this struggle is a matter of pure metaphysics: no one is able to calculate, predict, plan, or assess either its course or its results. Hence the direction and nature of this struggle somehow places it in the hierarchy of ethical values and moral significance. On the horizon of the moral problems of twentieth-century man there again looms *intention* as a half-angelic, half-demonic premise of thoughts, feelings, and actions, a psychological and moral category which we thought had been buried along with Victorian literature. In view of the general impossibility of doing anything positive, correct, wise, or useful for oneself and society, sheer intention begins to count as an integral and autonomous value, that is, as something a man can still set store by.

Probably it was applied for the first time to Marx and Engels themselves when it became apparent what a gap was opening between what they had wanted and the mess that was being made in their names. "He means well" was said of Lenin when you could wash your hands in the blood around the headquarters of the Soviet political police in Moscow and Leningrad. The same thing was said in the thirties by intellectuals stupid with fanaticism about Stalin, when he finished off his closest henchmen, who had earlier got rid of other henchmen on his orders. The societies of Eastern Europe, exhausted by war and the Nazi occupation, wanted to believe in someone's good will and at first were inclined to give credence to the Communists and their siren songs about the new paradise on earth which their power would bring.

It soon became obvious that there was simply no way of finding out whether the Communists meant well or not, but it was as clear as daylight to everyone that whatever their intentions, the results were fatal. Political dignitaries in government offices have particularly long lives under communism because their careers are determined not by their actual accomplishments, but by the Party's favor. A political worker may cause catastrophe after catastrophe and ruin the most thriving areas committed to his charge, but if the Party regards him as a faithful son, nothing will ever happen to him; in fact, his promotion will be assured.

Records for longevity in office were broken by the Polish premier who held that office for twenty years. He even enjoyed a certain popularity in society because of an unusually perfidious propaganda tactic. His factotums, whom he guaranteed lucrative positions, would proclaim everywhere how much he wanted for the people, but how his fellow Communists who ran Poland would not let him do what he wanted. In answer to this they often heard that decade followed decade, and despite the premier's fine intentions, things were getting worse and worse. His extollers, in turn, replied that without him, things would have been even worse, which, of course, could not be verified since Poland had existed for twenty years under him and could not know how things would have been without him. Other Communist statesmen build great careers by winking an eye at society or at their eventual supporters within the Party. This winking is supposed to imply that they know what to do to improve conditions, and will do it immediately as soon as they can. Consequently, they should be supported and encouraged, and their wielding power should be made easier. Sometimes the technique of winking an eye leads to real tragedies. At times a Communist politician really does mean well; he wants to relax censorship, put more consumer goods on the market, and restrain the political police. But then he enters into negotiations with the supervisors of orthodoxy (more simply, the Russians), without whose approval nothing takes place in the satellite countries. If he does get minimum concessions in these bitter struggles, he turns to his society with the suggestion: Stop demanding more and be glad we got what we did, because it wasn't easy to get and it took our last drop of strength to get even *this*. One section of society will then say that the fellow means well; another section will say that the fellow meant well, but broke down and sold out. Both will be right in a way, because protecting the minimum by any means, including repressions, police coercion, etc., is a capitulation before the unyielding nature of the general supervisors of the purity of communism. And here we have the tragedy of the man who meant well.

Karl Marx himself thought of his work as a defense of man suffocated by the social system. Later, in Marx's name, other people constructed a system which made man more defenseless than ever before in history, defenseless not only before the force of insane, bureaucratic structures, but also before human rottenness and sneakiness, which make the abuses of capitalist laissez-faire look like a friendly rustic idyll. The system of values and the mechanism of goals in communism put a premium on pettiness and meanness and reward these qualities with various forms of success, to an extent unknown in other eras. Everyone who lives within the system knows it is evil and rotten and that it depraves people, who become evil merely by trying to exist within it. Everyone who comes into contact with it is infected with evil, and since surely everyone comes into contact with it in some form or another, those who are good must perish in its gears. Everyone knows that communism has mankind hoodwinked and that what generations of dreamers, idealists, and writers said about it before it took shape was the usual abuse of the public's good faith. Its worshippers promised the triumph of truth, and instead it brought the sanctification of the lie on an unprecedented scale. They guaranteed justice, and instead it became a giant incubator of injustices big and small. They announced that it would bring true freedom; instead, it brought the perfectly constructed enslavement of every manifestation of life and every cell of society to an extent unknown to tyrants of old. They dreamed out loud about how communism would ennoble man once he was freed from the fetters of exploitation. But instead, communism degraded man and caught him in a web of stupidity, base instincts, mediocrity, insipidness, and destruction, with a refinement previously unknown. So it is difficult to be surprised at the fact that intention in this world becomes a rare treasure and a synonym for virtue.

The abyss of moral pitfalls in communism means that the man who means well must do evil effectively and for a long time in order to ensure his actions a minimum of results. This is the only way he can get sufficient authority to wear as armor when he goes forth to do good. Such authority is a double-edged tool: it may indicate steadfast loyalty to the Party for idealistic motives and it may also indicate an unbounded readiness to commit any filthy act at the Party's bidding. A moral critique of authority in itself is meaningless; only its results count. In practice, however, the following scenario takes place: In order to get the authority needed to do good, the idealist and the cynical pragmatist alike must be responsible for so much evil through their actions that the formula "He means well," for the sake of which he embarked on his struggle, gets lost somewhere along the way, and the lover of the good, harnessed to life's routine, becomes a docile executor of coercion and lawlessness for the rest of his life.

Nonetheless, a position we can define as Talleyrandism is the model of moral behavior that attracts many thinking people of good will in communism. Let us briefly recall what Talleyrandism is. The name comes from the life and actions of M. de Talleyrand, a French aristocrat and diplomat who served, in turn, the Bourbons, the French Revolution, the Directorate,

Napoleon, and again the Bourbons. At the bidding of each successive ruler, he committed every possible infamy and atrocity from the influential political and administrative position which was his the entire time. At the same time, when asked about his conscience and his self-respect, M. de Talleyrand always declared that he considered himself a man of above average virtue and decency since throughout his life he served only France, not its rulers, ever mindful of the principles of mankind in general. His contemporaries, moreover, testify that he always had the fresh complexion, perfect digestion, and spiritual serenity enjoyed by people who are unflinchingly convinced of their own honesty, and that any feeling of guilt was absolutely foreign to him. Communism is swarming with Talleyrands, or rather, his more or less successful imitators. As a result, people who to all appearances are completely alike in their existential profiles—alike in belonging to the Party, in the foul deeds they commit in its name, in their stupidity and venality—are spoken of in quite different terms to the point where absurd polarizations of opinion exist. This is simply a result of that strange social arrangement in which only intentions count—whether someone means or ever meant well and gave proof of it.

In a Western democracy the political-moral element functions only on holidays and special occasions, and no one will vote for a politician *only* because he arranged a loan at the bank for a bankrupt merchant who got back on his feet again as a result. In Communist nations this litmus test is in daily operation, and every day discloses a new choice, a new need to evaluate, different in every circumstance and in every affair, but always in terms of conventional ethics and with respect to the interests of other people. Whence the tremendous ambivalence and the total irrelevance of general labels. A person is good who is good today, here and now, and in a concrete matter. If a political worker helps a war invalid get a newspaper concession and news about it gets around, he will gain popularity and the reputation of a person who means well. His action is fraught with consequences, sometimes dangerous to him, since his enemies, who are working for his downfall, can always charge that the invalid lost his leg in the anti-Communist partisan struggle, and thereby ruin both the invalid and his benefactor. Moreover, news of the political worker's good deed will probably never receive wide enough circulation for him to take any great advantage of his popularity, if only because the political worker himself, aware of possible intrigues and dangers, is not willing to give his action too much publicity. It is enough that now and then people speak well of him, since a Communist politician is not answerable for his program, which by the nature of things is dogmatically rigid, but rather for his everyday decency, which is his only trump card in the eyes of society.

This bizarre paradox can best be observed in the atmosphere of elections. Elections are a farce in communism, but a farce which is not without broad significance. You vote only for one ballot, which is composed of five or six names in every district. The names are those of people who belong to the Party, or whose loyalty and obedience are above suspicion though they are not Party members. The voter, then, has no choice and his right to cross out any name he wants never effects a change in the team which is chosen to sit in the quasi-legislative organs. Nonetheless, those who want seats deliver election speeches and the cleverer candidates know that the voter is guided in his actions by the hope that the elected representative will *not* realize what he promises in his program. In other words, that he is decent enough not to put the program he embraces into effect. So there are endless prospects for Talleyrandism, albeit vulgarized, and by rights every district Party secretary who christens his child in church regards himself as a Communist Talleyrand.

Communist psychology, in which the works of Freud, Adler, and Jung are all prohibited, has to its credit some major achievements completely unknown to the West. For example, it has investigated in great detail the correlation between the actions, words, and thoughts of a so-called authentic person. In this case, "authentic person" means an individual whose manner of thinking, behavior, impulses, and reactions conform to what the Communist Party expects from him. For it appears that the truth about a man is not closely and logically connected with his ac-

174

tions, words, and thoughts, and that these things are not dependent on each other. Dostoevsky and many writers after him demonstrated quite convincingly that a man's actions do not necessarily tell the truth about him. Nor do his words, since everyone knows how a political activist can speak from a tribune draped with a red flag and not believe a quarter of a word of what he is saying. On the other hand, a man can pull the most inexcusable and nasty tricks, but if he regarded them as nasty when he pulled them, and communicated his doubts in a whisper to trusted friends, then they are no longer considered nasty. And here we come to another aspect of the elevation of intention onto the pedestal of virtue. Under prevailing conditions the fact that some one *means well* is transformed into a moral virtue, though a virtue precarious and risky for everyone around him. For it is enough that someone meant well, but things didn't work out for him, so he committed a nasty action, but . . . The moral decalogue of life under communism will grant him absolution; the very fact that he thought of it as a nasty action, that he was aware of it, means his sin does not count. There is no possibility of fighting evil, so millions of people live doing evil unconsciously, as blind instruments of the system. Hence the *awareness* and the *evaluation* of evil as evil is a virtue. Even the traditional Christian moralists who were prepared to absolve unconscious behavior ("He didn't know what he was doing") would be shocked at accepting the thesis that someone is innocent because he was fully aware of what he was doing and even consciously discussed his doubts and suspicions about his actions with his friends over vodka. Unfortunately, these moral principles have made deep inroads into the societies ruled by the Communists, and the worst scoundrels and opportunists have built their careers on them, together with various distilling apparati to diffuse their own meanness and chicanery.

Probably the most pathetic and immediate demonstration of the principle "He means well" was one I came across one day in Zagreb, Yugoslavia. Down the main street there proudly and defiantly marched a parade of well-organized Communist youths in red ties, with red flags, in a sea of banners and amidst continual shouts of "Peace! Peace! Castro! Tito!" They held one another's hands and arms, and took each other by the waist, demonstrating that artificial fraternity put on for show, the ostentatious love of everyone for everyone else, the mindless happiness of chanting slogans. From the crowd on the sidewalk there cheerfully emerged a drunkard, overcome by the wave of universal affection. He was an old, poorly dressed alcoholic, crumpled up from an all-night bender, but the extent of his emotional involvement in the excitement of the moment was beyond all doubt. He was touchingly sincere. He also wanted to fraternize, to solidarize, to participate; in a word, he meant well. He shouted louder than the rest, called for peace and victory, and cheered them on, giving it everything he had. Two strapping youths in red ties pulled him brutally from their ranks and pushed him so that he staggered and fell on the pavement. Afterward he sat on the curb, covered his face with his hands, and began to cry.

## 22 · How to love

LOVE IS the only basic element of existence before which communism is helpless. At the very beginning, immediately after the Revolution, voices were heard proclaiming that love was a relic of bourgeois civilization. Their impotent absurdity, however, qualified them only for the sideshow of revolutionary fanaticism. Still, the problem is not as simple as it might seem and cannot be dismissed with the argument that it is nonsensical. Communism is a monistic world view in which there is no room for anything equal to itself: there exists only the supreme principle, and everything belongs to it. If even common sense tells a Communist that a man must leave room in himself for loving other people—women, parents, a child—something in an ideal Communist who is shaped according to the prescription for the Communist absolute still revolts against such an exception. The Party is the supreme giver of all good, so all feelings belong to the Party, at the very least the feeling of unconditional loyalty and unbounded trust. From here it is only a short step to love, and an absolute Communist is convinced that the Party should be loved above everything else, and that other emotional ties have no right to exist. There are more absolute Communists, or Communists who proclaim their absolutism for their immediate gain, than one might think. Most of them are in the political police, a sacerdotal organization whose job it is to keep the sacred fires of love for the Party alive in the citizens' souls.

At this point we must make a crucial distinction. Christian love implies a love for God which inspires one with love toward other people, toward his neighbor, in order to bring about the kingdom of God on earth. That is, it expects one to love his fellow man because he is a man. Love as proclaimed by the neo-utopians in the West in the sixties, though stemming from a chaotic hierarchy of values, has an even more concrete goal and meaning: love is a value in itself, and we should love everything without distinction: people, cats, the sky, flowers, or music. In comparison with these principles of love, the postulate of communism seems appallingly impersonal. Communism enjoins exclusively love of faith and ideology; its catechism makes no mention of people. Moreover, it refuses to recognize those who reject it as fellow creatures, or neighbors; a Communist accepts only the existence of those who are like himself, the others have to be annihilated. Man should love the Party, production, the system set up by the Communists, and dead and canonized Communist leaders. As far as the living go, feelings have to be regulated by current Party policy. The Party decides who should be loved as well as who should be hated. It is characteristic that whenever hate is involved, its symbols are always people, never ideas. One should hate imperialists, Trotskyites, Social Democrats, spies, capitalists, liberals. The object of one's hate should be, above all, the Pope in person, rather than Catholic hostility to progress. Stalin, who identified himself with the Party, demanded love for himself. The instructor in a Communist school organization who required its members to report on what their parents said at home would add, "After all, you love Stalin more than your father and mother," and would rarely be contradicted. During the era of the Stalinist trials, an examining magistrate who wanted to force a tortured prisoner to denounce his wife would ask, "What's this, do you love her more than Stalin?" and would have been shocked to hear an affirmative answer. It would have shaken his world view, even if he were a cynical thug.

In communism feeling is a retreat. It is the only value of

existence that is not determined by conditioning and environment, the only one shaped exclusively by a man's individual characteristics. Love between a man and a woman can be as beautiful and as tormenting in a Communist society as anywhere else. But its beauty exists *despite* communism, despite the universal drabness, the everyday inconveniences and annoyances, which sometimes makes this beauty stand out and embellishes it with memory. On the other hand, its ugliness and torments are ofttimes the *result* of communism. They arise from the overall misery and the impossibility of getting human living conditions, from living in one-room apartments for entire families in which there is a complete lack of privacy and intimacy—conditions in which love fades and has no chance to develop.

In such a system the feelings arising from love undergo strange metamorphoses, and one must admit that in this area communism can boast of many singular accomplishments. All Warsaw knew about the case of a certain writer who had won fame, large printings of his books, and even the respect of his fellow writers. Apart from this wonderful good fortune, the writer had a young, charming, and talented wife, and also a beautiful apartment with a separate bedroom, which was the envy of his friends and acquaintances and the most emphatic proof of his success and his excellent relations with the Party authorities. But his wife had a lover. This lover had everything the writer lacked, namely youth, good looks, and indefatigable strength, but he did not have his earning power or his connections. He was a nice fellow, quiet and good-natured, who really did not wish to hurt the writer and was willing to make all sorts of compromises. The writer was very concerned about hiding this stain on the picture of his happiness, so he, along with his wife and her lover, avoided all ostentation and all three lived in harmony and on good terms, happy in their discretion. All Warsaw, however, had no doubts about the nature of their mutual relations, so much so that eventually everyone even became tired of gossiping on the subject. There would be nothing extraordinary about this, for literature has recorded such situations from life as anciently as cuneiform writing in early Sumeria, were it not that the writer somehow antagonized the Communist authorities who, in order to punish his recalcitrance, declared that the writer had too much living space and decided to either lodge another person with him or take away his bedroom. Whereupon the writer's wife went to the government housing agency where she declared that someone was already living in that bedroom and demanded an official placement for that person. From then on, the three of them lived in the apartment, violating, to be sure, traditional concepts of honor and jealousy, but enjoying universal recognition and respect for their unbending position in the fight against Communist arbitrariness.

# 23 · What a government office is

A GOVERNMENT OFFICE in a Communist state is the place where an applicant is absolutely certain that he will not get what he came for and what he rightly or legally deserves. Franz Kafka's great work, his contribution to modern literature and our knowledge of life and the world, prophetically describes, in fact, a Communist government office. Day-to-day life under communism confirms Kafka's vision at every step. If someone does not get something from a government office, he begins to search within himself for his mistake or guilt, even if he is as honest as the day he was born and as careful as an adding machine, because the Communist government office exists beyond guilt and error.

The complaints against the bureaucracy heard in the Western world have numerous grounds and reflect a profound anxiety about the progressive regimentation and depersonalization of administrative functions. Such complaints, however, remind one of grumbling over bad weather. Bureaucracy is an inevitable consequence of a society and social organizations which are continually growing more complex. The more of us there are on earth, the more need there is of offices to sort and classify the problems arising from our number. The key to taming the monster of bureaucracy and forcing it to serve man is the internal moral directives in the name of which a bureaucracy develops.

The American bureaucracy, so far, still replies to letters, that is, it reacts to stimuli from outside—and this guarantees its eventual health, despite the excrescences of dehumanizing mechanization and computerization. Its superiority over the bureaucracies in West European nations, which are also democratic and liberal, lies in the prevailing belief that its offices are not directed *against* people. For all its shortcomings and the difficulties it gives rise to, no one believes that the purpose of its existence is to hurt citizens. On the contrary, people do believe that its *raison d'être* is the general good and that its purpose is to make life easier, despite the stupidity and blundering it exhibits at every turn. This belief is imparted to the bureaucracy itself and to the frame of mind prevailing in its offices and mollifies its attitude toward citizens and applicants. A Frenchman or a German no longer has this unshakable conviction that his civil service does not exist primarily against him. In these countries the tradition of the autonomy of the government office makes the fact of its existence a *raison d'être* in itself, releasing it from an obligation to serve people or make their lives easier. The original idea of a Western European civil service is to serve order, organization, the correct division of what should be divided, and the supervision of the correct function of what should function without paying too much heed to people. Nonetheless, this position seems extremely humanistic in comparison with the status of the government office in Communist countries and the position it occupies in the minds of their citizens.

Under communism the general conviction prevails that the purpose of the government office is the blind and unthinking destruction of everyone who comes into contact with it or within the range of its activity. The fundamental reasons for having dealings with a government office, such as want, necessity, or the logic of a given problem, are not in the least relevant here. When the popular imagination looks for comparisons for the role of the government office in the life of the masses, it most readily falls back on the ancient legends about an insatiable dragon which demands endless victims and cannot be slain. This is an extremely apt metaphor since it is easy to see on closer examination that the Communist bureaucracy lives off the *sufferings* of its petitioners; their harm is its circulatory system, the driving force behind its activity and its reason for existing. The applicant who has been wronged writes appeals, protests, and complaints, which new civil servants, new offices, new buildings, and new authority over the applicant's fate are needed to examine. In this fashion a Frankenstein-office, or a lethal office, a broken machine grows up like a horrible mushroom. An idea is not born out of immediate need, but is artificially worked out in the office and becomes fatally bureaucratized. We should not forget that communism itself is one big office, the incubator of ideas which were born behind a desk, not engendered by life. It is not accidental, and perhaps is even symbolic, that the main command and executive center of Communist governments is called the Politburo.* The concept of capitalism developed organically, from experiences in fields, in workshops, in stores, and in factories. Communism was born on paper. It is not surprising, then, that in communism Parkinson's Law acquires the characteristics of an animated cartoon. Capitalism humanized itself once it discovered that self-restraint was not destroying it, but was revealing virtues previously unsuspected. In this way, the *welfare state* arises, an institution which is contaminated by the inevitability of bureaucratization, but the antibureaucratic essence of capitalism is not disappearing or being liquidated. Communism knows quite well that self-restraint means its atrophy and death. Hence it is condemned to blindly rushing forward, destroying everything in its path, and to the hypertrophying of bureaucracy like a cancer in the organism.

The cannibalism of the Communist government office is best investigated in the area where modern man is becoming a regimented being. In a democracy the offices created to issue documents, such as birth certificates, driver's licenses, and passports, exist for the purpose of issuing such documents. An applicant may meet with various obstacles and difficulties because of the

---

* Politburo: Abbreviation of the Russian *politicheskii biuro,* literally "political office."

183

nature of bureaucracy itself, but no one denies these offices have their proper function. In a Communist society these offices exist in order *not* to give the document to the person who needs it. The order of reasoning is automatically reversed: If a man needs something and this something is legally his due, he must not be given it. There are numerous reasons for this rule; we will list only the most important.

1. Annihilating, crushing, decomposing, and reducing a citizen to a helpless nonentity awakens in the individual and social consciousness a peculiar mystique of the office, which Communist authorities encourage and regard as a didactic tool for educating man in the proper way. A man who is confronted with the mysterious invincibility of the government office becomes aware of his own insignificance and no longer revolts.

2. When a man comes for something and is not given it, despite the fact that he is legally entitled to it, what is called his "case" begins. His file is put together: papers, documents, certificates, and endorsements. The office becomes a fact of the man's existence and his case. Under communism the purpose of a tax is not to accumulate money, since money has no value and the government can print as much as it likes, controlled neither by the free market nor by other economic laws. But when this same tax is not paid, it is a *case against* a man, and the true ideal of communism is to have a case against every one of its subjects in order to have them totally in its power. An unpaid electric bill is not simply an unpaid bill, but an element in an eventual court trial in which the prosecutor, proving the political unreliability of the defendant, can always refer to the unpaid bill as part of the accused's filthy machinations to rob the state, representing the community property of the workers and peasants.

3. Last, but not least, denying a man what is officially his due often produces in him the desire to buy what he cannot rightfully obtain free. Officials, moreover, must live on something other than their salaries. As a result, corruption and bribery in Communist states have reached proportions which make South American republics look like oases of puritanism. Com-

munist authorities avert their eyes, because in their never-ending struggle against man and humanity they prefer to have the government office and its formidable power on their side. Their mistake lies in the fact that ultimately bribery is a sign of humanity, and there is nothing they can do about it. So, as is always the case with everything human, we find ourselves going around in a vicious circle.

In other words, within the government office, an apocalyptic monstrosity, man's ultimate hope lies in his relations with another man. Pity and weakness, snobbery and the desire for gain, come to his aid. Defenseless before the blind desire to subdue and degrade him and the humiliations he is subjected to by the Communist civil service, all concepts of legality and illegality, principles and arbitrariness, are dashed to the ground. A man's only defenses are the pitfalls of human nature. And the dignitary, the sovereign of the office to whom flattering lies and humble obsequiousness are mandatory while the defense of Copernicus' theorems is impossible if to this day he believes the sun moves around the earth, is often so abject that you can call him a man.

# 24 · How to be a playboy and play around

I N ITS DAY the following story went around Warsaw: At the
Warsaw Polytechnic, technological experiments were con-
ducted which required a large supply of very thin rubber. Numerous attempts to get the necessary material from the unfathomable depths of Communist industry had failed, when one
of the professors hit on the idea of simply buying a sufficient
quantity of imported condoms, which could be found in state-
owned drugstores. Thereupon his assistant went to the largest
drugstore in the city and asked for condoms. The salesclerk asked
how many he wanted. The assistant replied as many as he could
buy. The rather surprised salesclerk brought a case containing a
thousand condoms; the assistant paid and asked for a bill. The
salesman asked who the bill should be made out to, and the assistant answered, "The Warsaw Polytechnic." "Aha," said the
salesclerk with deep understanding, "does that mean there's a
big dance at the Polytechnic next Saturday night?"

The salesclerk's conclusion would indicate that he was aware
of the abyss of debauchery which society lives in. The question
then arises: Is sexual dissipation really an attribute of Communist societies? And does it fundamentally differ from the freedom of morals currently prevailing in the West?

The answer to these questions is not simple. The relaxation of
morals, called by its ideologists the liberation of man from the

bonds of false morality or convention, which is undoubtedly a result of growing sexual equality, appears to represent a worldwide phenomenon. However, the increased relaxation of sexual morals in both Western and Communist civilizations appears to have different motivations and different characteristics. In the West it is closely tied up with the profound revolution of ideas deriving from moral and social convulsions and changes, and is the result of radical ideas about the fate of the individual in today's world. As always is the case with solutions based on the mass diffusion of a problem, certain values are sacrificed and there is no doubt that the overriding feature of the universalization of sexual life in the West is its devaluation, the decay of values sanctified by centuries of restriction, its debasement and cheapening. There is something paradoxical in the fact that the capitalist West applied a moral-social criterion to the sexual problem, whereas communism, an ideology built on social conditioning, is experiencing a sexual inflation which is based on a hedonistic premise. In the West the deluge of sexualism is accompanied by rationalizations, never-ending dialectics, and rather boring discussions on the theme of openness, sincerity, psychoanalysis, and neoinnocence rather theoretically conceived. In Communist societies sex is an escape, the only available scrap of epicureanism, the only real and widely available pleasure in life, an authentic charm of existence, a genuine value. It is the only area in which communism is on equal terms with the West, since the beauty of girls and erotic talent are elements that are not subject to Communist regimentation and Communist economic mismanagement. Though everything in communism is so much dramatically worse than in capitalism, this one aspect of life, this one attribute of enjoying life, escapes the overall stagnation, grayness, and defeat.

But the general grayness and inferiority of life under communism cannot be escaped even in this area. Inferior soap, inferior cosmetics, inferior underwear create an atmosphere in which everything, even passion, becomes slovenly and threadbare. Inhuman overwork for a minimum livelihood takes away all a man's desires except the desire to rest. Poverty or semipoverty, that is, a state of chronic vegetation in which there is nothing to live on near the end of the month, just before payday, fosters prostitution and semiprostitution. Prostitution is officially prohibited but Communist cities are better supplied with this commodity than many metropolises traditionally famous for it. Although professional prostitution is illegal, it is visible at every step. Its purely physical countenance is horrible: the age, appearance, and general condition of the Communist daughters of Corinth strike terror in decent citizens and a man must be in a state of unusual blindness of the senses to avail himself of their services. However, this is not at all necessary, since Communist cities are filled with girls representing a peculiar moral mixture in which Communist rhetoric about emancipation, actual professional independence, the all-pervading atmosphere of permissiveness, and the agonizing desire to escape a one-room apartment usually shared with a large family combine to produce casual availability. Every foreigner from the West knows how few of the trappings of the so-called good life need be invested in a passing, easily formed acquaintance in order to get something that in capitalism would cost much more.

The moral and social pattern so exploited by nineteenth-century realist and naturalist literature in which an oily, lustful, fat, degenerate capitalist, landowner, bourgeois, or bigot seduces and corrupts a lovely young maiden, a child of the people, has not at all disappeared from the picture of life in these countries. The capitalist and the bourgeois have been replaced by the factory director, the head of an office, and the Party secretary. The child of the people has remained and has even undergone a significant statistical increase: the abused servant girl, governess, or poor relative has been replaced by the entire female staff of a factory or office. It is not an accident that the saying circulates in Communist countries that sexual intercourse is the most primitive form of man's oppression of man. The sexual-social status of a director's secretary is no different from her status in capitalism. Of course, in communism, as anywhere else, professional stratification is known, and some professions are traditionally more sexualized than others—the natural territories of playboys and women interested in all aspects of life. The theater, the movies, and rest and vacation resorts are by the nature of things conducive environments, and it is easier for an actor, say, to be a playboy than for a miner.

The official attitude of communism toward pleasure, entertainment, and alcohol is crafty, cautious, and ambivalent. Most expounded are hierarchies of virtues which would win the respect of the most proper bourgeois positivist of the last century. In the code of Communist values sex is a matter involving reproduction and a demonstration of deep feelings. Treated otherwise, it becomes a source of indecency and base instincts which distracts a citizen from his social goals and from working for the state and the collective. The libertine literature of turn-of-the-century revolutionaries and socialists which was so esteemed in preparing for the Revolution and in the struggle for power was thrown out as garbage once power was won. The authentic, free men and women of Russian proletarian literature of the revolutionary period were transformed into Party catechism teachers and Party housewives. But from time to time, in moments of crises and breakdowns, Party authorities relax their hold and proclaim the benefits of taking a drop and suitable recreation. This is called the humanization of reality. The people, however, have another name for this kind of ideological instruction. It says that whereas once the synonym for pleasure was wine, woman, and song, now, according to the recommendations of some Party leader or other, everyone must have vodka, asses, and accordions in their spare time. The triteness of this ideological command is best demonstrated in the drunken hiccough and the saying, "Everyone, after all, is a human being," which is proclaimed from political pulpits as the dialectally canonized justification of the hiccough. This enlightening observation is the official formula of Party epicureanism.

Petit bourgeois puritanism and Communist bigotry found their strongest ally in the poverty and shabbiness of existence. This ultimately gave rise to a situation in which the supply of physical love is the only thing communism overproduces and it falls victim to shameful dissipation. Question number one for

189

anyone interested in making love under communism is: Where? Everyone registering at a Communist hotel is obliged to present personal identification. In many cases the hotel reception desk demands to see a marriage license before it will register a couple who do not look quite right. Hotels in Soviet Russia carry their zealous vigilance to the point of having supervisors reside on each floor. Of course, this protective net against sin has holes in it, and position, influence, and money can always stretch it. However, to people who are concerned about their reputations, which under communism means concerned about their careers, this net represents a tricky obstacle which must be skirted, not forced. How? It's simple—you must know someone who has an apartment which is sometimes empty.

This side of life under communism is still awaiting its Flaubert and Dostoevsky, as well as its Maupassant and Feydeau. Its mechanism and complications can fill up one's life completely. An empty apartment usually belongs to a person who lives alone, and it is only empty when its occupant is not at home, that is, when he is at work. This means that one's sex life must be organized in such a way that its ecstasies are obtained when the rest of the country is pulsating with the feverish process of production. The delicate intricacy and miracles of synchronization of these requirements cannot be conveyed in this study. What happens is that, first, the man must get the key from the lender in his office in such a way that no suspicions are aroused in the crowded, desk-filled room. Then he goes for the girl, who must obtain a leave from her job at exactly that time. Then he takes her to where their hearts are drawing them both. Later everything repeats itself in reverse order, returning the girl, the key, etc., but a great literature is needed to explain such riddles of existence. We must point out that transportation in these countries is in terms of speed and efficiency, reminiscent of the horse-drawn streetcars used in New York at the beginning of the century, so that this entire cycle is real torture, unless one has his own car. But if he does have his own car, the problem almost solves itself, since Communist metropolises have only embryonic suburbias and come to a definite end at a certain spot. So for those who long to be alone, there are fields and woods which have many virtues and one fault: they can be used only in good weather. But when the weather is bad, even the most cramped car seems a hundred times roomier than one's own home, filled with one's own wife and children.

The complications of fate which arise from the lending of apartments would impress even Sophocles. In one of the East European capitals a strange story occurred, filled with unexpected compensations and expiations. The political police in this city used the services of a specialist in electronic bugging devices who was distinguished by his high ideological probity and his fanatical devotion to the Party. One day he received an order to install a bug in the apartment of a man who had saved his life during the war. A short conflict of conscience was resolved in favor of his unshaken loyalty to communism and the job was done. The person being bugged was a quiet bachelor who from time to time lent his apartment to a friend. There his friend slept with the specialist's wife. The tape which came into the specialist's hands was filled with their amorous dialogues and sighs. The specialist, of course, destroyed the tape, but was unable to explain this act to his superiors. So he was accused of collaborating with the suspect, who was being charged with a deep antipathy toward the Communist regime. I don't know the end of this story, but if Euripides was ever set to work on it, probably in a thousand years children would still be studying it in school.

# 25 · The police, or conscience

THE LAW has always had two faces: one protecting the given order of things, the other protecting man from evil, violence, and crime. Police were established to uphold the law. From the beginning of their existence, they were a double-edged sword, and it has never been clear which they defended more zealously: order or man. Communism solved this dilemma once and for all. Man does not concern the police in the least; he simply does not exist for them. The only job of the police is to maintain order, in other words, the system of government. In this way, an institution which was created to protect people against evil was transformed into an institution to protect evil against people. The defender became a supervisor.

Communism is called a police system and the Communist state a police state. These terms are not very precise as far as society in general goes, since they confuse the principle of political-social totalitarianism with the principle of police rule. It is closer to the truth to define communism as a reality in which the police play the role of conscience. Ever since people first began to discuss conscience, it has always been the most slippery and treacherous weapon in a man's struggle with his own imperfection. Christianity tried to make conscience an instrument of prime significance in renovating the world. It wasn't very successful and today few people ever discuss the problem of conscience in terms of moral decisions. In its early phase communism tried to reactivate conscience under the name of "class consciousness." However, when it saw that nothing good was coming out of this and that its authority was just as shaky among people with an awakened class consciousness as among those who did not have the slightest idea what it was, it hit upon an epochal idea. It took conscience away from the individual and built massive, gloomy buildings for it, equipped with everything modern technology has to offer for effective torture, for the psychological and physical vivisection of man, and for the most efficient ways of finally destroying him en masse. It trained and organized a huge army to service these establishments and installed conscience in them. From then on, it was called "proletariat conscience," "social conscience," or even "the conscience of mankind," depending on the circumstances, and was strictly binding on everyone. Individual vacillations and conflicts disappeared; confession no longer meant trifling with intimacy and became the property of the collective. The police—political, secret, public, uniformed, regular, criminal, and traffic—which were first conceived as the defenders of the Revolution and its conquests from its enemies, now became specialists in the technology of conscience. Or the guardians of a value which was so deformed that no one, even its masters and rulers, knows its true face.

This ultimate and abysmal ugliness of an idea and an institution resultcd in its becoming overgrown with contradictory legends. Embittered writers, especially anti-Communist ones, or those who suffered at the hands of communism, see in it the mysterious power of a demonic genius, organized and run by obsessed scholastics of evil with the minds of philosophers and white pampered hands who delight in torturing humanity. Pro-Communist apologists and panegyrists see it as a masterpiece of logic in handling problems, a difficult social service performed by people with a sublime sense of honor and dedication. These people personify such a supreme genius for good that they do not hesitate to plunge their hands into blood and, perhaps, perpetrate an occasional injustice which is called the decree of history. A nation ruled by the Communists sees them as moronic imbeciles and stubbornly insists that the only qualification needed to serve in the Communist police is absolute stupidity. I once spoke with a decent old streetcar driver who had three sons. The first was a mechanic, the second studied medicine, the third became a militiaman, that is, a regular policeman. "You know," the old man said to me, "when I asked him why he wanted to join the police force, he answered, 'You see, Dad, I like to catch fish. But why go to all that trouble? When I'm in uniform, I go where people are fishing, say that fishing there is prohibited, and take what they've caught.' It makes you shudder to hear such a thing . . . a complete idiot."

Of course, the truth lies somewhere in between. After fifty years communism has produced a human type known as the employee of the security authorities. At the lower rungs he is essentially a mechanized creature trained to take orders automatically and to carry them out without the slightest participation of his own psychological functions. Innumerable jokes circulate about him, such as the following.

A police recruiting board examines candidates:

QUESTION: How much is two times two?

ANSWER: Three.

QUESTION: How much is two times two?

ANSWER: Five.

Result of examination: Accepted. Candidate has an open mind and a bent for investigation.

QUESTION: How much is two times two?

ANSWER: Five.

QUESTION: How much is two times two?

ANSWER: Five.

Result of examination: Accepted. Candidate displays great strength of character.

QUESTION: How much is two times two?

ANSWER: Four.

QUESTION: How much is two times two?

ANSWER: Four.

Result of examination: Rejected. Stubborn and a smart aleck.

Or: Policemen patrol in pairs the world over. In Communist countries there are always three policemen in a patrol. Reason: One policeman knows how to read, the second knows how to write, and if there are two intellectuals together, someone must watch them to make sure they don't rebel.

Those in the upper echelons of the police, that is, the political police or the security service, can, of course, read and write quite well, and even know how to use the most complex organizational and technological techniques. This makes police work the only area of life under communism that functions efficiently. In an environment where dogmatism, inefficiency, and the antipathy of everyone toward action have given rise to a surrealistic chaos, it is the only branch of state and social life functioning according to modern principles and coherent rules. It is, above all, a branch that *functions,* effectively, purposefully, in keeping with assumptions agreed on beforehand, and based on theoretical models, so solidly and faultlessly constructed they could have been developed in the best American institutes for the study of organization and efficiency. An outside observer or a victim of the political police may sometimes think that some of its actions or moves are the products of accident, disorder, lack of foresight, or error. This impression is totally false. In the early 1920s a few of the best brains of the Russian Revolution sat down and worked out a plan for the political police which to this day is the most perfect product of communism in terms of ingenuity, functionality, and utility. All the features of the era, the eternal human soul, the feeling of fear which is always the same, and the ethnic and geographic characteristics of Russian society were scrupulously considered and synthesized into a monumental work which has no counterpart in the history of other civilizations on the planet. Its durability, its capacity for adapting to new, perhaps even all, national and social conditions, and its continually enriched utilitarianism confer the hallmark of fundamentalism upon it. Various aspects of life display deviations from the Russian norm within the Soviet empire and in the Communist countries outside it. Only the political police is constructed in exactly the same way everywhere and operates on the basis of the same principles, in China as well as in Yugoslavia and Cuba, though the range and nature of its activities vary depending on the political coloration of the time and place. Because of the soundness and rationality of the whole structure, what distinguishes the policeman from the rest of society in communism is the meaningfulness of his life and work. Under communism the policeman is the only normal and psychologically healthy man, who acts on the basis of clear-cut, precise, logical, and readily understandable premises and moral norms. This gives him a sense of the meaning of his own life and achievements, spiritual balance, and the feeling that he is not wasting his time, i.e., his life. Thus it frees him from the most tormenting obsession of man under communism. Complexes and frustrations are unknown to him, and when he feels alienated from society, he attributes it to the righteousness of the path he has chosen and his ideals, insofar as he has any. The policeman is that rare man between Vladivostok and the Elbe who springs briskly to his feet in the morning, whistles cheerfully as he shaves, enjoys the sun and good weather, and flies eagerly to work where he knows that the satisfaction of true productivity and effective action, always with a cause and an effect, a beginning and an end, awaits him.

As everyone knows, state holidays and the anniversaries of the great men or historical events of communism are celebrated by means of so-called increased civic actions. Bricklayers lay more bricks per hour without extra pay, stevedores unload more goods, farmers mow, milk, and sow longer. The police also take part in the joyous and intensified effort of society, and cases are known, though never written about, of interrogating staffs pledging to submit the prisoners to extra tortures to celebrate May Day, or of prison staffs arranging for whole columns of prisoners to stand special hours in the frost in honor of Lenin's birthday. How much simplemindedness and psychological uniformity, without the slightest chinks or worries, is needed for such a brilliantly robust interpretation of the concepts of good, usefulness, and duty! The only regret a policeman may feel under communism is that his efforts and his inventiveness are not repaid with suitable publicity and sufficient renown.

The role of the police as conscience is only possible when certain attributes of existence, formed by five thousand years of Judeo-Christian civilization, are doomed to annihilation, such as personalism and individualism, or a man's right to be himself, or the idea of man as an autonomous psycho-physical whole. The age-old relationship between what is properly public and what cannot be expressed and is a man's exclusive and inviolable right to possess in private must be completely broken down in order to meet the condition of subjection which the police require in aspiring to the role of conscience. Everything we know about individual free will and its attribute of choice counts for nothing in this life. The openness and candor the police want are, in practice, unfeasible and unattainable, even by the most perfect and most exact invigilation apparatus. Hence from time to time openness and sincerity have to be fabricated in the confessions of the police's victims. The primitiveness of these fabrications and their vulgar contempt for the intelligence of the society for whose benefit they are prepared are usually striking. Here lies the weakness of the whole marvelous apparatus, and the police are aware of their inability to attain to absolutes of openness and perfection. Consequently, they fight not for a certain state of affairs, but for the need of this state of affairs; not for an ideal, but for their right to fight for an ideal; in short, for an atmosphere in which they will be able to demand anything while the entire society agrees with the necessity of their demands.

Their most effective weapon in this fight is to so poison the atmosphere of society that every act of honor, decency, courage of one's convictions, heroism, and incorruptibility is depicted as the opposite—as capitulation, meanness, hypocrisy, conformism, cowardice, and venality. This creates a situation in which the harder someone fights for his independence, honesty, and decency, the easier he comes under suspicion in his immediate environment. The more openly someone voices his opposition, the easier it is to suspect him of collaborating with the police. Often the police themselves are the source of rumors about a person. This is the best demonstration of the closed circuit of totalitarianism; everything can be explained so easily in terms of itself. Everything becomes suspect, even suspicion itself. In such an atmosphere the wildest lie can be fabricated without any difficulty and nothing requires more than one explanation. People in the West are surprised that Communist leaders make such improbable charges in their showdowns with each other: Trotsky is an agent of the Gestapo or Tito an agent of the CIA. But it would not occur to anyone living there that probability can play any role in the three-way relationship between state, society, and the individual. A well-known Warsaw joke provides, I think, the best illustration of this setup. A new prisoner appears in a prison cell and its occupants ask him what sentence he received. "Ten years," he says. "For what?" they ask? "For nothing." "You're lying. For nothing they give at most five years."

Of course, the police are infallible. This kind of deification is obtained through various little tricks which are extremely innovative with respect to the old traditions of Western civilization. Generally, because of the long and rich history of these matters, we are accustomed to think that immunity from punishment is the privilege of the powerful while the little man pays for the abuses of his superiors. Under communism things are reversed. The great occasionally perish in bitter power struggles and the mighty fall for the sin of overeagerness or for shortcomings which could be tolerated in mining or diplomacy but never in security work. On the other hand, small fry enjoy complete immunity regardless of their mistakes, cruelty, or misuse of power. Because of the solidarity among the coarsest thugs, society remains in a state of permanent hypnosis, like a humming bird before a snake, and a metaphysics of helplessness pervades every cell of society, and every individual. Legality violated is never rectified, no one ever has a chance to question injustice, and a man killed by a security officer by mistake is simply a man killed without any follow-up. If his family sues, it will be informed that the man killed was a CIA agent, even if he were deaf, dumb, and legless from birth. The man who killed him will receive a decoration for vigilance in the fight against the enemies of the people, since it is an ironclad principle that the rule of law should be violated by means of ever more intensive violations. There is no such thing as innocence, runs the basic principle of the Communist police's philosophy; everyone is guilty of something and we know about it. Only ideas are innocent and pure, such as the idea of protecting communism from its enemies. And we are the guardians of this innocence and possess the esoteric knowledge needed to protect that purity, a knowledge which cannot be shared and is subject to the control only of those whom we serve. This dialectic is put more simply in the well-known joke about the dog who escaped from Czechoslovakia to West Germany. Here he met another dog who asked him why he left his country. "Because they murder rabbits there," the Czech dog replied. "But you're a dog." "Well, but how do I prove it? They know better."

The knowledge at the police's disposal on how to distill fear is infinite. A person can, for example, be arrested without an actual arrest. Someone receives a summons to present himself at the police office in order to make a statement about a car accident he witnessed. He arrives punctually, gets a pass at the entrance, and goes to the designated room. The functionary sitting there takes his pass and tells him to wait in the hall. In the hall the man sits down on a bench and waits. He waits half an hour, an hour. He knocks on the door of the room where he was supposed to make a brief statement. When he opens it, he sees with amazement that another functionary is sitting behind the desk, who asks what he wants. He explains. The second official politely explains that his colleague had to leave on an important matter but will return at once, and that he should not get upset but wait calmly. The man returns to his bench. Another hour passes. He has already smoked all the cigarettes he had on him. He knocks again at the door. No answer. When he pushes the handle he finds the door is closed. He is seized by panic. He cannot leave the building because he does not have a pass. There is no telephone he can use to call home or the place where he works. So he sits hunched on the bench and waits. He is tormented by terrible thoughts, pictures, and visions. He knows he will be in trouble at work since he told them he was only leaving for a while to make a statement to the police. He will be accused of playing hookey and may be fired. Within the next two hours the first functionary reappears. He apologizes for the delay, shows him into his room, and offers him a seat. The statements concerning the accident take ten minutes. The man stammers that he would like some proof of where he spent six hours on a working day for the place where he works. The functionary says that that's no problem and gives him the necessary form. Then he adds, "Oh, by the way, it just occurred to me that we are interested in certain things connected with the place where you work and would be very interested to know what you think of them. Perhaps you could drop in and see us now and then." He smiles pleasantly and hands him a pass allowing him to leave the building.

This simple little scenario makes an easy introductory exercise in a security worker's textbook. As he studies further, he comes across a whole store of knowledge on how to deal with society and the individual. This knowledge is not too complicated and is based upon dividing people into three categories: those who are in prisons, concentration camps, places of isolation, or labor camps; those who have already been there; and those who will be there. Other people do not exist.

# 26 · What a commission is

FROM THE BEGINNING of time it has been said that two heads are better than one. Whenever there was something important to decide, a few people would sit down in a conference. This conference was usually of great significance and dealt with weighty matters. Monarchs, chiefs, and presidents, provided they were wise and restrained, would seek the advice of others. Decisions were made on matters of war and peace and acts of power and justice. On the other hand, the act of cooking soup or the problem of what kind of shoes to wear was usually left up to individual citizens to decide for themselves.

Under communism everything is decided collectively—except for acts of power and justice, which are usually the result of a telephone conversation between two people, or at most three. On the other hand, problems involving soup, shoes, medical prescriptions, and the packaging of sugar are decided at large gatherings which consist of a few dozen representatives of various areas of public life, the economy, and, naturally, the Party authorities. It is strange how the brilliant career of the collective counsel of wise men was the cause of the complete decline and atrophy of the decision, the ultimate result of a conference. In innumerable cases the transcendental mystery and incomprehensibility of what is happening around a man in communism are due precisely to the omnipotence of a commission which is in no position to do anything. This is tied in with the problem of responsibility.

The following story gives an extremely accurate picture of what the idea of responsibility looks like under communism. A beautiful Western sports car belonging to a hotel guest pulled up in the protected parking area in front of a large and elegant hotel in Warsaw. A uniformed hotel employee came out of the hotel and informed the guest that he could not park there. The guest parked the car a half a block away, and when he came out of the hotel a half hour later, he found that his car had been broken into and some valuable movie cameras had been stolen. He went to the police, filed a report, and then went to a garage to have the damages repaired. Afterwards, he returned to the hotel and pulled up in the hotel parking area. The same employee came out and told him that parking there was not allowed. The guest said, "But it says that this is the parking lot for hotel guests. When I parked down the street, I was robbed!" "Well, you see." The hotel employee smiled proudly. "In that case it's your problem. But if you had parked here, I would have been responsible."

Exactly the same frame of mind prevails in commissions. Commissions decide everything, or rather, decide nothing. Suppose a margarine factory has produced a new kind of margarine. Packaging is needed. So the directors of the state enterprise the factory belongs to call in a commission. The commission is made up of representatives from the factory, from the branch of industry the factory belongs to, from the ministry the industry belongs to, from the workers' labor union, from the trade enterprise which will sell the margarine, from the artists' union whose members will design the packaging, from the printing shops which will turn it out, from the Communist union of women (since margarine is used to cook family meals), from the censorship board (since packaging has writing on it which must be checked), and, of course, representatives of the Party, without whom nothing can take place. Agreement on anything seems completely impossible in such a large body representing such divergent interests, but this is not the worst problem. Worst of all is that when some concrete decision seems imminent, someone, moved by that sense of responsibility formed by life under communism, described above, will suddenly say, "But I wouldn't approve it." Then a deathly hush falls on the meeting and everyone feverishly thinks to himself, "He must know something. There must be something politically unsound about it. I'm not going to stick my neck out and fight for God knows what! Later it may turn out that I approved something that wasn't correct." Voting begins, and everyone votes against the packaging plan. The margarine, unable to pack itself, lies around for a few years until it goes bad, and instead of going into the frying pan, it becomes grease for the wheels of horse carts in the countryside. Later, Western tourists are amazed that in Communist countries there are more horses than tractors.

## 27 • What a passport to go abroad is

---

NEARLY TWO HUNDRED YEARS after the French Revolution and the American Constitution, and over fifty years
after the Russian Revolution whose goal was the freedom of all
people, a Russian peasant, to whom the country and state allegedly belong, must get a pass from the secretary of his *kolkhoz*
if he wants to visit his brother in a city fifty miles away. This
pass, issued by the local police authorities to the *kolkhoz* authorities, represents a passport, without which the peasant has no
right to move outside his own *kolkhoz*. If he is stopped in the
city and cannot prove his identity with a pass, he is threatened
with prison or a concentration camp. Such a pass is often called
the authorization for an official business trip in order to camouflage its true nature. The facts about travel restriction *within*
Russia are little known to advocates of communism in the
West and are worth closer examination. Such restrictions represent the last known vestige of feudalism or semislavery on the
European continent and no camouflage can hide the truth.

I don't know what things are like in China, but nothing of the
sort exists in the countries of Eastern Europe. The satellite countries, and even the most fervent Communists in them, look
with scorn upon Russia and many of its practices and consider
themselves a part of Europe. So it's out of the question for a citizen of these countries to be constrained in his desires to move

freely around his own country—he can go wherever he wants. But if he wants to cross his country's borders, it's another matter, and here there opens a field for deep and complicated reflections.

The leaders of a Communist country are in principle opposed to their citizens, residents, or subjects making trips abroad. Throughout the world, when someone wants to leave the country of his birth or residence, he goes to the appropriate office where, provided he has not committed any serious crime, for a fee he receives a document attesting to his citizenship and entitling him to go where he wants. In Communist countries you must file a special application and request for this document—despite the fact that legally it belongs to everyone—and even then, you probably will not get it. You must wait years for an answer explaining the refusal, though generally you will not get that either.

Let us try to reconstruct the method of reasoning that leads to such a state of affairs. Generally, a Communist ruler believes that people should not be allowed to do what they want or what they feel like doing, but rather that their business is to sit in one place, work, and praise the ruler for making this possible. This conviction is reason enough not to issue anyone a foreign passport and can easily be justified by the so-called interest of the people's state. Moreover, the Communist ruler regards communism as the culminating achievement of the human race. Thus the idea that someone living under communism wants to leave it seems first of all unnatural, and then blameworthy to the ruler. Of course, the ruler must admit the possibility that someone may want to leave the country not to abandon it, but for other reasons, and also that there are other Communist countries to which one might want to go, certainly without abandoning communism. Still, the ruler feels that each of his subjects should feel most at home in his own country and under his rule. If someone doesn't feel this way, there must be something wrong with him and he had better be watched.

The next stage of reasoning somewhat contradicts the preceding. Although the ruler regards communism as perfection, he prefers that it not be discussed outside Communist society. He also rightly assumes that someone who leaves even on a short trip will be asked about communism and that what he has to say is not really suitable for conversations with foreigners. They may be incorrectly informed by the traveler, since only the information from the ruler himself is suitable for distribution outside communism. In addition, he is more than certain that the person who wants to leave communism for good will not praise it. Consequently, it is better to forcibly prevent him from leaving rather than run the risk of a bad press, since it is a lesser sin to extinguish human dreams, hopes, and plans, and even to imprison one man or millions of people, than to jeopardize the good name of communism. In a certain sense the ruler is completely right. Knowledge of a Communist state begins with those who come from it, not with those who visit it to see what it is like. Before the war the eastern part of Poland, which bordered on the USSR, was the poorest section of the nation, and at the same time the most anti-Communist. In every little village everyone had relatives who chronically escaped from the other side of the border to Poland, so that people knew *what it was like there*.

Certainly, in every Communist country there are a number of people who simply want to leave communism once and for all. This does not necessarily mean that these people are opponents of communism, but communism thinks they are. Communism keeps those who openly oppose it in prison, so that every opponent of communism tries to hide the fact that he is one, especially when he submits an application for a foreign passport. But instead of determining who is an opponent and who isn't, communism, aware of how many people don't like it, found a simple and brilliant solution: it simply closed its borders, turning even the most beautiful country into a great prison for all those who want to leave. Anyone who has lived in a Communist country has not the slightest doubt that at least one third of his fellow citizens would leave at once if they were allowed to do so. Wherever possibilities of escape exist, people simply escape. Throughout the fifty years of its existence refugees from communism may number in the millions: from East Germany alone three and a half million people escaped, nearly one quarter of the population. *True* knowledge of communism begins with those who escape from it, and communism cannot let this knowledge be disseminated abroad. Hence we have the Berlin Wall, mined borders, barbed wire stretching for hundreds of thousands of kilometers, dogs, and machine-gun nests. When Communist power was being consolidated in Poland, people were allowed to swim only in specially marked-off beaches on the Baltic Sea. The other beaches were put off-limits by the police in order to make escapes to Sweden difficult. Footprints in the sand of these areas alerted the police to begin immediate pursuit if some daredevil decided to escape by raft or perhaps by swimming.

As a result, Russia and China, the two biggest Communist countries, are closed societies. People leave them only for the purpose of maintaining the nation's contacts with the rest of the world, which is an unavoidable tribute to the importance of world civilization in the twentieth century. The people allowed to leave are only those considered most trustworthy, diplomatic or foreign trade personnel whose loyalty has been proved, sailors, pilots, or people who must occasionally be displayed somewhere for propaganda purposes—pianists, athletes, mathematicians, as well as secret police to watch them. The travelers as a rule leave their families at home. This is the primary condition for issuing them a foreign passport, since the Communist ruler, for all his modernity, always exercises his power on the basis of ancient methods—in this case, the tried and tested method of hostages.

The problem looks different from the standpoint of the East European countries. After the disturbances of the post-Stalinist era, Poland was the first country which decided to issue passports to people who wanted to visit their families abroad. By the end of the fifties other countries had followed suit. Of course, this was like an invitation to exodus. A huge percentage of the people going to the West ostensibly to visit relatives or as tourists refused to return to their Communist homelands which, however, were apparently no longer upset by it. At times, 80 percent of the tourists on excursion boats going from Rumania to Italy would escape. Why the East European regimes thought it expedient to deviate from one of the most sacred canons of educating society in the spirit of communism is not too clear. We may assume that permanent economic crises made them look with a favorable eye upon population decrease. Perhaps they regarded this outflow as such a valuable way of discharging political hostility that it was worth raising the curtain and risking damage through foreign propaganda. On the other hand, this new system fundamentally changed the role of the passport in the lives of the citizens of Communist East Europe. The political police, which is in charge of issuing or denying passports, came to the conclusion that under these modified conditions, the passport represented a powerful weapon against people, their rights, and their peace of mind. From then on, it changed from a constitutionally guaranteed but never issued document and to an object of reward or punishment. The situation appeared to be different from that under Stalinism and the mass turnover in passports was incomparably greater, but by a strange coincidence those who could obtain passports most easily were those who could get them even under Stalin, while it was most difficult, or generally impossible, for those people who could not even dream of getting one then to get one now. Naturally, the process of issuing or denying a passport is not regulated by the rule of law. When it is denied, the unfortunate applicant receives a poorly printed form informing him that the appropriate authorities (read: the political police) have decided not to issue him a foreign passport, justifying their decision by referring to paragraph four of the Passport Code. If someone were to check paragraph four in the official decree, he would find that the authorities have the right *not* to issue a passport if they think it advisable. The matter ends there; it is forbidden to ask any more questions and no answer exists.

For centuries we have been accustomed to calling certain eschatological denouements tragedies, so the fact that someone cannot go abroad does not seem to fit our idea of tragedy. But the elements of tragedy are subject to historical reevaluation, and the new inevitability of catastrophes, the supersonic revenge of fate, or cybernetic fatalism can undermine characters and break morality no less than Oedipus' *moira*. So it is not hard to imagine a tragedy involving the citizen of a Communist country in which the denial of a passport leads to events as bloody and irreversible as any in Shakespeare. From the moment a passport becomes a sign of the state's opinion of a man, the measure of his situation within a system where approval or condemnation become the main element in a human destiny, the problem of a passport takes on the dimensions of one of the elemental problems of existence. It is a sentence passed without a trial, without an indictment, without the possibility of defense, without proofs of guilt, without witnesses. The only question a man may ask himself after receiving a refusal is: Why? He will never get an answer, because the decisions of the political police are a state secret, even if they involve a two-year-old child or a ninety-year-old man. People who are proved enemies of communism—and there are many such people in intellectual, literary, and artistic circles—at least know why they cannot get a passport, and this certainly makes their lives somewhat more logical. But an ordinary wage earner with no ambitions of opposing communism who merely wants to live his life as far away as possible from the problems of social existence under communism is overcome by a sort of paranoia when he receives a refusal. He is obsessed by the tormenting question: Why? He does not know where he is at fault because no one has accused him of anything or proved anything against him. Nonetheless, he is guilty of *something* because he did not get a passport. Not knowing what one is accused of provokes him to think of an infinite number of possible accusations, all false, but how can he defend himself when he does not know what to answer for? Slowly the conviction is born in his mind that because he does not know where he is at fault does not mean he is not at fault but rather represents his vote of nonconfidence in those who pass judgment on him. From here it is only a step to feeling guilty because *they* found him guilty. Who *they* are and what *guilt* is remain hidden behind a Kafkaesque wall of mysterious ignorance which it is better not to delve into. No one who has not experienced this state of mind and these feelings is in a position to understand them. They contain depths of tortures as shameful as they are subtle, tortures of the heart and mind, psychopathic states of desperation which are all the more painful in that they are completely incommunicable to those who have not experienced this condition. These tortures are completely devoid of pathos and nobility, all that loftiness of suffering sanctified by the tradition of unjust suffering which sustains the dignity of the suffering person. Ultimately, it is only a fight over a scrap of paper which allows a person to move between one spot on the earth and another, something that in normal societies is obtained by standing for fifteen minutes on the right line. This suffering destroys the soul just as the unventilated interior of a prison destroys the body, complexion, and respiration.

In Eastern Europe the gypsies who accost people in parks to tell their fortunes don't begin with the ritual words, "You will be rich . . . You will win in a lottery . . . You will get married." Rather with, "You will get your exit visa and go abroad in the near future."

## 28 · How to be a Jew

I T's HARD to be a Jew under communism. It has been ground into the consciousness of the masses, especially in Europe, that Jews are that section of society which wants communism for its own selfish ends. There are numerous and complex reasons for this conviction, which has been vaguely and incompletely explained and is full of contradictions but still persists. It is more important, however, to reveal the consequences of this prejudice than to explain its causes. In a country where communism has taken over, a Jew begins to live in an atmosphere of psychological-moral pathology, regardless of his personal attitude toward communism. The pressure of the popular belief in an organic connection between Jews and communism is so strong that whatever happens, even in an area of life most remote from him, a Jew feels it is his fault. A Czech, a Russian, or a Pole undergoes communism. A Jew takes the responsibility for it, even when he hates communism and sees in it his mortal enemy.

A general characteristic of communism is that wherever it has appeared, it has placed its practicing disciples in unequivocal and uncompromising situations, the upshot of which has been totalitarian coercion and often crime. In official language this is called the active defense of ideas, or ideological struggle, and it inspires the conquered nations with blind hatred and resistance to the death. Once the idea has been permanently instilled in the masses that communism is a "Jewish" cause, the Jews are automatically incorporated as an entity—ethnical, racial, religious, and, above all, distinct—into the concept against which the widespread defensive hatred of militant communism is turned. Hence in twentieth-century communism the situation is the same as in the Middle Ages when the Jews were a priori responsible for epidemics, crop failures, earthquakes, and floods.

Degenerations of social consciousness are sinister and lead to historical tragedies. An investigation into their causes is complicated and difficult so that often attempts are made to explain them by mythologizing events. Jews are not free of the tendency to reverse the principles of causality and often tend to see anti-Semitism as a phenomenon which lacks a cause, explicable only in terms of the absolutization of separateness and hatred. The connection of Jews with communism is, however, a phenomenon as concrete as it is ill-fated. Even the most irrational and vulgar interpretations of this connection would not have taken root in the consciousness of the European masses without some cause.

Marxism is the work of a Jew. Jews were among its earliest and most important apologists and champions. Its most influential reformers were Jews. Russian Bolshevism and communism which, rightly or wrongly, proclaimed themselves to be the only consistent continuators of Marxism, were to a large extent framed by Jews. Jews held important posts in post-revolutionary Russia and often determined the practice—bloody and inhumane—of communism. In a country and among a people where anti-Semitism was an animalistic, almost instinctive impulse and the word "Jew" was a synonym for contemptuous abuse, Jews were among the most visible and ostentatious propagators of communism. The Russian Communist soon realized that they would not be able to liquidate hatred of the Jews, encrusted in the Russian soul for centuries, overnight or within a definite time. There then arose a conflict between principles and tactics, which was quickly resolved in favor of tactics with the consent of authoritative Jews. And so while Engels, Bebel, and Bernstein had borne their Jewish names with the pride of true faith in their professed ideals, the Russian Communist Jews recognized that

they would have to sacrifice the pride of moralism and fundamentalism for the good of the Revolution. Hence Trotsky,
Bukharin, Sverdlov, Zinoviev, Kamenev, Litvinov, Radek, etc.
It took Joseph Stalin, however—another person who had
changed his name—to show the Jews their mistake, to make this
tactic look like a villainous act, and thus to make anti-Semitism
once again an instrument of political infamies as absurd as they
were deadly. For the first time in the history of anti-Semitism,
Stalin accomplished an unusual thing: he planned and set in
motion persecutions of Jews of a terrible intensity while at the
same time he avoided having them branded as anti-Semitic by a
substantial number of Jews in the world—those Jews who de-
luded themselves, and still delude themselves, that salvation lies
in Marxism, that is, in the vision of one of themselves, which
was so easy to turn against themselves.

Stalin's perfidy in using anti-Semitism inspires amazement
because of the simplicity of the idea, the profundity of its historical prospects, as well as its cold murderousness which far
surpasses the clumsiness of the Nazi extermination in its precision. The countries of Eastern Europe are traditionally anti-Semitic, though in a different way from the pogrom-style brutality
of Russia. Toward the end of the Middle Ages Polish kings
offered shelter and privileges to the Jews who had been suppressed and persecuted in Western Europe. For four centuries
Poland was the center of a flourishing Ashkenazy civilization
which extended over Germany, Austria, Czechoslovakia, Hungary, and Lithuania. The Jews, who did not merge with the surrounding societies, acquired a powerful economic position in
them, which finally in the nineteenth century turned existing
religious and social animosities into acute anti-Semitism with an
economic basis, especially in Poland where Jews had grown to
10 percent of the general population. The demographic situation
in Hungary and Rumania was similar. But in these countries instances of physical attacks on Jews were rare and pogroms on
the Russian and Ukrainian scale were unknown. Nonetheless,
social barriers pushed the Jews to the fringes of life; their opportunities for development were limited and entry to many fields

and professions was closed to them. The intelligentsia of Jewish origin, which was growing in numbers and significance, did not receive equal professional rights and was subjected to restrictions and harassments. At the turn of the century this state of affairs converged with the growth of social movements, socialist ideas, and the political awareness of the working classes. Marxism and its offshoots assured them of their unyielding striving to eliminate nationalism, ethnic differences, and the privileges based on them. So it is not surprising that both the pauperized Jewish masses and the Jewish intelligentsia, which had not been able to find an outlet for its abilities, saw in socialism, and later in communism, a savior which was consistent in its promises, and joined the Marxist parties in a proportion much higher than the native societies. Consequently there arose in the anti-Semitic consciousness of East European nations an ambivalent image of the Jew as a plutocrat and a Communist, a capitalist exploiter and a godless subversive rolled into one. Anti-Semitic feelings intensified in the period between the wars, stimulated by the proximity of Fascist Germany and its mythologization of anti-Semitism which sanctioned the impending genocide. At the same time pro-Communist feelings increased among Jews, to whom nearby, but rigorously isolated, Russia appeared to be a paradise of freedom and equality. Even then many Jews—fanatical Communists—played the role of a Soviet fifth column, intensifying the ill-will of Poles or Rumanians, and blind to the truth about the Soviet Union where Zionism was banned, synagogues desecrated, and every citizen of Jewish origin had to have "Nationality—Jewish" written on his passport, even if he regarded himself as a Russian or merely as a man. Then Hitler invaded Poland, and the Jews began to flee en masse to Soviet Russia, where they were taken in without any trouble. There Stalin was waiting for them with his plan.

Five years later when the Red Army began to sovietize Eastern Europe, a Jew stood at the head of the Czechoslovakian Party team, a Jew gagged Hungary, a Jewish woman ruled in Rumania, while Poland had as its leader a figurehead Pole behind whom in key positions stood Jewish Communists who carried out the Kremlin's most ruthless orders with fanatical devotion. Behind the leaders stood loyal ranks of Communists of Jewish origin who were the only ones capable of getting the economy and administration moving in Poland, Hungary, and Rumania— peasant and petit-bourgeois countries where anticommunism was a sort of national religion. Stalin knew all this. And he knew that only Jews, who were fanatically devoted to communism, could perform that preliminary and not too clean work for him. This was part one of his plan.

Did the Jews as a group realize what was in store for them? They must have had some foreboding of the catastrophe which was to be their fate as a sequel to the catastrophe which preceded. Soviet Russia, which they got to know from its worst side in Siberia and Kazakhstan, was a dismal, eye-opening experience for many of them. Proof of this is that over three quarters of the Jews who returned to Poland from Russia immediately after the war set out at once for the West, mainly to Palestine, thereby giving the best testimony of their attitude toward communism. But the Communists stayed behind: they had learned nothing in Russia, and had not noticed the fate of their German Jewish comrades whom Stalin had handed over to the Gestapo during the Molotov-Ribbentrop flirtation. They still believed that the end justified the means, believed in the stainless purity of an idea which no infamy could besmirch. Before them lay Poland, Hungary, or Rumania, where communism had overthrown all barriers of origin, realizing the age-old dreams of Jews for absolute, unconditional emancipation and equality.

Using national minorities as a means of controlling the Communist Party when it takes over somewhere is a perfect trick. It creates the impression that those who were formerly discriminated against have been totally liberated, and at the same time makes them slavishly dependent on Moscow, which alone is capable of protecting their high position from the hatred and anger of the natives. Thus Lithuanians, White Russians, and Ukrainians dominated the Polish Communist Party in the initial stage of Communist power in Poland, a Hungarian was vice-premier in Rumania, a Slovak in Hungary, while Jews were everywhere. With overzealous enthusiasm they threw themselves into the sovietization of East European societies, the building of socialism, and tightening the Communist noose around the necks of old nations which were hardened against violence and experienced in the fight for psychological independence. With their zeal they ruined the greatest chance Jews had had in this part of the world since the Middle Ages. For, despite their traditional anti-Semitism, most of the people in these societies were shocked by Hitler's crimes. Anti-Semitic Poland, along with numerous displays of shameful abuses, exhibited many acts of heroism and self-denial in saving Jews, this despite the fact that the occupying Germans' treatment of Poles bore all the marks of genocide and the execution of entire Polish families for hiding Jews was the order of the day. Anti-Semitism, though still present, was drying up at its sources. Only a small fraction of the Jews returned, representing neither a demographic nor an economic threat. New generations grew up which knew the Jewish problem only as an example of Fascist brutality. Under these conditions the servility displayed by Jewish Communists in serving Soviet imperialism created the impression of suicidal madness. The microbes of anti-Semitism began to come to life again and to grow on a new food, despite official condemnation. And a person would have had to be completely blind to think that their deadly strength would not, sooner or later, be used by the Communists for their political ends. To what extent the devoted Jewish Communist represented only a blind instrument of Stalin soon became apparent. As a prelude to a general showdown with the leaders of East European communism, the purpose of which was to establish principles of unquestioning obedience by means of terror (in the aftermath of the schism with Tito), Stalin ordered that the first secretary of the Czechoslovakian Party, Rudolph Slansky, be imprisoned and executed. A man who had spent his life fighting Zionism was accused of being a secret agent for international Jewry within the Communist movement. From then on the word "Jew" became a political expression in the interparty struggles of East European communism. Anti-Semitism received an official safe conduct for its subcutaneous existence. And this was part two of Stalin's plan.

The third part was put into effect not long ago, a tribute to Stalin's political astuteness and the scope of his outlook in planning evil. It also provides an insight into his gloomy forebodings about the fate of the idea in the name of which he murdered so many people. The erosion of the empire in the nearly fifteen years after its founder's death seems unquestionable. The process of disintegration is complex and slow, but is quite apparent to an observer who is not blinded by faith. National, economic, and social contradictions are weakening the organism of the empire with suppressed but continually renewing schisms and ideological heresies. The heirs of this bankrupt estate waver between hypocritical pseudoliberalism and pseudoenlightened absolutism, between inefficient mirages of pragmatic consumerism held in check by repressive bureaucratic autocratism. Disillusioned Jewish Communists are now among those who are rebelling against the degeneration of the idea and the system. So what could be simpler than to take full advantage of Stalin's foresight and direct the people's anger against them? Anti-Semitism as an antidote to inhumane policies has never disappointed anyone, particularly in Eastern Europe.

Despite what the gullible and the fanatic believe, such an undertaking has a solid logical and dialectic basis. In Russia it is not needed. "Social life in that country is a permanent conspiracy against the truth; a person there who cannot be deceived is considered a traitor," the French writer and traveler Astolphe de Custine wrote in his *Lettres de Russie* in 1839. From the beginnings of the Soviet state, the fate of the Jews was that of a national-social group systematically destroyed because it represented a separate entity, but also because it did not do so to a sufficient degree, because it both wanted a distinct identity and to escape a distinct identity by assimilation and merging with the milieu. Right after the Revolution Lenin wrote, "There is no such thing as the Jewish people. It does not exist now and never will exist." But in 1949 Stalin established the mythical category of "cosmopolitan" as an object of persecutions and the main target of repressions in the Communist demonology and ordered that there be published a list of the names of intellectuals of Jewish origin together with their former Jewish names in brackets. He thereby proclaimed the Jews in Russia, a country which from time immemorial has been ready to trample on people not approved by the regime, an object of political and civil assassination. A physical hecatomb soon followed. The Jewish Anti-Fascist Committee, which had been so necessary to Stalin during the war with Hitler, was shot almost to a man or liquidated in concentration camps on the absurd charge of wanting to separate the Crimea from the USSR. According to incomplete figures, 238 Yiddish writers perished, 106 Jewish actors, 19 musicians, and 87 painters and sculptors. At exactly the same time the Communist parties in the West, which were to a large degree led and unreservedly supported by many Jewish intellectuals, launched a crusade against postwar America called by Stalin, its conceptualist, the "peace movement." Pro-Communist circles within the Western democracies then played an epoch-making role; they activated cold war Soviet "anti-imperialism" and supplied it with the atom bomb. The overwhelming majority of them were Jews, appallingly blind to the fact that right after the destruction of the Anti-Fascist Committee came the so-called Case of the Jewish doctors who were accused by the Soviet political police of conspiring to murder Soviet leaders. This provocation defied reason just as much as Hitler's most primitive exegeses of the mechanism of the world and the existence of nations.

The question arises: Does Marxism, as a philosophy and an intellectual movement whose progressiveness and mission to free mankind from ignorance generations believed in, contain within itself the organic prerequisites which make such monstrous degenerations possible?

Like every monistic system which regards pluralism with scorn, Marxism is a despotic system which sanctions the despotism of an idea and a faith. An intrinsic feature of every despotism from its most ancient embodiments to fascism and communism is that it bases its morality on the principle of collective responsibility. A man is showered with privileges or thrown on the garbage heap of history depending on his group connections, his racial, class, ethnic or religious affiliations. Marxism, despite all the provisos of rationalism inserted into it, also *agrees* to evaluate a man according to his group classification. From here it is only a step to any abuse and crime. Jews have always suffered more than other peoples from the principle of collective responsibility and Marxism, as it turned out, did not do anything to change this state of affairs. Communism, regardless of how far certain circles of enthusiastic revisionists have gone in a purely theoretical "humanization" of the young Marx, has become permanently fixed in the mind of twentieth-century man as a morbid obsession with power at any price and the insane pursuit of super-human authority. The *casus* of Communist anti-Semitism, horribly deformed in its motivations and justifications, is the ultimate and blatant proof of this. In the Communist empire the position of the Jews as a group at the end of the sixties represented the following equation: According to the sanctified orthodoxy of Marxism, communism, its offshoot, eliminates all differences of origin among people. When, however, it is to communism's advantage to do so, these differences can and even must be *creatively* reactivated and used to explain setbacks or necessities. In order to get the leveling of differences they are entitled to, Jews must serve communism blindly and faithfully, thereby arousing the hatred of the nations subjugated by communism. Communism is their defense against this hatred, but makes no secret of the fact that if it thinks it necessary, it will freely avail itself of this hatred. In other words, it demands of Jews that they accept its position as a persecutor and a defender against persecution rolled up into one. This ambivalence contravenes the intellectual criteria of twentieth-century man in the womb of Western civilization but, strange to say, it still finds forgiveness in the minds of many Jewish Communists living outside communism. In Poland, where after the last war there arose possibilities for extinguishing anti-Semitism in subsequent generations or at least reducing its sources to a socially harmless minimum, the above equation led to an outburst of persecutions whose result was a neo-hitlerian social climate. Using the political configuration—the Arab-Israeli conflict—as a pretext, Polish Communists proceeded to dispose of the intelligentsia of Jewish origin and the rest of Polish Jews in general, creating psychological-moral situations reminiscent of Germany in the 1930s. It is hard to say whether the inspiration for this thoroughly considered and ruthlessly carried out action came from ideological headquarters in Moscow or whether it was the product of a purely Polish, deeply rooted anti-Semitism. But it is not hard to see that the goals and methods of both possible sources are identical. Nor is there any doubt that the Polish model, effectively tried out on Polish society, will receive a general imperial patent as the best method for allaying ideological unrest, the protest of the masses, and heretical rebellions. Aging and deteriorating Communist propaganda has long been in need of a transfusion of fresh, catchy slogans. The old, tested, chauvinistic Fascist lies suddenly turned out to be uncannily vital in this part of Europe and so were applied with the Kremlin's blessing where they would prove most useful. Reasoning does not play a major role here: the Stalinists' maltreatment of the remains of the Czech reform of 1968 went on to the tune of anti-Jewish invective, despite the fact that all the Jews living in Czechoslovakia at the time could be put into a single movie theater.

The Polish model dismally reveals the degeneration of doctrine. It is, however, more modern and more functional than the Russian-Ukrainian pogrom pattern. Poles do not murder or shoot; in other words, they do not simplify the problem. The abusive and crude method of liquidating Jews by means of a terminology reduced to absurdity, so instrumental in the climate of Stalinist paranoia when the epithet "cosmopolitan" often meant execution, has undergone complications and become politically elevated. "Zionist" became a synonym for the political archenemy, like "imperialist," and a person so proclaimed becomes an outlaw: any act of violence or expropriation is permitted against a Zionist, who has no right to defend himself. In a totalitarian state violence is, like everything else, a state institution and no one can kill people on the streets without state approval. The Polish Communists did not stage acts of the so-called wrath of the people, which were too extreme, knowing full well that even the most carefully worked out mob action can get out of control. Instead, they channelled this anger into breakneck dialectic acrobatics and told the society they ruled that the Zionists were the most stubborn, hidden, and insidious enemies of Communists and that they had perfidiously tried to get control of the movement to shamefully misuse and exploit the proletarian masses for their own ultrachauvinistic ends. The centuries-old Jewish octopus, extending its bloodsucking tentacles, this time from Tel Aviv, entwined the world with its deadly embrace and the historical mission of the Communists (as it was once that of the SS boys) was to cut off the poisonous polyps by mercilessly and courageously (?) demasking the Zionists in their own ranks. It remained to establish who was a Zionist, but this turned out to be easy: every Jew who did not proclaim his obsequious attitude toward the current rulers of Communist Poland in a degradingly servile manner was one. This formula practically represented the apogee of fascist "science," that the Jew does not exist as an individual but is *per definitio* a particle and exponent of some antihuman super-power, the annihilation of which is the duty of every German, Pole, Russian, etc. On the whole this was a risky undertaking, because knowing the hatred of Poles for communism, one might expect that all Poland would flare up with ardent love for the Jews and their anticommunism which had suddenly been revealed *ex cathedra*. But the Communists counted on the fact that anti-Semitism is stronger among the Polish masses than anticommunism, and they were not wrong.

This objective decline of ideology soon turned into a fantastic distortion of the ideological exegesis. A whole pleiade of Polish Goebbels and Streichers began to prove that there are no fundamental antinomies between "healthy" nationalism and communism which was "cured" of Jewish miasmata. The Jews were the only obstacle on the road to national communism (again, this sounds strangely familiar) and the liquidation of their influence would allow a symbiosis of the element of national aspirations and ethnic quality with the prime tenet of Marxism—the struggle to liberate the masses. The madness of Fascist syncretism again emerged in all its splendor from the columns of the Polish Communist press. Once again, a Jew was a plutocrat and a revolutionary in one person and his Janus-like face was a cunning device to deceive and subjugate peoples in order to break their wills and make them passive victims for the sake of the age-old interests of Israel, Judaism, the Sanhedrin, and the Elders of Zion. There was an upsurge of semi-intellectual "historical" hypotheses that the Slavs had been Marxists at the very dawn of their history, that their prehistorical culture indicates many ties with the later theses of Marxism-Leninism, that the early Slavic communities anticipated the advanced socialist economy—and it was the appearance of the Jews in the historical arena that brought on the class struggle. This "scientific" equal sign between "people's" and "Communist" led to a farcical obscurantism, such as the argument of an art historian who wrote that old Slavic ornaments and jewelry met the requirements of socialist realism, whereas the Jews, through Christianity, contaminated European gold work and artistic handicrafts with cosmopolitanism.

Today many people the world over ask themselves the question: How could things have come to this? At what point did Marxism, which is the result of strict reasoning and the product of learning and moral principles, turn into a phantasmagoria of ignorance and political banditry? The antihumanistic and totalitarian element contained in Marxism has never appeared with such force as in the Communist version of the anti-Semitism of Poles and Russians. And undoubtedly the difficult and complicated answer to this question and many others lies in this fact. Of course, these questions will be resolved with the acids of doctrinal sophisms, but the fundamentality of many of them does not permit evasive answers. For example, when does a Jewish Communist's usefulness as an instrument in the struggle for power come to an end, and when does his utility as a sacrificial goat in the process of propping up by force a regime which does not have the mandate of those it rules begin? Many of the Jews in non-Communist countries, blinded by their own extremism, ofttimes by ambition and simple cock-sure stupidity, should ponder deeply over these questions. Today American universities take in Jews who worked for the political police in Eastern Europe for twenty-five years, during which time they assiduously persecuted people, including other Jews, who were fighting for their right to an independent conscience. Today these Jews hide behind their once so easily forgotten Jewishness. The fact that in 1968 in Poland they were suddenly and brutally reminded that they were Jews is a horrifying and disgusting fact which should be condemned. But it does not make them worthy of respect or even sympathy nor does it mean that we should in any way solidarize with them. At the grave moment when the age-old forces of darkness threaten and attack, a careful distinction must be made between defending and protesting in defense of those Jews who suffer *only* because they are Jews and those who are merely victims of the power struggles between Communist politicians and the talmudists of Marxism. The Polish Jews, spat on, kicked around, and deprived of the means of existence, are paying for the careers and mistakes of those other Jews and for their intoxication with usurped power. The latter do not have a moral right to defense because they were the unremitting architects of the reality in which, after twenty-five years, things could reach the point of such caricatural degenerations of thought and ideas, and the engineers of that structure in which it was so easy to make monstrous lying a principle of life. It is hard to forget their fanatical faith in evil which they proclaimed in Communist newspapers, articles, books, and films, regardless of whether that faith was a pure faith or whether it had its ambiguous rationalizations. The former Communist dignitaries who flee from Poland are insincere when they revile Polish Communist anti-Semitism. They denounce and curse it in the name of fundamentalism and their lost positions, hypocritically raise their eyes to the heavens and call upon the frustrated spirits of the Jewish creators of the law as witnesses. In substance, however, anti-Semitism is a salutary deliverance for them in the face of coming to terms with themselves. They will never again experience the bilious taste of defeats which come from serving lies and crime; they have suffered an *undeserved* defeat because of their origin.

They were oppressed *because* they were Jews, not because they extolled and realized violence, slavery, and infamy. They will never be called to account for their own crimes; they have been saved by stupid anti-Semites who trampled on their birth certificates and thereby redeemed their humanity. Every honest Jew is by nature a passionate opponent of the principle of collective responsibility. But only certain Jews from Eastern Europe whose lifework made them common scoundrels in the service of totalitarian communism hide behind this principle after fleeing to America and try, in the eyes of the world, to shift their responsibility, or rather their lack of it, onto their circumstantial Judaism.

Every deception is a trampoline from which it is easy to jump into the abyss of metaphysics for the demi-intellectuals. To the anti-Semitic mob's imagination, the Jew decides, draws up, disseminates, fertilizes, swaddles, and with his own hands sets in motion acts, movements, and whole complicated political and social processes together with their antinomies, vectors, tendencies, and wealth of components. How a Jew or even Jewry does this, no one bothers to explain. Realism is not the favorite epistomological method of either crowds or totalitarian regimes. The narrow boundary line separating metaphysics from intellectual limitations has plagued mankind from pre-Aristotelian times. It is not intellectual rebellion, criticism of existing reality, or even slavery and poverty which thermodynamize protests, moral unrest, and revolutions, but death merchants, the CIA, the Elders of Zion, the Masons, Wall Street executives, Israeli intelligence, or an anarchist-Trotskyite cell in the London Jockey club on Pall Mall. Everything seems to indicate that *every* offshoot of Marxism, once an honorable philosophy, is today in a position to attain these limits of institutionalized paranoia. Before our eyes the Marxist and neo-Marxist left and what is today called the New Left are rejecting the tenets of rational thinking for increasingly trashier metaphysics. Communism as practiced in Eastern Europe uses the cheap argument that the "restlessness" of the Jewish mind (as if there were anything new in this!) "obstructs" and even "destroys" what the Slavs, Germans, Hungarians, etc., constructively try to build up in spiritual serenity and according to the inviolability of the faith proclaimed by Marx, a Jew. Whether Marx came to it by the strength of his own restless Jewish mind is a point which is not discussed today. There then arises the most tormenting of all questions: Must all ideologies created by Jews, conceived by the Jewish spirit, and in the name of its moral norms in the end be turned against the Jews, despite the fact that their goal is the defense and salvation of *all* people, Jews as well? But perhaps this is the reason? Perhaps the broadly conceived spectrum of humanism which the Jews have fought for for centuries cannot be accepted by a humanity which never wanted it and never will want it? Can a narrowly conceived tradition be the only safeguard of the Jews' historical fate, while every effort to link their destiny with a more universal idea means suicidal catastrophe? Does, then, every Jewish attempt conceived by the Jewish intellect in the long run mean self-destruction?

It is my conviction that every totalitarian doctrine must violently turn against the Jews in its assumptions and rationalizations. Totalitarian ideologies are by nature utopian and their ultimate goal, theoretical as well as practical, is to create a definitive vision of the world and life, to establish a static model the finality of which is subject to neither criticism nor modification. But the Jewish mentality will never go along with this. Life is dynamic, while thought is the fruit of life and should serve life not an abstraction. This was known to the Jewish creators of the most brilliant abstractions. Their fate has been the age-old torments of ambivalence and relativity, which in turn made them always the most agile brains of humanity. Throughout history humanity has felt the power of this agility, succumbed to it, and cursed its intensity. So once utopia had reached the stage of realization, and showed the bottomless pit of human limitations and cruelties and the blundering which accompany the incarnation of the absolute into an existential form, the Jewish mind threw itself into revising concepts and reevaluating values. It produced layers of devastating criticism and destroyed everything it had only recently fought so fiercely and drawn blood for. Hence anti-Semitism was always and remains today the most easily produced weapon for the defense of totalitarian utopias—

while the inevitable sequel of all threatened totalitarian regimes is always the same.

Discussion has been going on for a long time about whether the American New Left is the natural incubator of an anti-Semitic backlash by the very fact of proclaiming its ideas. This is a mistake. Any eventual anti-Semitism in America will be found not in the antennae of a society which is hostile to New Left trends; instead, it is an immanent factor in their totalitarian tendency. All the experiences of the distant and recent past indicate that anti-Semitism will arise sooner in the very nucleus of American leftist thought than in the society surrounding it. For the present, a situation in which today's prophets of the New Left, most of them Jews, begin to feel the need of anti-Jewish (not to be confused with anti-Israeli) ideological formulas and oil their ideological machine with vicious anti-Semitism seems surrealistic. However, history knows of a situation in which anti-Jewishness became an immanent motive and even the essence of powerful spiritual activities (and other kinds) which brought to life the great ideological organism created by thirteen Jews. In twentieth-century Marxism as promulgated and practiced by the Russian and Polish Communists who proclaim the need of annihilating the Jewish spirit, we can see for the second time that such an absurd conception is not the illusion of sick minds but becomes a concrete fact of reality. Why should it be different anywhere else?

# 29 · The upper class and its *dolce vita*

THE SET OF VALUES a Russian Communist leader operates with is quite different from that which an East European leader uses. The latter rules his society within the same power structure as the Russian does, but if he wants something from the ruled masses of his nation, he must appeal to another set of values. These values have been crystallized by centuries of a pan-European Christian civilization in which the ideals of individual dignity and the quest for social virtues are deeply rooted. Also, the objects of desires, ideas of happiness, and the concept of individual success are different from those in Russia and in Asia. Communism builds Potemkin villages everywhere, but only in Russia does society either believe in their reality or recognize their dialectical necessity. In the East European countries they represent the subject of a joke.

The look of the streets and the girls, night clubs and theaters, fashions, housing, and the types of conversation—these are the things which in the opinion of Western correspondents distinguish Russia from Eastern Europe. This is a correct, though superficial, observation of the symptoms. They are ascribed to the relative liberalism which is a consequence of so-called national communism and the gradual winning of independence from Russian ideological headquarters. At the same time these things are essentially a specific subculture on which the post-Stalinist thaw conferred only the marks of publicity and universality. This subculture in turn is largely the product of an upper social class which represents a special phenomenon and is one of the main features of communism in Eastern Europe.

Like any other upper class, the East European upper class has its own mannerisms, its own way of dressing, and its artistic and recreational likes and dislikes which permeate the rest of society, becoming sought-after and imitated models of fashion. It also has its own jet set, which is universally admired and slandered. A Western correspondent or political scientist notices the elegance of the women there and the particularly free satirical cabaret (which he thinks must be embarrassing to the regime), but he does not associate these phenomena with the existence of a definite social group which produces them as its own subculture expressing its needs and requirements. So the genesis, functioning, morality, and influence of this group usually remain a secret to the Western observer.

A common mistake in the West is to identify the Communist upper class with the Communist ruling class. The upper class is a phenomenon of morals and manners. Its individual members may also be members of the ruling class and play major roles in politics or the economy, but its general characteristic is a lack of power and an importunate stressing of its political impotence. Power means traps and perils, and that spoils the picture of the good life—the main goal of the upper class. But it incessantly looks for political *influence,* which is not easy to come by. A totalitarian ruling apparatus is not subject to the influence of any opinions, either in public or behind the scenes.

The ruling class is made up of revolutionaries and lifelong Party members, mostly of low social origin. They are devoured by the imperfections of the system they themselves created. They live in never-ending bitter struggles for power, in eternal fear of Party discipline, of making a mistake, intrigues, and the denunciations of careerists who want their positions. The absurd organization of the state and the permanent economic chaos makes them work sixteen hours a day and die early of heart attacks.

They are nobodies, not very bright, and live modestly and unassumingly.

Relations between the upper and the ruling classes are characterized by mutual contempt and hatred. The ruling class scorns the upper class's avoidance of responsibility, but envies its freedom in enjoying the fruits of its success and privileges, which it is in no position to consume itself. The upper class hates the iron harness it has voluntarily put on its own back and is used by the ruling class to force it to lies and humiliations. It is obsessed with a complex about its own impotence; it hates its masters most because it does not represent a threat or a danger to them. It gets compensation by mocking the political failures and intellectual limitations of the ruling class, to which it contemptuously applies the term "quarter-intelligence."

When the Communists took power in Eastern Europe they were confronted with a disastrous shortage of cadres. Parties were miserably small and lacked roots in societies which were predominantly peasant and petit bourgeois, conservative and religious. The guarantee of their power was the garrisoned Soviet Army, their allies were careerism, opportunism, and arivisteism. They had enough of their own people to fill the highest positions in the power and terror apparati, but alien elements had to be admitted into the fields of culture, science, and diplomacy. The Communists promised themselves that they would soon produce replacements from their own social milieus. After some years this turned out to be unnecessary: the alien elements had become theirs. They made careers for themselves and created an upper class connected with communism to the death.

The reservoir for this recruitment was for the most part the intelligentsia, the social class whose intellectual qualifications provided a substitute for the traditional lack of capital in Eastern Europe. This never produced astonishing economic results but it allowed the intelligentsia to live comfortably before the war in alliance with the possessing classes.

Money has exactly the same function and importance in communism as everywhere else since its invention by the Phoenicians. It represents the goal of aspirations and the implement of attainments. It is true that in communism money is cheap and not much can be got for it, but without it one can get nothing at all. So the advantages arising from its possession are unquestionable. Money was probably the main reason a part of the intelligentsia actively supported the new regime. As people living off the activity of their own intellects, however, they could not keep from fabricating euphemistic excuses which in the end they themselves came to believe. So they called their own conformism the force of attraction of a victorious doctrine, the merciless logic of history, or bitterness toward the West which had betrayed them. Those who before the war had nurtured Fascist sympathies found a fine field for action in Red totalitarianism. The most cynical called this the only prospect for development, and these were the ones who reached the highest levels. In the early period, moreover, the Communists acted with moderation: they proclaimed the intelligentsia the ally of the Revolution, flirted with it, and drew it in. One of the legends about communism is its unrelenting hostility toward the possessing classes, which it needs in the struggle for power when it calls itself the spokesman of the proletariat's interests. In reality, it is an unrelenting enemy only to those who do not want to give in to it and accept its lies and crimes; the submissive and the useful can always count on favor and employment. So those who were able to offer the new rulers some talent or some propaganda advantages found their way into the upper class which was then forming.

This does not mean, however, that everyone who declared his readiness to cooperate immediately got an entry pass. The criterion for entry was the rulers' confidence. Those who were granted it were people with certain carefully checked out character traits such as cowardice, a readiness to support any vile act in ideology and politics, and above all, a blind fear of the drabness of life without readily available luxuries. Many who were willing fell by the wayside, while the most submissive and venal were elevated.

The power of the present-day upper class began during the

years of the Stalinist terror. Its beginnings were grotesque. Communism needed figureheads who would camouflage its actions with their names and positions for the benefit of stubborn nations and a mistrustful West. It needed historical aristocratic names which would appeal to nationalists, Catholics who would declare that Stalin loved the Church more ardently than the Pope, leaders of peasants' parties who had never been in the countryside in their lives, prominent writers and artists who would show that lies are truth and the truth stupidity, and scholars who would prove that two times two is five. Flexibility and skill in such mental and moral gymnastics guaranteed these people profit and honors. The better someone could explain how the sun moved around the earth, the greater was his reward. Names which are highly valued in the West today were signed to articles which declared that Harvard University gave PhD diplomas to CIA agents only or that Stalin was a more brilliant physicist than Einstein. Today some people maintain that they were pressured by threats and unexplained necessities, even outright attacks by the political police. They had to do it, everyone did it, and no one was any better than they. This is a glaring distortion of the facts. No one had a pistol placed at his forehead and the best proof of this is that the majority of intellectuals survived Stalinism without resorting to such compromises, only they lived in poorer apartments, used worse means of transportation, and did not travel abroad. Advancing to the upper class was an imperative and it permanently sanctified a category of people who were elevated and singled out for prosperity. The feeling of one's own productivity is the supreme psychological luxury in communism.

I say "permanently sanctified" because a major characteristic of the upper class is its stability. The supervisors from the ruling class perish in relentless power struggles, fall from the heights of power to prison cells or miserable retirements. Intellectuals, diplomats, and artists from the upper class remain unchanged in their positions once they have acquired them. Access to such status is an automatic guarantee of stability because it signifies the choice of an opportunistic attitude and therefore functions

universally and is applicable in any conditions and serves anyone at all. The more cynical their servility, the greater is their
assurance that they will survive all changes and political upheav-
als.

The upper class is never closed and entry to it is always possible for new Rastignacs. The mechanics of entry is the result
of either an active or a passive position. In the first case, a dec-
laration of faith is required. This is a carefully worked out technique of hypocrisy because those who declare themselves usually
scorn communism even as they apotheosize it in their writings
and speeches. However, they avoid being primitive about it; they
skillfully externalize their resistance and reservations, their ostensible concern over the imperfection of Communist practice
(theory is sacred!), publicly vacillate, and worry intensely about
the so-called sincerity of their decision. Finally, however, they
will discover—also publicly—the deepest deposits of humani-
tarianism, wisdom, and justice in communism, and their hon-
oraria in turn will grow to fabulous proportions. During the
Stalinist period the pattern of demonology was simple: on one
side there was the Satan of American imperialism and its local
embodiment, the rich peasantry, the bourgeoisie, and the agents
of the CIA; on the other, the Communist angel, in other words,
the Stalinist apparatus of power. Today things have become
more complicated: the demands of those who pay have to be
appeased, but the public—more reluctant and skeptical—must
not be scared off by clichés. Consequently, a CIA agent has a
toothache or his vileness may be just as much the result of a
hard childhood as the Pentagon's orders, while a good Communist may be loaded with faults and character defects, which is a
measure of his humanity. Because, however, the latter thinks
dialectically, he will ultimately defeat the frustrated agent.

Sometimes a member of the upper class is an orthodox Marxist, but this is a rare occurrence. An orthodox Marxist who lacks
a sensitive conscience will be a member of the ruling class. If
an upper-class Marxist is burdened with a conscience, he will
soon become a disillusioned critic, whereupon he will fall from
the upper class and come down to the level of the rest of society,

sometimes even undergoing more violent persecutions than militant non-Marxists. When he exists, a Marxist writer from the upper class can afford to take greater pains with appearances: he does not portray agents or *apparatchiks* in their fashionable disguises, but alienated intellectuals who do not feel comfortable in communism but finally are convinced that Western democracy and its philosophical prescriptions such as Christianity or existentialism are worse in every respect.

A person can also become a member of the upper class by taking a passive position. This leads to the accumulation of money, honors, and privileges with as few servitudes as possible. Music is by nature ideologically neutral, but a composer who calls his symphony *Holiday of Spring* can win at most an artistic success. If, however, he calls it *Holiday of the Revolution* or *Cantata of Lenin,* he will be showered with awards and continual performances on the radio and in the concert hall. Everyone within the upper class will smile knowingly, aware of the composer's contempt for the Revolution and Lenin. But the fact that society will regard him as a careerist is a matter of complete indifference to the composer because he sees himself as a charismatic artist to whom everything which serves his own creation is permitted.

An actor who frequently and wholeheartedly plays roles in socialist realist plays and films can be sure of enthusiastic reviews regardless of whether or not he is a good actor.

The production of a mass culture gives rise to a multitude of semiartistic and auxiliary professions: architect-designers, cameramen, authors of popular songs and lyrics, and sound engineers. The pay here is considerably better than in other professions and all that is needed is skillful lip-service in an interview granted or a turn of phrase in a song carefully calculated to appeal to the taste of the ruling class, to stand in the full glare of publicity, and thereby win a ticket to the upper class.

Advertisement and promotion play a major role in the continuous formation of the upper class but this role is quite different than in free societies. Popularity is decreed. It can be acquired neither by personal value nor by the attractiveness of one's talent. It cannot be bought; it can only be obtained as a reward for services rendered. When the mass media are all concentrated in the hands of the ruling class, an interview with an author, an actor, a scholar, or an inventor is not the result of either his merits or his popularity but exclusively a measure of his usefulness to the rulers. A person can become famous and idolized overnight, not because this was the public's verdict, but because the Party decided it. Western publicity cannot match the efficiency in fashioning pseudocelebrity of the Communist mass media.

Personal popularity is neither the goal nor the cause of publicity and does not determine financial success. The purpose of publicity is to bring a given personality in line and show him in such a light that he can be showered with privileges and rewards from the favor and cash registers of the ruling class. Sometimes a young writer, actor, or pop singer will appeal to the broad taste of the public. Then he will be carefully checked out by the ruling class for his political-propaganda usefulness. If he is recognized as harmless and his product or personality can be used to illustrate the ostensible freedom of culture and entertainment, then he will gain entry to the upper class along with fame and fortune. If, however, he insists on his independence, he is fated to be totally ignored and passed over. Newspaper editors, radio, and television directors, and therefore the members of the ruling class, will not make the slightest allusion to his existence, even if the public tears his books out of the salesclerks' hands or records him privately on their tape recorders. For the most ambiguous and sophisticated feature of the upper class which makes it a priceless instrument in the hands of the ruling class is its ability to produce artistic and intellectual contents which appear to be free, liberal, and a threat to communism, but in fact are not in the least independent or threatening. The literary cabarets of Poland and Czechoslovakia seem to the West to have potentials of criticism and satire which are a threat to communism. This is a cardinal error, because they are merely an expression of the upper class's ambivalence and opportunism. If they were a real threat, they would not exist.

The passive position is characterized by the cynicism of cautious and dubious engagement. At every step the musician and actor emphasize that their arts are neutral, unengaged, and freed from all responsibility. An upper-class writer would consider it a supreme disgrace to be on friendly terms with the director of the censorship board, despite the fact that the latter is actually his ally who defends him from the competition of more honest and more talented writers.

In most of the East European languages the upper class is called the "profitariat." The Poles refer to it as "the owners of People's Poland." So profit and property defines them most clearly in the consciousness of these societies. What, then, does their material luxury, their "dolce vita," look like?

It rests primarily on the difference between them and the social environment. An American millionaire, an English aristocrat, or a successful French artist has a quite different standard of living from his society. Nonetheless, the differences are quantitative and qualitative, not objective. In the final analysis, almost every American, Frenchman, or Englishman who wants a car, a one-family house or a trip abroad can achieve his goal by means of work, even by physical labor. Rich people simply have better cars, bigger houses, and take more frequent and longer trips. In a Communist country the possession of a two-room apartment is out of reach for the overwhelming majority of society, a car is a sign of supreme affluence, while a trip abroad is a complicated undertaking which is planned for years and usually never materializes. These problems and concerns do not bother the members of the Communist upper class.

Residential poverty is the Egyptian plague of communism: two people living in a small bed-and-living-room is the general norm. Excluded from this rule are: the ruling class, a microscopic group of people who have kept the remains of their former estates, doctors, scientific specialists whom communism must tolerate and pay highly even without political testimonies, and the upper class. The latter gets special assignments to special apartments where the usual degree of crowding does not prevail and two to four people live in three or four rooms. Financial prosperity enables the upper class to build one-family houses or villas without the interference of the income tax authorities. In the event that a wealthy doctor or someone else possessing the funds decides to build a home, the tax agency will begin an investigation of the source of his funds. As a rule, it discovers certain "excesses" and eliminates them by unauthorized taxes which it has the right to levy arbitrarily, independently of the fiscal codes. If the doctor is not a Party doctor and well connected, (if he is, then he belongs to the upper class), his private practice is destroyed. The upper class escapes such annoyances.

When he is sick of his own apartment, a member of the upper class has at his disposal the so-called houses of creative work for musicians, writers, journalists, etc. These are for the most part old palaces transformed into comfortable *pensions*. The rates are low in relation to current market prices and the food supply comes from special sources. When a country is going through one of its periodic food crises and long lines are forming in front of stores in the cities, the representatives of the upper class go en masse to the houses of creative work where no restrictions threaten them and they can write poems in peace about equality and brotherhood, the abundance of goods under socialism, and the hunger of exploited colonial peoples.

Political conditioning is not the only obstacle to traveling to the West. The currency of the Communist countries has no exchange value in the West, so a trip is dependent on getting hard currency which only the state possesses. Only the upper class receives the means to travel without any difficulty. This has been true from the very beginning, for the East European ruling class, as opposed to the USSR, never cut itself off from contacts with the West. The West is a profitable trading partner and its Communist parties and leftists are a missionary terrain and a potential ally against Soviet hegemony. And membership in Western civilization is a powerful never-extricated longing of the East European masses. Lastly, the Communist governments in these countries were the outcome of an understanding between the West and Stalin, and the West must be assured it didn't do something wrong in trading off these nations for Soviet promises of security. So the upper class travels—to congresses, conferences, festivals, and to serve on the juries of international contests. The ruling class is not running much of a risk in allowing these peoples to leave, because where could they live as well as at home? And the West regards them with respect, enraptured over how well true intellectuals are doing under communism. The poor West! It has no idea of what exact instructions these people get before leaving about making a show of nonconformism. Moreover, the ruling class leaves its subordinates a fair amount of latitude for private enterprise. Journalists are known to have offered to write articles about Western airlines in the Communist press in exchange for expensive and exotic trips. The airlines give them free tickets and all the trimmings; the journalists go, come back, and write bitter Anti-American articles. When their sponsors reproach them for not keeping their agreement and for not even mentioning the airlines which treated them, the journalists refer to the censorship which allegedly did not let them write positively about Western businesses, depicting themselves as victims of the lack of freedom of the press. Of course, as prominent members of the upper class they never have any trouble getting an exit visa and act in concert with their superiors in the ruling class who call this little game "making anti-Western propaganda with Western money."

Frequent trips and the judicious handling of official travel allowances are a source of Western cars, clothing, television sets, long plays, and other trappings which make life sweeter. The Western observer often is amazed to find what an elegant crowd surrounds him at parties; the way the men and women dress does not depart from London and Paris fashions. Material purchased abroad with state money is given to a tailor who for a modest fee dresses a person from the upper class in hand-tailored clothes.

Cars, clothes, social life, and a great deal of free time means that sexual life flourishes. The striking social contrast attracts pretty young girls from underprivileged environments and makes them an easy prey. The most attractive and enterprising of them enter the upper class as wives. Once here, they behave like the wives of husbands belonging to the possessing classes everywhere: they are prone to shallow, safe adventures and escapades.

237

In countries of an official puritanism, where hotels scrupulously check the civil state of every couple, sexual morality must look for other facilities. The roomy, comfortable apartments of the upper class, its cars, and its telephones (difficult for an ordinary citizen to get) provide these facilities and marital triangles and rectangles are easily sanctioned under these circumstances and within the framework of extremely flexible morals. Perpetual divorces are the rhythm of social life no less than in Hollywood or on the Riviera. Homosexuality flourishes, excesses and orgies in tightly closed circles are not unknown. A practice involving certain high officials in the Hungarian civil airlines was once notorious in Budapest: they poured melted chocolate on naked girls and vied in licking the sweet liquid off them. They might still be enjoying this innocent amusement today if they had not been denounced by someone who grudged the waste of so much chocolate. He felt a pang of conscience as the subject of a system where food is harder to get on the market than pretty girls.

The upper class does not capitalize on its earnings. The reason is both fear of the ruling class who would look askance at the accumulation of estates and a lack of confidence in Communist money. The upper class lives high off the hog, but without security, from one day to the next, not stinting itself anything in the country. On the other hand, it becomes an insatiable beast of prey where foreign exchange and dollars are concerned. Its members are capable of any infamy and any risk to get them. Salaries and awards in foreign currency are the summit of their dreams, the supreme success and the cause of deadly enmity on the part of the rest of society. Various illegal transactions and tricks are undertaken to get it and often end in a loss of privileges. More often, however, the ruling class manages to forgive the abuses and to cover up any scandal.

It would be wrong to look at the life-style of the members of the upper class only as a pursuit of material satisfactions. The driving force behind their actions is their hunger for recognition and the need to raise themselves above others. Proof of this is their care and caution in displaying their own success and celebrating it. It is a principle that it should be revealed to one's inferior neighbors, but discreetly, arousing not their jealousy but only their admiration, which is necessary to self-esteem. Then too, many people believe in the exceptionality of their talent and feel that all possible means are justified to bring it to fruition because in a hundred years time no one will ask whether a creator was a political hypocrite but only what he left behind him. So many talented people were and are doomed to silence during their whole lifetime that others are willing to make a deal with the Devil himself and sell their souls for the mere opportunity to write, paint, compose, make movies. However, toadyism and humiliating submission before those who are stronger do not seem to provide a fertile climate for creativity and so far nothing worthy of survival has been produced in East European culture.

Both the passive and the active positions are the result of a free choice, that is, an original acceptance of cynical servility. Members of the upper class do not hide or deny this in private conversation. In looking for excuses they emphasize the coercion they are subjected to. Judging from their words, this coercion is ambivalent: on the one hand, it is the brutal pressure of the ruling class; on the other, their duty to the nation, the fatherland, and to culture in general. In the second case, the member of the upper class is a priori assuming his genius, i.e., his indispensability to the nation, culture, etc., which forces him to accept the conditions of the ruling class. This casuistry leads to various kinds of psychological complications. Members of the upper class want the alleged violation of their consciences to be noticed and recognized as such by their societies and by intellectual opinion in the West, thinking that this objectification of their inner torments assures absolution. There can be found in this yearning a deep nostalgia for moral purity and a need for excuses, and therefore an awareness of guilt. Complexes arise in these people because the upper class, in glaring contradiction to the ruling class, are ashamed of their careers and hide this shame behind nonchalant intellectual clowning and moral acrobatics. These are accompanied by an ever-present effort to represent their careers as the result of force and themselves as the victims of "something." The upper class works on nothing so feverishly as on the myth of "persecutions" which it supposedly suffers at the hands of the ruling class, a myth the West believes. Nothing gives them greater pleasure than to boast about these "persecutions" and to hear the expressions of sympathy for their sufferings or praise for their uncompromising adherence to principles and their integrity which some Western intellectuals shower upon some members of the Communist upper class.

The upper class exercises a profoundly negative influence on the societies around them. For two centuries the peoples of Eastern Europe were accustomed to see their intelligentsia as a moral compass and to obtain their categories of honor and decency from them. The upper class, as an offshoot of the traditional intelligentsia, is generating new categories and models which are unworthy of the noble tradition of this social class. What is worse, by active support of the ruling class, it has deceitfully usurped for itself the right to represent the *entire* intelligentsia. By the sneaky technique of projection, which communism uses to show societies their own image, the upper class conceals those who defend themselves and do not submit to corruption or depravity. The false dialectics of victorious communism have imprinted on the social consciousness the law that what cannot be seen does not exist. Nations which are deprived of the sight of struggles for the independence of minds and characters become morally indifferent and soften in their resistance. Sooner or later they accept the upper class as the object of their jealous sighs and gossip and their methods as a sure-fire prescription for individual success in life.

We must, however, beware of oversimplification. The upper class consists both of Party members and non-Party people; a Party card means nothing in assessing and describing it. The upper class is not the equivalent or the representative of the intellectual elite and does not represent culture. Certain areas of culture have been leased out to it, and it does have ambitions of exclusivity and hegemony. However, it has never managed to get a monopoly on culture anywhere. During the post-Stalinist thaw in Poland and Hungary, and later in Czechoslovakia, culture managed to escape the ruling and upper classes' grasp and for a brief period became the domain of liberals, nonconformists, and rebellious youth.

A comparison with the Western upper class will reveal similarities and differences. In both cases, belonging to the upper class is determined by money, success, and a life of ease and pleasure. Under capitalism these advantages accrue usually either from an inherited estate or from pandering to the indiscriminate tastes of the masses who demand neither intelligence nor brilliance. They can, however, also be the result of a success which is truly deserved. Under communism success is the result of cynicism and intellectual shrewdness which are nonetheless inseparable from genuine brightness. The Western jet set is made up for the most part of the idle rich, deprived of any ambition except to cut a brilliant figure, and stars of the stage and screen whose intellectual dullness and crudity are embarrassing while their press interviews reveal unimaginable stores of spiritual vulgarity. In this respect comparison is to the advantage of the Communist jet set, which is thoroughly educated, witty, and interesting. It is a real pleasure to associate with its members, who on the whole are extremely charming people, masters of irony and sarcasm who carry on fascinating conversations. They remind one of Renaissance and Rococo courtiers, clever, bitter, initiated into all the mysteries of life, and perverse self-mockers and flatterers. There prevails in their midst the cult of the joke at any price, even at the price of relinquishing what is left of their own dignity. The Western jet set, despite its intellectual shallowness and moral and ideological indifference, is independent from its ruling classes and at times brings itself to provide useful patronage of the arts or philanthropy to science. It does not demoralize its societies. Youth has a contemptuous attitude toward it, but if a young person who sings well, for instance, sets as his goal material prosperity, then he must only learn to sell his talent equally well or to pander to the public's taste. This may destroy the individual morally but it does no social damage. The Communist jet set is the helpless client of the ruling class, while the only thing it has to offer as a regulator of its success is conformism, turning itself into an unyielding corrupter.

The West, particularly certain of its intellectual circles, sees the upper class in Communist countries as its ally. The false theory prevails that cynicism is the source of Communist splits, schisms, and heresies, that the scarcity of worldly goods will finally force the strict dogmatists of the ruling class to make concessions while the main standard-bearer of consumption is the upper class. Its readiness to sell itself provides, in the eyes of certain political scientists, an opportunity for infiltration, the injection of political ideas and conceptions and the infection of these societies with the West, its culture and its civilization. Even more superficial and naive Western observers accept the upper class's declarations as sincere confessions of their faith and convictions and believe in their ostensible liberalism and cautious opposition. They underestimate the degree of the upper class's loyalty to their ruling class. This loyalty is not, of course, sincere, but rather a calculated move which has been tested for achievement for over two decades. No one in the world can give these people a better life than their ruling class. Why, then, should they jeopardize something it is easy to give a pseudomoral justification to? Even in a moment of the most merciless confrontation and recapitulation of his own miseries, failures, and humiliations, an individual belonging to the East European upper class believes that by his presence he is humanizing, beautifying, and mollifying something which is dangerous, dirty, and inhuman. He regards himself as a rose in the barrel of a gun pointed at humanity and mankind.

# 30 • Of what use are sports?

U NDER COMMUNISM sports are used to show the superiority of communism over democracy. Such an important end justifies any means available, so that those who are in charge of sports in the Communist countries—and this means huge institutions in many-storied buildings filled with thousands of employees—do everything possible to enable Communist competitors to win in competitions with athletes from the non-Communist world. The simplest method is, as always, common cheating, based on representing professionals as amateurs, and as everyone knows, in today's world of specialization an amateur is in no position to compete with a professional who has devoted his entire life, all his time and energies, to polishing his form. A young man who has the necessary physical requirements chooses the career of an athlete, and if he shows talent and results, the state takes all further responsibility for his life. It rewards him much more generously than anyone else, guarantees him a *dolce vita* available only to fate's elect, takes care of his family, showers rewards upon him in the form of comfortable apartments, cars, free vacations in the best hotels, to say nothing of such a trivial bonus as the money that comes to him as lucrative salaries from fictitious positions in factories or offices he never sets foot in. His only duty in exchange for this horn of plenty is to beat competitors from the democratic countries who run, jump, swim, and row out of ambition, the desire to compete, or simply because they enjoy it. They receive no payment except travel expenses. Why Western athletes since the Second World War have taken part in the operettas and masquerades called the Olympics remains a mystery to many sports fans behind the Iron Curtain.

Someone may rightly observe that young men in America who have the physical requirements and show the necessary talent and results choose to make a career in football or baseball and earn a pile of money. But football and baseball are the only athletic activities in which the Communist countries do not compete with America. They thereby do not run the risk of catastrophic defeats. Even if they did learn to play football and baseball, they would probably refuse to meet the Green Bay Packers or the Orioles. Because according to the Communist system of explaining phenomena, the latter are the product of capitalism which pays filthy lucre to corrupt athletes for brutal displays of strength.

# 31 • Culture, or total disbelief

"A KNIFE, a fork, and a spoon," a Polish writer once wrote, "are civilization. And the method of using them is culture." If science, art, and literature in the traditional interpretation represent that part of civilization we call culture, then communism looks for more precise classifications. The Communist definition of culture includes only the methods of using science, literature, and art for its own ends. Thus the objective complex of opinions, norms, criteria, and evaluations which compose cultural life in democracies does not exist in communism and is replaced by something that is called "cultural policy." Cultural policy is an unusual symbiosis of dogmatism and caprice. This may seem impossible or a paradox but it constitutes reality in communism. Caprice, that is, capricious transformations as frequently as possible, or the acceptance of something which only the day before was held to be a mortal sin, must be pushed to the point of surrealism. Communism's strength, as a certain writer once remarked, lies in its own fantasticality. So if the controllers of culture under communism announce that yesterday's genius is to-day's idiot, it is only because *such* a fantastic about-face is likely to make the consumer of culture shrug his shoulders and say to himself: Why not? For the statement that yesterday's genius is perhaps not as clever as he appeared is an invitation to polemics and polemics do not exist in communism. There exists only discussion, the rules and prescriptions of which are tightly defined. A participant in a discussion is only allowed to change adjectives, so that if one debater declares that communism is good, the next may agree with him, or disagree and declare that communism is beautiful, while a third participant has the right to contradict them both and say that communism is both beautiful and good. This example may continue *ad infinitum* since it is precisely this bitter argument about whether communism is more beautiful than good that represents the heart of cultural policy.

Dogmatism is the natural counterbalance to caprice since either affirmation or negation in the name of idiocy must be equally rigid. Until 1956 William Faulkner was characterized by Communist literary criticism as a pervert and a sadist, Hemingway was a warmonger, while John Steinbeck was a cheap pornographer. After 1956, which, as everyone knows, marked the beginning of the era of so-called peaceful coexistence, Faulkner was recognized as a great moralist, Hemingway was promoted to the last great romantic, and Steinbeck became a great *écrivain de moeurs.* Ten years later, the official doctrine of cultural policy was based on the assumption that the cold war does not actually exist but that peaceful coexistence involves only foreign policy. Every other sphere of life and thought is a field for relentless ideological war in which the imperialists will use any method to bring about the moral and psychological disintegration of socialist societies. Faulkner thereby became a sophisticated defender of the remnants of feudalism, Hemingway an animalistic behaviorist, and Steinbeck sunk to the depths of psychologism where every rotten liberal ignominy can be justified by relativistic psychoanalysis. The works of all three, though nothing in their biographies indicates any connection with American intelligence activities, are nonetheless objective tools of the CIA, whose job at the present stage when the USSR, in the opinion of the dogmatists, is stronger militarily than the USA, is to poison and corrupt the spirit of the nations that have chosen socialism. The proofs for this are obvious: Hemingway and Steinbeck's books are torn out of the salesclerks' hands in Czechoslovakia and Hungary and disappear from the stores in a single day even when they are printed in editions of 30,000. In Russia Faulkner is copied on private typewriters and circulates among university students in typescript, or in the *Samizdat,* the underground, illegal form of distributing literature officially banned by the Communist authorities. It seems inconceivable that there could exist a society where a worker can buy only one pair of shoes with a month's salary, Trotsky is proclaimed an agent of Hitler, and one generation is taught that the same writer is both degenerate and a moralist. But, as the writer mentioned above adds, the Communists *created* a fantastic world which one cannot believe in—and in this lies their strength.

Cultural policy is an activity the highest goal of which is to generate knowledge about how people should think and feel. The Communists do not possess this knowledge but they try to get it at any price, regardless of the material sacrifices, wasted individual lives, defeats of reason, and the absurdity with which they cover themselves at every turn. A Polish writer of genius by the name of Stanislaw Ignacy Witkiewicz wrote a brilliant novel in the 1920s anticipating the philosophical essence of twentieth-century totalitarian regimes even before communism, the most menacing of them all, had revealed its still imperceptible mechanisms to the world. Witkiewicz describes the career of a Malaysian prophet by the name of Murti Bing who preaches a new faith which is supposed to represent the quintessence of subduing a human being. The basic element in propagating this faith is a little pill, distributed by fanatic advocates of the faith, which must be swallowed, like the quotations of Mao Tse-tung today. The swallowed pill changes a person's outlook and enables him to accept painlessly, even enthusiastically, any crime and any madness which are presented to him as justice and wisdom. Communist cultural policy is fundamentally based on the formula of Murti-Bingism. Once someone has accepted the Communist host, he turns into a passive consciousness, ready to accept statements and orders that defy the most primitive exigencies of reason. The person who refuses lays himself open to mental tortures whose scope and depth cannot be explained to anyone from outside. Because in no sphere of life does the night-

247

mare of absurdity appear with such force as in the field of thought and intellectual creativity, that is, in culture.

The cultural politicians start from the assumption that the world is as the founders and theoreticians of communism knew and described it. If reality does not conform to their prescription, so much the worse for reality; it must be changed. This set of principles makes sense in politics, and though it leads to tyranny, it is nonetheless logically coherent. In culture, however, and especially in artistic creation, it leads to a chaos of mutually exclusive ontological and epistemological categories of an unparalleled intensity. So far no one has been able to come to terms with those depths of that laboriously thought out simplification and flattening of the world, to which dialectics lend the external characteristics of dignity and majesty and is officially called the Marxist-Leninist pantheon of thought. The principle of literary creation known as socialist realism proclaims that the world should be depicted not as it is, but as it should be, according to the ideas of Communists. The question then arises why such a creative method is called realism, which means the reproduction of reality in keeping with the most universally accessible knowledge about it. To this even the most intelligent Communist will reply that since doctrine has acknowledged that the world should be *so,* then the world is already *so*—which puts an end to rational discussion. Of course, this method of reasoning is sublimated into many different subtleties and sophisms: true socialist realism is said to be the discovery of deeply hidden tendencies and vectors of development, which means that even if the world *looks* objectively different, the truth about its future corresponds most closely to the laws of doctrine, which represents a sort of realism with room to grow. Years later it becomes apparent that everything is different from the way the guiding principles of development had envisaged it a few years earlier, at which time it had been described as the realism of the future. And once again, everything turns out to be colossal nonsense, which is easily forgotten when there exists a censorship that will not let a word of remembrance get through.

The following two concepts designate creativity as a whole

under communism and represent the main guide lines of cultural policy even if their names change or they are taken out of circulation for a while. One of them is "formalism," or the theory that only that which serves ideology and politics is literature, art, theater, etc., while everything else is empty form without any value for culture. The second is called "cosmopolitanism" and explains that only the recognition of the preeminence and exclusiveness of those who laid the foundations for the Communist future of the world—that is, the Russians—offers protection against succumbing to the toxins and microbes of alien and enemy ideologies. Thus a person who thinks that Shakespeare gave more to the world than Pushkin is an insidious cosmopolitan, while someone who firmly insists that Lenin is greater than Einstein and Gandhi put together is an internationalist, actively promoting the brotherhood of nations.

The lunacy and perversions of socialist realism committed in the struggle with formalism and cosmopolitanism are most visible in the plastic arts. A cow grazing on a pasture in the light of the setting sun is, of course, a formalist picture, but if it is indicated in the title of the same picture that the same cow is the property of a *kolkhoz,* then the picture becomes a work of socialist realism. If, on the other hand, a critic as schooled in agriculture as in dialectics discovers that it is a cow of a Dutch breed, thereby coming from a country belonging to NATO, then the artist who painted it will be accused of cosmopolitanism.

Cubism, tacheism, and abstractionism were proclaimed the formalist poison of imperialism, as were constructivism and functionalism in architecture. I was once a witness to a discussion among some famous Marxist philosophers of art and aestheticians during which it was maintained that the shape of a rectangle conforms to the tenets of socialist realism, while the oval and the circle are contaminated with a formalist and cosmopolitan tendency. I no longer remember the proof of this axiom, but I know it was distinguished by its scholastic subtlety. At the other pole of discussions on art must be placed the once notorious opinion of Marshal Voroshilov, the chairman of the Supreme Soviet of the USSR who, when visiting the National Museum in Warsaw, muttered through compressed lips at the sight of the canvases of a famous Polish post-impressionist, "Such an artist should have his hands cut off." Fortunately the painter was no longer alive.

In Eastern Europe in the 1960s cultural policy has undergone far-reaching changes and has eliminated the caricatural excesses of socialist realist orthodoxy. The terminology of literary and artistic criticism avoids Party jargon, while "formalism" and "cosmopolitanism" have lost their magic charm and their power to destroy people, their works, and their projects. But we must not forget that the elementary interdependence of caprice and dogmatism is still the only determinant of culture as a sphere of life. Cultural policy changes but remains an inviolate function of general state policy in the sphere of culture. As long as this state of affairs continues, there can be no talk of the creative independence of intellectuals and artists under communism regardless of what forms and manifestations of boldness in criticism and research are allowed. No matter what terminology currently holds sway in the literary press, or whether praising Proust and mentioning Dostoevsky are permitted, a book under communism is always written by the writer, his editor in the publishing house, and the censor at the final stage. Aristophanes, Pascal, and Dickens can never be sure whether in the quiet of the editorial offices a few of their sentences will not be skillfully operated on, after which their meaning will completely change. Then they may be interpreted in a scholarly preface as the true and untouched text of a great writer, proving his devotion to the cause of the people and the social revolution, which had previously been ruthlessly effaced by his feudal or capitalist editors and commentators. No one will be able to speak up for his rights and his violated property, while it is doubtful whether scholars at Harvard and the Sorbonne will track down forgeries in Bulgarian translations of Aristophanes or Rumanian editions of Pascal. Even if they do, so what? I myself was witness to the rewriting of the dialogue in the Polish translation of the novel of a contemporary Australian writer who was also a fanatical Communist. "But after all, he's a Communist and a loyal writer," I said. "But not of the sort we need *now,*" was the reply. "Can't you ask him for his permission? Perhaps he'll agree." The editor smiled indulgently. "He won't understand what the matter is," he replied.

It would be easiest to regard people who contribute to culture under such conditions as masochists, but this definition would not be very accurate. Roughly speaking, such people can be divided into three categories. The first are those who have a boundless faith in communism. There are very few of them and they are the most stupid and least talented, but they do earn the most money, receive the most honor and fame, and the newspapers write about them incessantly. The second are those who are against communism in an overt and fundamental way. These, too, are very few and no one has any idea whether they are doing anything or not because no one publishes their books, no one performs their music, no one exhibits their pictures, no one gives them any money, no one ever writes about them anywhere. To all intents and purposes, they would not exist at all were it not for the fact that they are known to exist and to have their fixed standing in a rumored hierarchy which exists outside the compulsory reality. The third and most numerous category are those who are in the middle. This middle is an extremely complicated mosaic, full of ambivalencies and contradictions, and its only common feature is the desire to participate. It is as if half of the Murti-Bing pill were swallowed: the swallower accepts, but does not lose the bitter awareness of participating in some sinister imbecility in which he somehow *wants* to take part. And he wants to for the most varied reasons: because he believes a little, but not in everything; because he is in point of fact against, but not totally; because he wants to publish his books, exhibit his paintings, hear his compositions, and not waste his life in sterile resistance which seems to have no chance of success. This position can easily be called selling oneself in exchange for purely material advantages and successes; it can also be called cynicism. In both cases the name will not *completely* conform to the truth, although both cynicism and selling out are components of this position. A certain East European writer has called the circles of these intellectuals, writers, and artists a *court,* and this definition is amazingly apt. These people are courtiers of communism, and just as the courtiers of the Renaissance, the baroque, and rococo absolutism, exist and prosper at the courts of their rulers, lords, and tyrants. Their job is cynical flattery for which they receive an expensive ring and the title of favorite which they themselves make fun of in the corners of salons. Their tactic is the cunning conformism of a gentleman-in-waiting who is quick to grasp what the ruler needs and knows how to give him as little of it as possible in return for the greatest possible reward in favors, money, and privileges. They get their satisfaction from the joys of subcutaneous understandings, from getting jokes and associations in a flash, from witty, mocking bon mots, from the winking of an eye, a grimace of the lips, the helpless but all-knowing gesture of people who understand everything, forgive everything, and are capable of everything. Their moral stance is an ironic shrug of the shoulders and the formula, "But we know, we know that all this is rotten, disgusting, and idiotic. But how amusing it is! Anyway, what can we do against their power?" And in keeping with this deep conviction, their names will be found the following day under essays and poems singing the praises of these crimes and nonsense in elegant words, brimming over with poetic inspiration. They consider what they do *unimportant* and, especially, as not being subject to outside judgments, as isolated from both the social context and common sense, and therefore escaping judgments and criteria. They consider people who regard their lives as subject to any social and moral judgment as fools and say, "We know that what is happening is one great paranoia and this knowledge of ours is sufficient for you to appreciate us, for we do carry something important through times of contempt. And one must live . . ." They thereby grant themselves irrevocable absolution. And when they go to the West—and they are constantly going because as favorites they have access to all sorts of privileges—they make public speeches or have confidential conversations with their professional colleagues in which they assure them of their abiding loyalty to principles, their crystal-pure honesty which must assume the *appearance* of opportunism, their sufferings in the name of the ideals of literature, art, truth, and humanity. They run no risk in doing so. After returning to the ruler's court, they will tell him, splitting their sides with laughter and provoking his mirth, about the naiveté of his enemies, who will be so easy to defeat because of their gullibility. And at times the ruler believes them, which perhaps is the only thing to their credit. Among them are archmasters of perfidy who deceive everyone, including themselves, and virtuosi of endlessly complicated intrigues. A certain Russian poet who is celebrated in the West as an unyielding nonconformist has a reputation for writing letters to the rulers protesting some of their moves. Marvelous legends circulate about these letters, about their courage, the sharpness of the wording, the heroic challenges contained in them, and the poet's readiness to make sacrifices in the name of truth and justice. These are letter-poems which jar the autocrats' consciences and put their author on a level with Socrates and Galileo. The only thing is that no one has ever seen these letters. The poet talks about them in secret to acquaintances he meets on the street and rumors begin to spread. Where are the proofs? There are no proofs and there can be none, because in the final analysis one is living in totalitarianism where everything is destroyed, falsified, or hushed up, where no fixed value or fixed element survives the onslaught of lawlessness. Later the poet, the archmodel of the courtier, the confidant and the factotum of the tyrants in the Kremlin, leaves on a new trip abroad with instructions on how to imitate an independent Soviet poet in New York and Acapulco. Immediately before his departure he whispers in the ear of an acquaintance who is seeing him off that he is being forced to leave the country in order to neutralize the effects of his protesting letter which provoked a terrific impression in the Politburo circles.

The court has, however, its own concepts of honor and dignity, which may seem surprising in this picture of degradation and servility. In its internal conflicts, animosities, sympathies, antipathies, and admirations, the measure of value is one's degree of conformism. Immediately after the war the non-Communist resistance movement against the Germans which had made history in Eastern Europe did not exist in the official picture of the recent past. The Communists vehemently eliminated any chance of mentioning that the principal burden of the struggle against fascism had been borne by millions of people who had nothing to do with communism, and had been murdered or taken to Siberia by the Red Army which occupied Poland, Czechoslovakia, and Rumania after driving out the Germans. So these people, whose heroism and sacrifices were known to entire societies, were missing from the postwar literature of these countries, while books and films were full of Communist partisans whom no one had ever seen during the war and had no idea even existed. The societies which read these books and saw these films built in themselves a permanent mistrust of everything Communist and learned to coexist with the fantasy which was binding as reality in culture. So when a certain Polish court writer, and after him a certain film director, got the idea of introducing in their works the negative figure of a non-Communist partisan, made hateful in keeping with the recommendations of Party dialectics, but endowed with credible features, the success of the book and the film with the public reached a zenith. The reader and filmgoer couldn't have cared less how the partisan was shown or characterized (they had their own opinion on the matter), but the fact that he existed in the pages of a book or on the screen meant a certain challenge hurled at the command from above. Of course, nothing appears in a Communist country without permission from above, so the authority which granted permission had perceived certain advantages for itself in it. In the final analysis, the public gets its satisfaction from seeing its partisan; the regime is happy that it has calumniated that partisan in a more subtle way than before; the writer or director basks in the glory of being an instantaneous nonconformist because he thinks he has outwitted the regime and forced it to make concessions, and the grateful public must know this and will never forget him for it. And everyone accommodatingly forgets that one more big lie has been told about the partisan, his heroic struggle, and what it really was like.

In the period of change which followed the death of Stalin,

filmmakers in Eastern Europe used a special tactic which they called the struggle to broaden creative freedoms, namely, when they were shooting their servile, conformist films about Communist partisans, or about workers struggling to raise production efficiency in keeping with the most obscurantist socialist realist scenarios, they would dress their actors and especially their actresses in the fashions currently popular in the West. Hence the heroines would discuss topics which sounded more like the lead articles in *Pravda* than normal dialogues, while on their heads they would have the latest hair styles out of Paris *Vogue*. Of course, the filmmakers regarded this as proof of unusual courage and creative independence, since the censors were so sharp in catching any detail which they felt was incompatible with the purity of a Communist film that the filmmakers had to wage a mortal struggle for every sweater and every curl. But the viewer was not aware of the censor's iron grip; he did not listen to the dialogue and was not concerned with what the actors had to say. He saw only the curl and the sweater and was happy that he could get a little look at such a manifestation of pro-Westernism. The filmmakers basked in the glory of being nonconformists and regarded themselves as inexorable fighters against the brute force of totalitarianism. Their belonging to the court had so desensitized them morally and intellectually, so reduced their dignity and their ability to see things in their proper light, that the merit of the views, words, or behavior of a character in a film no longer had any meaning for them; only their accessories did.

The fruit of cultural policy in communism has been an atmosphere of total mistrust of anything, of any fact or any value produced in the name of Communist culture. This mistrust embraces the producer and the consumer of culture alike. Literary characters who are conceived as immortal models to imitate and persistently pushed by all possible media as symbols of civic and personal virtues become the objects of universal jokes. The results of this state of affairs are amazing. A year after Polish television had bought some old and cheap American serials for entertainment programs, 90 percent of the boys polled about the ideal of their dreams replied "Zorro." And to the question, "Which literary or film character you have come to know in recent years would you like to meet in life?" millions of Polish television viewers replied, "Doctor Kildare." Lamenting this phenomenon and inveighing at its eventual results, the official organ of the Polish Communist Party wrote, "Why does *that* truth win thousands of worshippers and sympathizers among us?" The answer to this question is extremely simple, but it can be neither printed or publicly stated in Poland. In any case, perhaps there's no need to do so.

## 32 · What revisionism is

THE ORTHODOX in Marxism still keep declaiming about how the masses make history. The practicers of communism regard the masses as manure. But actually, things are different. In capitalist democracies, where the masses are absorbed in television and worrying about how to make the right use of their weekends, the masses do not make any history. In democracies history is made by politicians and intellectuals consumed with ambition, militants and activists inflamed with their own passion, unwashed fanatics with half-baked ideas whom no one stops and who are free to do anything, and relatively cautious technocrats and specialists with a solid education. In capitalism entire industries live off the interminable discussions and polemics of all these people. In communism individuals and entire politburos crazy with an excess of power lay down the laws of inhuman systems, but the actual masses, a beaten, formless, apparently directionless pulp, terrorized and practically mindless, determine history by the weight of their passivity. The masses hate communism, but even if they merely disliked it, the weight of this individual aversion multiplied by hundreds of millions of human lives means that despite the most perfect system of terror in history, everything dissolves, smears, and turns into the dung of grotesquely messed-up economic plans. The West is able to take note of the street disorders in Berlin, the uprisings in Budapest and Poznan, the invasion of Czechoslovakia, and the trials of recalcitrant writers in Moscow, but it cannot recognize this particular form of *nonacceptance* of communism, this *lack* of support by the masses which gives rise to the passive resistance of the masses. There are many explanations for this state of affairs, none of which is entirely satisfactory. There is the abhorrence of doctrine and methods. A feeling of superiority and a weakly defined but truly existing knowledge of how things *should* be can be sensed in every Hungarian, Czech, or Pole and gives rise to an almost new form of indirect, disorganizing, and alienating resistance in these countries. In Russia, Rumania, or Bulgaria the masses lack this feeling of superiority with respect to their Communist governors, so that in those societies aversion occasionally assumes the form of Westernization, but does not represent an element in the liberalization process. A Polish or Czech student looks for bell-bottom trousers or a psychedelic shirt and such a search is clearly linked to his scorn and hatred for communism and its systems. A Russian *stiliaga* or hooligan hates only the policeman who persecutes him for the cut of his pants, but as far as communism goes, he does not have his own, well-formed opinion. Current Polish and Czech apathy derives with a strange ambivalence from the goals which were only partially realized during their respective thaws as well as from frustration at their unproductive attempt to make things better. This looks like a contradiction but it isn't; it is only a peculiarity of these new forms of resistance through nonacceptance of the credo. Hence it is easier to send a rocket to the moon in the Communist countries than to organize a health service which would satisfy even 2 percent of the needs of a society where no one gives a damn about anything. A few grams of apathy, frustration, and smouldering resentment toward the environment, multiplied by millions of people, is already *something*. In this way there arise troubles which bring foam to the lips of Communist dictators and also lead to the uncomfortable squirming of more intelligent Communists, which is elegantly called by well-disposed researchers, "revisionism," or the unrest of Party intellectuals.

The problem of the former Stalinists and those who actively

cooperated with the most savage period of communism—from a variety of motivations, ranging from sincere belief through hypocrisy to cynical indulgence and selfish conformism—remains pivotal for the feelings and moral positions of entire generations. Stalinism spread a network of human interdependencies with a moral infrastructure full of nooks and crannies, which has not to this day been examined. So often what some people represented with fraudulent dexterity as a conflict of the consciences of the epoch turned out to be common ideological and intellectual fraud. So often ostentatious vulgarity turned out to be the only possible attempt at preserving one's own dignity. Today in the West, under conditions of free research, many romantics in sociology, sentimental political scientists, and speculative psychologists fervently rummage through the endless stories about the ideological existences of former Stalinists. The fact is that these Stalinists produced a gigantic literature about their beliefs and sufferings which is full of such sheer euphemisms that one could speak about neosophistics as a regenerated branch of philosophy. To people who live under communism, these abysses are childishly easy to fathom and their utter shallowness is more ridiculous than striking. The glaring nature of the truth is found in the street and is affirmed by every lie in the newspapers and on banners. Knowledge of *what it is like* makes up the fabric of everyday experience, the structure of existence.

Some people are inclined to equate a former Stalinist with a revisionist. This is correct to the extent that a generation which has no actual ties with the recent past and expresses a desire to reform communism has not yet come on the political scene. Even the youngest known revisionists today spent their youth in Stalinist school organizations. Experience teaches us that those who mechanically repeated formulas in their youth have remained the same repeaters. The best material for disillusioned people is always idealists, so one must assume that today's young revisionists were not so long ago rabid Stalinists. Thus they know hell to a certain extent from the side of the supervisors, which makes it relatively easy to believe in the sincerity and honesty of their conversions. Whether, however, a generation will arise which refuses to accept communism altogether rather than trying to fight for it in another form remains to be seen.

So a revisionist is a Communist from the bosom of practical communism who has realized that communism started from correct assumptions but became corrupted, disgraced, and did terrible things during its fifty years of existence. And that it must be changed or corrected. In other words, he wants another communism, but communism all the same. One may agree that many revisionists are honest people who believe in their convictions and in their own intentions. But communism has created an extremely complex social and moral reality, and human reason and motives have not been amenable to lucid classifications for a long time. It is worth quoting the words of a certain Polish authoress on the subject of the elite who rule the Communist state. "They are people who yesterday believed and today have stopped believing. Despite this, they have not given up their membership in the elite, have not voluntarily handed in their resignations. Just the opposite—they continue to preach a lie. Officially they preach it with great conviction; privately they joke and make fun of everything sacred. The refined cynicism of these people is considered a mark of good tone." We should add that there are also those who have stopped believing but pretend they believe, while this pretending and the profits, glory, and good life derived from it are called the "improvement" or the "humanization" of communism. We must not forget that lack of belief does not mean revolt and that long years of service create a complicated system of vested interests, the maintenance of which can be identified by many as the right fight for the good cause. People living under communism are fascinated by the sight of the perverse, extremely well-camouflaged indulgence of the orthodox toward the revisionists. Extreme cases of revisionism are relentlessly exterminated, as the fates of the leaders of the Czechoslovakian reformation and the Polish and Yugoslav schismatics show. But revisionism in Eastern Europe in the sixties was already a universal and everyday phenomenon. It cropped up at every session of every basic Party organization in institutions distributing milk, where whoever wanted to question the methods of delivering milk used until then, and justified his questions by more general theoretical arguments, citing the classics, was liable to be charged with revisionism. Then the masochistic tendency toward forgiveness on the part of the strictest Communist Catons is striking: they punish the guilty, but as a father or a brother. This is not, of course, a matter of pure feelings. East European communism, continually threatened by the power of the masses' passivity, understood the benefit to be derived from *its own* rebels and saw the advantages accruing from the possession of *inauthentic* revolutionists, angered and embittered, but *its own*. Authentic opponents were and are, as always, trampled into the dust, liquidated, crushed, imprisoned, and deprived of the means of a minimum existence. But the door is always open for the return of former brothers who are never seriously injured because, as history teaches, only a few heretics are burned at the stake; the majority, after years of rebellion, return to the bosom of the orthodox church.

So in almost every case the roots of revisionism lie in former Stalinism and its moral or pseudomoral transformation. The weakness and ambiguity of this position and this process lie in that the ex-Stalinist demands absolution only because he has *stopped* being something evil. In the overwhelming majority of cases, he cannot cite any proofs of his own resistance to evil; his anti-Stalinism begins with the death of Stalin and the revision of ideas about Stalin and his deeds. The ex-Stalinist does not show contrition at having served evil but demands immediate recognition, respect, and sympathy for *no longer* serving evil. In other words, he is in a way capitalizing on his bad faith and evil deeds and demanding dividends for them. The setup of the intellectual establishment in present-day Eastern Europe is based on innumerable shades of revisionism, on semi-revisionisms, and quarter-revisionisms, on various pseudo-nonconformisms and never-ending versions of opportunism. Its homogeneity stems from the fact that one and all fall into the category of ex-Stalinists and thus of those equally trained in the practice of the lie in the service of a scholastic of violence. Participation in this congregation is based on a rule frightening in its power and persuasiveness and on the astonishing norm of evaluation that those who never made mistakes cannot be right, while it was a true value to serve evil and later to *stop* it and proclaim one's abused good will and imposed-upon wisdom. But what should be done with those who from the beginning did not want to be evil and stupid and, as it turned out, were right? Various works explain what is a difficult truth or what represents the supremacy of movement over inertia. Twentieth-century psychology took away guilt from the world; contemporary relativism in communism is not derived from philosophy, however, but from skill in juggling balls of different colors and with different writing on them. The result is such that today ex-Stalinists make up the most powerful Mafia in the world, better organized than the Cosa Nostra, international homosexuality, or stamp collectors. Their saintly community rests on the washing of guilt off each other and on brilliantly composed laments over their ill fortune and violated and exploited innocence. The result is amazing: fifteen years after Khrushchev's revelations, after the uprisings in Poland and Hungary and the heroic crisis in Czechoslovakia, the most assiduous attention and respect is given on both sides of the Iron Curtain to the people who had been the most eager to lick Stalin's boots and who helped him set up his moral, political, and intellectual systems. They withdrew from their past in a stereotyped way; that is, by claiming their childlike naiveté misled them, or they evoked the miracle of transfiguration and miraculously transformed their own faults and mistakes into their own immaculate glory.

One thing should not be forgotten: the revisionist does not stop being a Communist; that is, he does not reject totalitarianism. The truth he believes in and wants to preach is only a neo-truth and does not fundamentally contradict the cardinal blunders and mistakes of doctrine. Or, as a Polish literary critic put it, he demands the exclusive right to fix a watch for those who broke it.

# 33 • America, or the total lie

EVERYONE WHO KNOWS who Marx was knows that Marx was wrong. It is embarrassing to say it again, but Marx predicted that the Revolution would break out in the industrially advanced countries. It broke out in a backward agrarian country. Marx claimed that progress is a function of the development of the forces of production. Today we know that the unrestrained development of the forces of production does not have much to do with progress and may lead only to the disappearance of life on the planet. Marx believed in the polarization and growing antagonism between classes in the capitalist system, and that a hundred years after him, capitalist society would consist simply of a huge mass of proletarians and a small handful of their exploiters and their hired servants. A hundred years after Marx, democratic capitalist society is a complicated mosaic of interrelationships among ever-multiplying and objectively diversified social groups, whose variety and complexity give headaches to the sociologists who try to classify them. Lenin, the most important Communist theoretician after Marx, avoided prophecies and predictions when he saw what was going on. Still, he deeply believed and uncompromisingly declared that the proletariat, the working class, would always represent the vanguard of communism and the Communist Revolution and the loyalest army of the Communist Party. In the seventies in the

263

United States, the staunchest capitalist democracy, the working class is communism's most bitter enemy and the main obstacle to its activity in America. An American worker, who conforms to the classic descriptions of a proletarian deprived of the means of production, possesses material comforts and political influence on the fate of his country which a worker in a Communist country would not dream of in his wildest dreams.

Very little is known in America about what America means in the Communist countries. American diplomats and journalists know a little bit about this, but not very much, because communism has achieved marvelous results in isolating and misinforming all those whose job it is to know something about it. In any case, even if they knew absolutely everything, their knowledge would not be much good in informing America itself, since America does not know about communism for two reasons. The first is that it doesn't want to know, because communism does not concern it and does not seem to be especially different from any other alien geographical and ethnical entity. America looks upon Communism as a matter of national behavior and mores: its specific character appears just a matter of different customs and ways, as in cases of Moslems or Eskimos, which can and should be met with benign curiosity and respectful observance— like accepting leis from Hawaiians. The second reason is that diplomats and journalists, like everyone else interested in communism, examine, appraise, measure, and evaluate it using traditionally American criteria, norms, and intellectual standards. In other words, they apply the complex of ideas developed over the past five thousand years by Judeo-Christian civilization, of which America is the heir and the dynamic promoter. But over the past fifty years, communism has created its own civilization in which the relicts of the common European heritage continue to vegetate but in which the most fundamental concepts and criteria of good and evil, wisdom and stupidity, were long ago thrown on the garbage heap. Thus the scales and hierarchies of values that prevail in communism are usually in clear-cut conflict with those by which an American diplomat, journalist, or observer operates. In the final analysis, it is hard to blame him for this: he is yielding to the force of his own intellectual habits, which are very different from those he needs to evaluate communism correctly. Besides, he is being exposed to the unceasing emanation of the most finely constructed lies in the history of civilized societies.

We must remember that right from the start communism was pregnant with the effects of conflicts among its protagonists. Some insisted that only revolution on a world scale would ensure the historical triumph of communism; others, that it had to first be built in one sufficiently powerful country, and from that base spread out over the entire world. Both sides had at their disposal, a store of learned arguments and irrefutable proofs of their rightness. The second conception won, and in its name Stalin murdered the adherents of the first, headed by Trotsky. Nonetheless, he accepted one of his opponents' arguments and proclaimed it a dialectical and ideological dogma—that is, that as long as the so-called capitalist encirclement existed in the world, communism would be unable to be completely realized and its noble goals, the hope of all mankind, would have to wait to be fully implemented. This is one of the most amazing sophisms, impressive in terms of its functionality and intellectual impudence. On the one hand, the mechanism of history is declared to be inviolable in its sanctity, because in keeping with it, no force on earth can stop the ultimate triumph of socialism. The masses in the West, exhausted by poverty and hopelessness, have waited longingly for fifty years for the arrival of the Red Army, whose power, according to the decree of history, no one can resist. On the other hand, it is pounded into the skulls of Communist societies that if the whole world were already ruled from the Kremlin, but by some strange accident, Paraguay and Kenya remained in the grip of capitalism, communism would still be threatened and its masses compelled to remain in a state of mobilization, readiness, and actual slavery. As in every paradox, there is a valuable and essential truth to be read here. Communism has reached the state where it is not afraid of cannons; it is only afraid of ideas. It knows it cannot lose a war in terms of an unconditional defeat. But it also knows that as long as there exists the smallest place on earth where people can think and speak freely, its existence and *raison d'être* are in mortal danger. Even if this incubator of ideas were only Greenland, *Pravda* and *Izvestia* would proclaim it Enemy Number One, the cradle of imperialism and the capitalist encirclement of the socialist world. It would also accuse it of wanting to attack and conquer the USSR and of continually sending out agents disguised as penguins. So what must things be like when the cradle of independent thought is the United States, the greatest power of the world at the peak phase of its development?

Thus American divagations on the theme of the end of the cold war in the past decade are a one-sided affair and represent the transposition of politico-diplomatic thinking into the dialectical-ideological sphere, where it is worthless. "Peaceful coexistence" is a technical term defining the period of toned-down political maneuvers in the spirit of mutual courtesies and microscopic concessions. It has no other consequences in Russia than allowing a few American pianists to give concerts in Moscow and inviting a few writers whom only members of the Writers' Union and their families know about. On a global scale, the canon of American politics from the birth of the republic was and is the old liberal principle "Live and let live." Regardless of what the proponents of coexistence in America want, or think and write about it, the canon of Communist geopolitics is to destroy America. To attain this, they have never stopped teaching their children in school that the only goal of America is to destroy the USSR or that the great emaciated masses of the American proletariat, tortured by Wall Street capitalists, do nothing but wait for the arrival of the Red Army, its liberator. These two statements obviously contradict each other, but communism knows how insensitive children are to contradiction.

The whole problem looks somewhat different from the standpoint of Eastern Europe. Unlike the USSR, where the masses have been subjected to the most brutal indoctrination in history and where great power feelings play a major role despite the internal political nightmare, the East European masses are decidedly and distinctly anti-Communist. This is known in America but it is

266

not known that these masses are also frantically pro-American, and few people realize the degree of the intensity of their sympathies. If a public opinion poll were possible in Eastern Europe and the question were asked, "What do you want the most in public affairs," I am convinced that the vast majority would reply, "An American occupation." This is not a grotesque exaggeration: these societies have learned that in today's world, only the constant protection of the most powerful guarantees some material and social prosperity. It is only a question of who is the most powerful, and the examples of Germany and Japan speak for themselves. There will always be time for "independence" and "noninterference" once the Soviet threat has disappeared, East European Everyman reasons, and everyone knows how generously and delicately America treats those who relied upon her. The supply of concrete hatred in these countries toward communism surpasses the boldest American conjectures, but the Communists are well aware of this. They had counted on succeeding in getting rid of it, that life itself would somehow dispel and decompose it. This turned out to be a daydream, for the hatred has grown in a geometrical progression, and he who knows how to channel and use it will get control over the Communist empire in Europe.

The American principle "to make friends at any price," which constitutes the basic tenet of American foreign policy and diplomacy, represents the mechanical application of certain ideals of everyday American reality to politics and thus reveals the age-old, specifically American inferiority complex with respect to the aristocratic traditions of European diplomacy. In the propaganda jargon of communism, American diplomacy is incessantly accused of brutality, ruthlessness, cruelty, and vulgar self-seeking. This is a perfidious insult, a sneaky, insidious accusation and the projection of precisely their own sins onto the enemy. The true sin of a modern American diplomat is his sentimentalism and naive concern over manners and logic. He continually regards feelings and protocol as elements in the contest, and constantly thinks about what *they* will think, as if anything had any influence on *their* thinking apart from entirely real stakes such as strength, preponderance, or concrete action. On the geopolitical level, America desperately fights for recognition, sympathy, and symptoms of the feelings of the Bolivians and the French, the Egyptians and the Italians, who, feeling inferior and weaker than the Americans, can only fear and hate them, finding their only satisfaction in anti-American scorn. Nothing over the past fifty years indicates that America's allies have any other goal than to take political and material advantage of its power. Meanwhile, there are living on the earth tens of millions of people who are fanatical supporters of America, ready for anything, potential allies who see in America an ideal and an eventual crusader with whom they will one day wander to the promised Holy Land, though nothing indicates the approach of such a crusade for the time being. This is the only reservoir of allies whose enthusiasm knows no bounds, who cry in front of their television sets when an American athlete loses at the Olympics and get drunk with happiness at every American success. They all agree that America should wipe North Vietnam from the face of the earth because they *know* what the Communist lie is, and no humanitarian considerations play any role with them. The moment of the sweetest triumph in their lives was the landing of an American on the moon. Nevertheless, the answer to the question of whether hatred for communism is equivalent to love for America is complex.

It appears that America wasted a certain capital, much greater than it might seem at first glance, in conventionally assessing the importance of that part of Europe in the complex of geopolitical calculations. During the first five years after the Second World War, Eastern Europe conferred upon America the boundless love of a woman scorned who, despite the hurt, cannot forget the charms of her lover. During the Korean War pedestrians who passed by the American embassies in the East European capitals spontaneously took off their hats before the American flag hanging there. Secret police informers who lurked nearby would arrest dozens of people daily. In Poland a rumor spread that a conscription of volunteers for the fighting in Korea had been called. Crowds of people reported and openly discussed methods of crossing the front line to join MacArthur. The entire affair turned out to be a provocation of the political police who carefully taped/recorded/registered many of the "volunteers" before people realized what was happening. Caricaturists in official Communist organs used to draw MacArthur as a bloody hangman, his hands dripping with blood, decked out in Fascist swastikas, but always wearing sunglasses, which was supposed to symbolize Americanism. There was a time when all Warsaw went about in winter wearing dark glasses as a symbol of solidarity with MacArthur. Party secretaries assigned to places of work received an order to fire anyone who wore dark glasses, even if he could prove with a doctor's certificate that he suffered from conjunctivitis.

In 1952 an exhibition entitled "This is America," organized by the propaganda sections of the Communist parties, visited the cities of Eastern Europe. It was dreamed up as a gigantic indictment of what is imagistically called in Communist journalese the "wolf fangs of imperialism" or the "gutter of capitalist culture." But its organizers made a mistake. They filled it with authentic exhibits such as guns for spies, slides showing the persecutions of Negroes, *Brothers Karamazov* comic books, plastic gadgets illustrating by their garishness the vulgarity of manners in America. The effects of this exhibition were apocalyptic: the crowds that gathered at the entrances formed lines where one had to wait for hours; children fled en masse from school to spend at least a little time at the exhibition and only regular raids by police detachments took them back to their schooldesks. A Polish writer who escaped to the West in the late fifties remembers this exhibition in the following way: "People wanted to see something American—to look, if only for a moment, at things made across the ocean by people who would never help them. This was an unhappy love, a totally unrequited love. And I suppose it was the last love for those who were doomed to nonexistence in communism. . . . Our gesture of brotherhood toward the Americans was funny and pitiful and would never be noticed or understood by them. But it was the only gesture which was left for us. Perhaps our greatest hope lies in the absence of a promise. The Communists promised everything: bread, work, freedom, brotherhood. But he who promises everything in reality promises nothing." At that time people wore with passion old American suits and military coats from the war or from parcels sent by relatives in America, despite the fact that they were in danger of being expelled from school, the university, or work for this, and sometimes were even threatened with arrest and imprisonment But this was how America was loved then.

The cooling of this love came with the period of changes and reforms in Eastern Europe when the Americans, taken in by the appearances of internal relaxation, established new guide lines for their policies in this part of the empire. This was called placing their stakes on revisionism or on the erosion of power, as a certain American political scientist charmingly called it. In the restless East European capitals Americans suddenly felt most fascinated with communism, not with the real resistance to it. The changes within communism were recognized as the key to the future and as an eventual bridge to understandings. Of course, Americans understood these changes according to the traditional norms of Western political philosophy, unaware that changes in communism, even if they do emerge, have little in common with the idea of change accepted by *our* logic and *our* theory of cognition. Then an absurd situation arose in which the Soviet and American ambassadors supported the same people in every East European capital, namely, those Communists who created the impression that they had a decisive influence on what was happening in these countries. The Russians acted consistently with their own interests. All the Americans gained was the increasing distrust of those who had until then loved them. And they got nothing from the Communists in exchange for the gradual loss of the ardent feelings of their natural allies. To the loyalest of the loyal, who asked of the Americans mainly that they understand what it was really like, the Americans time and again served up worn-out and chewed-over slogans about steadfastness, freedom, independence, and heroism. More substantial feelings and proposals they saved for the Communists, who, in the opinion of the ideological planners in the State Department, had to be petted and caressed because they were ruling and would be ruling for God knows how long. Their attitude toward East European Communists underwent a fundamental change: no one sought any longer to argue with them about principles, even rudimentary ones formulated in an antiquated sentimental way. Argument was replaced by coquetry, subtle seduction, and temptations. Communists began to be showered with lucrative scholarships, invitations, free visits to the most attractive places in America, and contacts with its most interesting people. As if not understanding that every trip from Eastern Europe to the West paid for in dollars is a prize of kingly generosity, Americans began the action of bestowing their horn of plenty upon the worst among the Communists, those whose cynical jugglery with pseudo-nonconformism so positioned them in the eyes of the Party that it allowed them open contacts with Americans. Things got to the point where corrupt and opportunistic Polish intellectuals at the University of Warsaw enjoyed saying things like "If you are an exemplary Communist, you'll go to America on a Ford Foundation grant." Naturally, the societies under communism know better than the Americans who's who and what foul deeds are concealed under a facade of erudition, popularity, and intellectualism. So it is not surprising that the Americans' eagerness in rewarding Communists for their baseness would drive all those who loved America in a natural and simple way even farther away from them.

Where did the error of the American calculation lie? Largely in the application of a norm of reasoning from the sphere of its own civilization. By inviting and fêting people who were notorious for the terrible things they did under communism and people whose names often symbolized the lies and crime of the Stalinist period, Americans were acting in the name of equally antiquated concepts of idealism and realism.

American idealism stems from a belief in objective truth: every American, even the most skeptical one, in the final analysis believes that objective truth has an ultimate power of persuasion and that someone who is confronted with a concretely existing fact must accept that fact and agree with it. He therefore believes that if a Communist is brought to America and there shown freedom, the affluence of the worker, the rights of citizens, and social egalitarianism, the Communist will strike his breast, cry bucketfuls, and exclaim, "I was wrong! From this day forth I want to be a democrat. I will return to my homeland and work for common ideals." But the more intelligent a Communist is, the more he will smile pleasantly and not believe a thing. Often he will say with ineffable impudence that there is more freedom, equality, and prosperity under communism. Often, too, he will hate America even more deeply because things really are better there and now he knows it. But he will inevitably return to his country and spit on America with redoubled force, furnished by American money with new subjects to spit on, because that is the main reason he came here with his party's permission, though the American diplomats who sent him to America are not very aware of this.

A realistic motivation would look like this: We are inviting and paying for the visit of an opportunist and political wheeler-dealer to America. He serves the Communists and we know it, but he has influence and the respect of his Party bosses. By nature he is inclined to various machinations so perhaps we will negotiate something through him and reach higher and more authoritative centers of power. We will give proof of our approachability, which might favorably dispose them toward us. Let's invite the young, the enterprising, and the astute conformists. You never know what they will do when they get into power. Perhaps contacts with us will open a road to them after they get power. Let's invite the young, the firm, the ruthless, and the uncorruptible. Perhaps our strength will make such an impression on them that when they come to power, they will want something from us and will be willing to give us something in return.

From the standpoint of the rules of classical diplomacy and foreign policy, both arguments are correct. But in Communist countries their realization turns into a farce. In the USSR practically no one except those especially designated to do so speak to Americans. In Eastern Europe everyone talks to them. Many speak sincerely but just as many speak from the position of their own participation in the never-ending masquerade of servility and venality. Many are only artificially made up in the conflict of consciences of the epoch, in revisionism, in nonconformism, and in so-called national communism. Society sees clearly who's who but the Americans don't, so it's not surprising that they tend to take for nonconformism and opposition something that is only a crafty machination. The American obsession with those who have *influence* makes Americans even more defenseless because it is difficult to explain to them that the word *influence* has an entirely different meaning in a Communist nation than in America, and that those who seem to them to be influential are usually common hucksters, while those who apparently mean nothing count a hundred times more. Very few people in Communist East Europe still believe in communism, apart from those at the very peaks of power who will never enter into unofficial relations with Americans. But many people in communism live off the fact that they pretend to believe. For these people an American grant or a trip to America is a surrealistic reward for a lifelong fight against America and its ideals because Americans, often seduced by the freedom of their conversation, naively believe in their pseudoconversions and pseudomachiavellianism. A leading Communist journalist in conversation with the American ambassador will completely tear apart communism and its bosses. Afterward he will go to the editorial office and write an article utterly assassinating the character of America, just like the inflexible apologist of lies whom he mocked an hour ago. When he meets the ambassador again, he will discreetly give him to know that he had to do it, that he is in the clutches of terror, but despite this, the ambassador should not take offense, but believe that when the right time comes, the same journalist will play an appropriate role in shaping new relations with Americans. In return for this, the ambassador and his staff should arrange a luxurious trip for the journalist to America where by furiously saving on his daily travel allowance he will buy himself new shoes and new suits. At home these will assure him the reputation of a dandy for years to come

273

and will also bear witness to his excellent relations with the Americans. This will raise him in the esteem of his countrymen who perhaps may think to themselves that he couldn't be so bad if the Americans respect and entertain him. What the ambassador and his staff usually don't know is that the cynical, mocking, flashy journalist means nothing. His position is all tinsel and show. He suggests to the ambassador that he can do something, that he is in charge of a certain game and that it is worth playing with him—whereas in fact he is simply lying.

The last ten years have produced in Eastern Europe a caste of ruthless and cruel Communist *arrivistes* dressed in Italian shoes, French shirts, and English tweeds. Their battle array for propagating lies and running political affairs has undergone a similar camouflage. The West, mainly the Americans, sees them as the vanguard of progress, and as better representatives of power who are evolving toward better forms and the reforms wanted by the West. In reality, they are only a more dangerous incarnation of the same totalistic principle of seeing and ruling the world. They assiduously try to develop new, more threatening forms and to modify contents to maintain a doctrine which is on the decline. Their goal is to improve the functioning of the mechanism, but not to change its course of action; it is still supposed to act against man, truth, and freedom, only in a less brutal fashion. Americans greeted their appearance as a sign of change for the better. Instead of fighting them head-on and in full recognition of their nature, the Americans decided to try to buy them. This made the Americans look ridiculous to those whom they tried to buy as well as to all those who once loved them. The worship of oppressors, scoundrels, and opportunists which the Americans demonstrated at every step must finally have appeared to honest people as a sign of contempt for themselves. It is hard for an honest man to shake off a feeling of bitterness when he sees his persecutors honored and rewarded by those who are his objective allies. The question arises whether it is worth holding onto any moral values when a reward on the social scale goes to the person who violated them and continues to do so, only in a more complicated and underhanded manner.

In the final reckoning, Americans were practically saying to people in communism: "We want to talk with our enemies. We want to reach an understanding with them. Everything (shoes, new terminology, trips abroad, tweeds, etc.) indicates that they want people to live better. That's enough for us. And let us live, we in freedom, you in an improved, digestible communism."

So the Americans blissfully forget that communism has its own eschatology. Debate about the world is not ended by letting people have Hemingway, miniskirts, and rock music. Careerists come and go, aberrations pass; Trotskyism passed, as did national communism, schisms, and deviations. Communism remains, together with its integral enemies. They are the most durable bedrock of all passive resistance, the only power which forces communism to make concessions. By flirting with the enemies of the enemies of communism, Americans think they will succeed in maintaining good relations with the latter by appealing to the stale old pap of slogans which have long been invalid: that the Poles are loyal Catholics and cherish freedom, that the Czechs are sincere democrats, that the Hungarians are the nation of Kossuth and Petofi. Meanwhile, the Czechs, Poles, and Hungarians are waging a fight with modern communism in which all declamations on the subject of Uhlans, national honor, and inherited traditions sound like the height of infantilism. The world outside of communism does not understand the depth and complexity of this fight, while no one in communism itself knows much about it either since it represents a new and little-studied phenomenon. All that is known is that enormous human masses are involved in it and that these masses hate communism. The Americans have squandered the store of love they inherited from the Stalinist period and have not been able to establish either contact or a dialogue with the *new* phenomena of anticommunism within the societies ruled by the Communists, or with all those people *there* who are anti-Communist but have no connection with the traditions of cavalry spirit, resistance, and heroism from the past.

The question arises whether this wave of active anticommunism, which we observe in recent years, is equivalent to pro-

Americanism. The answer to it is hard. The last ten years of foolish maneuvers and the common blunders described above have led to a decline of America's authority in these countries. There can be no talk of love as it existed during the Korean War. Indeed, it can be said in so many words: America is no longer even liked there. The broad masses of people who hate communism want retaliation and revenge in various forms and guises. They want the Americans to behave like the hated Communists and the Russians, to reward value and virtue and punish evil and opportunism. They want to have the feeling that someone is standing behind them the way the Russians stand behind the Communists in the capitalist countries. If there can be no direct retaliation in the form of a crusade, let there be an infinite number of small, indirect retaliations in sports and in manners, in showing contempt toward the people who deserve it. But the Americans are doing just the opposite: they are treating the Russians as equals in sports despite the fact that everyone knows the Russians cheat. They invite and honor poets everyone knows are sellouts and obedient flunkies of the Communist regimes. It would be unthinkable for a hard-core Nazi professor, who had rendered open services to Hitler's regime, to come to this country and bask in favors and honors due to a scholar. American ethos wouldn't have held it out. However, it is common, of late, to see Communist intellectual thugs—known over decades as ferocious villifiers of America and persecutors of non-Communists in their respective countries—getting fat and honorable positions at American universities. An obscure but widespread rationalization is connected with this phenomenon: Americans must somehow consider that what those people perpetrated in their countries is neither the hosts' business nor anti-Americanism at all, although they would be quite resolved to deem any analogous Nazi behavior as both an American concern and utterly conflicting with American ideals.

America saves Americans. What they have ruined in Eastern Europe by their own bungling is corrected by what is going on in America. Those who hate communism and do not like America are still bound up in America as an objective ideal. They worship it for what is happening in it and what it does at home. This makes them dream of an American occupation; they believe unflinchingly that in a country occupied by them, the Americans would install the same kind of freedom that prevails in America, the same logic and efficiency of social life that makes America a land where everyone has an opportunity to develop. For the great masses living under communism, America represents a matchless political and economic standard, the symbol of a correctly and profitably lived life. But Americans have not known how to handle even this pro-Americanism. They have been unable to find the right way of uncompromisingly, skillfully, effectively, and productively supporting the true enemies of communism, those who most deserve it.

Despite these mistakes and blunders, everything still indicates that not many East European soldiers would fight against the Americans if there ever arose such a dismal thing as a war between the two worlds.

# 34 • What is the word?

THE WORD IN COMMUNISM in the public sphere serves first of all to hide the truth and then for communication among people. In the private sphere it serves communication and the hiding of thoughts equally.

When the head of a Communist state makes a speech, his subjects know perfectly well how much he is lying. They also know that a lie that has been stretched so far has, despite the appearance of idiocy, its concrete political function. They know, too, that on the following day the press, radio, and TV will strengthen lie with lie and nonsense with nonsense. Finally, they know that some time later there will ensue thorough denials of statements that were proclaimed to be absolutely inviolable, and some of these will be severely damned and branded as lies and nonsense. One need only know how to wait for this abjuration and condemnation. How long? Sometimes for years, but meanwhile, one can be quite sure it will come.

A lie in communism is always monstrous and awakens amusement in Western man. It expresses, however, a carefully thought-out political instrumentality. If a Communist journalist writes that in America children are eaten for breakfast, the fact that this is not true *for sure* is known only to his bosses and supervisors, to himself, and to a few thousand people who have been in America. The huge mass of readers think this is nonsense, but don't know for sure and cannot rely on any authorities, because even a letter to the editor that timidly questions this information will never be printed. And after reading every day for years about American breakfasts of infants, a man who by nature tends to hesitate will say to himself, "There must be something to it. In the final resort, who knows? They write about it and write about it, so there must be *something* in it." And this eventual succumbing is all the Communists were after. It is their only chance in societies where the universal conviction prevails that everything, absolutely everything, printed in a Communist newspaper is a lie. Of course, this conviction is not correct; it happens, for example, that the information that the movie theater "The Glory of the Revolution" is showing a movie called *The Dawn of Communism* does correspond to the truth. The weakness of this press is, however, that more often than not, even this item turns out to be untrue. Either the theater has not yet been finished, though according to plan it was supposed to be in use the previous year, or else the film is called *The Dusk of Capitalism.* (The manager of the theater, correctly thinking that the title is without much significance, has not published this title in the press for over a month.) It is also difficult to find out how many thousands of Arabs were murdered yesterday afternoon by the Israeli imperialists. But it is not hard to find in Lenin's *Collected Works* the famous sentence that the task of the press is not at all to inform the masses, but to form their consciousness, and that the highest goal of the printed word is to transmit the directives of the Party to the masses. In a certain sense the Communists should be proud that faith in Lenin's words is so deeply and permanently rooted in the societies they rule.

The ultimate corruption of the word in communism began a long time ago with Lenin, the greatest corrupter of semantics in the history of mankind. It reached the heights of cynicism under Stalin when the phrase "struggle with a dialectically false view" meant sentencing hundreds of thousands of people to life imprisonment in concentration camps while "the correction of a historical mistake" meant executing hundreds of thousands more.

"Catching up with the unfinished work of history" signified years of waiting in line for bread, while "peace will overcome war" meant Communist tanks trampling over South Korea, Tibet, and Czechoslovakia.

The perversion of the word as symbol of an idea has already been flawlessly recorded by Orwell. Interesting, however, is the Communists' nonchalant freedom in modifying sets of ideas. Every rise in food prices in Communist countries appears in the papers under a big heading "An Epochal Victory for the Working People!" Next to it is "A Drop in the Prices of Streetcar Rails, Elevators, and Locomotives!" and beside it, finally, in smaller letters, "Temporary Increase in the Price of Butter and Meat." It is hard for the man in the street to rejoice over a drop in elevator or locomotive prices because he does not buy either elevators or locomotives for himself every day, while it is even harder to bite into a rail for lunch. He also knows that the adjective "temporary" is meaningless because from the time Lenin first took a stroll around the Kremlin, food prices have never declined in the Communist empire but have steadily risen.

But the man in the street may think to himself, particularly if the laws of economy are familiar to him, that a drop in the cost of rails may mean a lowering of streetcar fares. It soon turns out that the price of streetcar tickets must depend on the price of butter, since they, too, go up, while the drop in locomotive prices apparently has an effect on the cost of movie tickets, which go down slightly. But in the movie theater the word, literature, and agitation prevail—here a man learns how much better his life is with every passing day, and what a marvelous future he is heading toward—and there is no end to this logical cycle, entangled in its own idiosyncracy.

The elections in which the huge, unnamed, and never defined majority are against the government and the regime are reported the following day in the papers as 99.89 percent of votes for the government and the regime. Thus if once the Communists published that 99.87 percent had voted for them, all Poland would be mad with joy over the fact that the Communists had lost the elections. The Soviet airlines, which also serve the Western world, once proudly printed the information that every pilot undergoes a preflight medical examination. This information is an amazing combination of truth and untruth. Soviet pilots do in fact appear before a doctor before every flight, but in order to check whether there is too much alcohol in their blood. Everything agrees with the information: there is an examination, it does reflect concern over the passenger's safety, it does denote a humane attitude toward the pilot. Only the vodka is missing from the total picture, a psycho-physical factor with a moral flavor.

The institution known as the censorship stands guard over the imprisoned, crippled, and dishonored word. People from outside of communism picture it as an agency that acts only on the basis of rigidly laid down rules and in conformance to the bureaucratic mechanism of commands issued by the Party and government leadership. It's true that there does exist an agency known as the Office of the Censor, but it is only part of a process which is constantly taking place in the minds of people involved in producing and spreading the word in communism. In reality, the act of censoring thoughts and words in keeping with the requirements of politics and propaganda begins at the desk of a newspaper editor or in a publishing house. An article or book undergoes a scrupulous examination and something is removed from it and something added. The author's consent is either not asked at all, or he can choose to relinquish publication of the article or book. If a book or article is irreproachable as far as the purity of its ideas go, something is still always added or removed because the editor is afraid that a higher institution, this time a Party institution, will regard a lack of interference as proof of apathy, carelessness, or stupidity. And this can hurt the editor's position and his salary. Thus if an absolutely devoted writer or journalist writes that communism is the hope of nations, the editor will if he really cares about his position, add that it is the hope and love of nations. The supervisor in the Party who reads the same text will add at least two adjectives: "radiant" to hope and "ardent" to love, because he, too, has his superiors, on whom his reputation as a vigilant and infallible supervisor depends, a reputation on which, in turn, his future career depends. Finally, the text goes to the censorship office, without whose stamp nothing can be printed, even a calling card with only a name on it. An employee of the censorship office does not have the right to add anything to the text and rarely removes something himself, but after reading the sentence quoted above, he would most likely phone the editor or the supervisor and say, "Listen, comrade, we don't like the word 'hope' very much. It means that feelings already exist and should be emphasized with the proper firmness now that the reactionary forces are on the offensive are being deferred till the future." Because the reactionary forces have been on the offensive since the beginning of communism and will never stop, and the employee in the censorship office is also looking after his position, the text goes back to the desk of the writer or the journalist whose job is to express himself more precisely.

If a traveler should happen to come to a Communist capital on the day of some state holiday, on the streets he will see crowds in a joyful procession, raising enthusiastic cries in honor of communism and its leaders. He will rarely associate this enthusiasm with mockery and usually will not be able to perceive the desperate jeering under the cover of applause. Words in this case are a function of the modulation and pitch of voices and take on undertones of exquisite ambiguities in the framework of which the cry "Long live——" becomes a definite insult to the ears of the crowd. Without this skill in coding meanings, the only defense of the oppressed, the foreigner has no chance of understanding what is really going on here. When someone makes a speech, using the most precise official Party jargon possible, the foreigner is inclined to think that the speaker is *for*. In fact, he is really against, and his listeners understand this perfectly. They know that it is neither possible nor worthwhile speaking against, which may mean prison or at least the loss of one's livelihood. Openly speaking against is regarded as flippant and stupid, as cheap striving for effect, or else as clumsy half-wittedness. A speaker should praise in such a way that everyone knows he is damning everything from A to Z, and he knows that they know it.

A foreigner generally looks at communism from the standpoint of an outsider, a visitor who can leave and return home, and thus can permit himself impartiality. It is precisely his impartiality that interests the Communists if he is a journalist, diplomat, intellectual, or observer. They are always able to show him things and facts not in terms of how they really are, but how they can and should be, or eventually will be one day. This arouses the foreigner's sympathy and activates his unbiased perspicacity in exactly the way the Communists want. The foreigner then cannot understand why his impartiality and objectivity are derided, loathed, and rejected by the non-Communists living under communism. Thus the overwhelming majority of reports written for the West by impartial, objective observers who are usually honest and intelligent people are primitive crudities in the eyes of people living under communism. Usually these reports awaken a feeling of helpless resentment in them and only intensify their feelings of desperate hopelessness.

## 35 · How to die

N° ONE IN THE WORLD has any illusions about old age. Everyone knows that old age means incurable heart-break, sorrow, and oblivion. In democracies modern humanists are always wrenching one's heart with pictures of unhappy, empty old age in literature and on the screen. Because there is no place for heartbreak, sorrow, and misfortune in socialism, according to official decree, old age *must* be happy there. This has nothing to do with reality, because old age there is even more dismal than anywhere else. An average monthly pension is sufficient for a few days of miserable living; what to do for the rest of the month no one knows, including the state and the Party. So the face of an old man on television or the voice of an old woman on the radio assuring people of their sunny lives and the happiness socialism gives them only makes one embarrassed.

Death is a problem which is complicated and political. The slightest mistake in dying turns against those who are near and dear to the dying person. One should die so as not to be a burden on them. This is especially true of prominent people whose lives were devoted to the work of the mind, to ideas, to creativity. Death puts them at the mercy of the Communists for the last time. For no matter what they have devoted their intellectual efforts, talent, and feelings to, the Communists will appropriate them for themselves and declare them to have been cooperative and ardent supporters of communism. The dead cannot defend themselves and their relatives and friends are afraid to defend their names and their life's work. Anyway, in the final resort, it is the living who need jobs and apartments, so why shouldn't they make the best use of something that otherwise would only spell disaster? And once again the censor encroaches on life, or rather on death. The obituary must receive the censor's stamp before it appears in print. In many cases an employee in the office of the censor politely but firmly advises what should be mentioned among the contributions of the deceased and what should not.

A state funeral is a catalyst of reactions and feelings. The greatest men of communism were buried in the presence of immense crowds which the official papers wrote about, exulting over how this was the highest proof of the love the masses had for them. But eyewitnesses have claimed that the elementary feeling, clearly perceptible to everyone in the crowd, was one of beatific joy. Good-naturedly drunk people would keep asking each other discreetly, "What's happening with the honored corpse?" to which others would reply with gusto, "Everything's O.K. He's already cold."

Sometimes a lesser light of the regime dies and the propaganda apparatus wants to have an appropriate part in the dialectic of death. So schools and offices are let out and the streets are again filled with contented office workers and delighted children. The next day the newspapers carry reports about how crowds of people were plunged into mourning, accompanying the luminary to his well-earned rest. They will write about the people's love for him and his faith. So in one way or another, death becomes a valuable and appreciated ally of communism.

# Conclusion

I N AMERICA a lot of books are written about how bad things
are in America. It is good they are written because they constitute a powerful guarantee that regardless of how good things
are, they will one day be even better.

In Communist nations, as well, a lot of books are written
about how bad things are in America. And even more books
about how wonderful things are under communism. This means
that the balance is upset. So I decided to contribute my share to
restoring the balance—and the result is this book.

It may be regarded as a collection of practical pieces of advice. It contains enough of the generalities which I deeply believe
in for this. And even if my deep belief doesn't predetermine their
correctness, it does give them a certain validity. The question
then arises: For whom was this book written?

Obviously for people outside communism. Perhaps the effort
of writing it was pointless since it seems impossible to understand what it is like there without having lived there. Life there
is in a certain respect based on the impossibility of living. Nonetheless, hundreds of millions of people live there, which at least
indicates that this type of life can emerge somewhere else. I
have always been amused by the divagations of Communists
who live outside Communist countries, and their sympathizers on
the subject, on how they would improve communism. In my

opinion, these are romantic daydreams; communism will be the same everywhere, despite its different make-up, which is determined by climate and traditions. The virus of communism is the same; only the chemistry of the different national organisms may be different. This only means that they will react to the illness in different ways, fight it within themselves differently, and produce various antitoxins. But the wasting and destruction of the living tissue by the virus will always be the same, as will be the final result. I have written about how people live under communism in lands where it has been established and tested by millions of people. I believe that life will be the same in any politico-social model that the totalitarian left is fighting for today.

So I did not write this book for Czechs, Poles, or Ukrainians, because they already know how to live under communism. I wrote it for the people of the democratic West who, when they meet refugees from communism in their countries, are amazed at their bitter, festering, inexpressible, and inarticulate hatred of communism, a hatred which is also full of wisdom. When the refugees are asked why they fled, they have so much to say that they are unable to give a simple, clear, and coherent answer. I deeply and humbly believe that struggling to show another man something one knows so well but one cannot express it constitutes a powerful force for propelling humanity forward. A force thanks to which humanity is sometimes able to distinguish good from evil.

Warsaw–New York–Peterborough
1964                       1970